**Funded by a State Legislature Grant
Senator Suzi Oppenheimer**

RYE FREE READING ROOM
Escape to the Library

Bloom's Modern Critical Views

Bloom's Modern Critical Views

Zora Neale Hurston
New Edition

Edited and with an introduction by
Harold Bloom
Sterling Professor of the Humanities
Yale University

BLOOM'S
LITERARY CRITICISM
An imprint of Infobase Publishing

Bloom's Modern Critical Views: Zora Neale Hurston—New Edition

Copyright ©2008 by Infobase Publishing

Introduction ©2008 by Harold Bloom

Consulting Editor: Brian L. Johnson

Bloom's Literary Criticism
An imprint of Infobase Publishing
132 West 31st Street
New York NY 10001

Library of Congress Cataloging-in-Publication Data

Zora Neale Hurston / edited with an introduction by Harold Bloom. — New ed.
      p. cm. — (Bloom's modern critical views)
Includes bibliographical references and index.
ISBN 978-0-7910-9610-9 (alk. paper)
    1. Hurston, Zora Neale—Criticism and interpretation. I. Bloom, Harold.

PS3515.U789Z96 2008
813'.52—dc22   2007049161

Contents

Editor's Note

My Introduction highly praises Hurston for her vitality, individualism, and freedom from ideology.

Folk sermonizing in *Dust Tracks on a Road* is noted by Deborah G. Plant, while Susan Meisenhelder addresses herself to *Mules and Men*.

Deborah Clarke credits Hurston for redefining African American rhetoric, and Laurie Champion locates some of Hurston's challenges to societal oppression in selected stories.

Seraph on the Suwanee, a minor Hurston novel, is interpreted by Claudia Tate as a "seditious joke on racialism," while John Lowe attempts to rescue Hurston's plays from neglect.

Dolan Hubbard centers upon Janie's sermon in *Their Eyes Were Watching God*, and Gordon E. Thompson examines personification in Hurston.

Daniel J. Sundahl defends Hurston's refusal to protest for the sake of protest, and Daphne Lamothe finds Vodou imagery in *Their Eyes . . .*

William M. Ramsey gazes at Hurston's own ambivalences toward and in *Their Eyes . . .*, while Michael Awkward and Michelle Johnson contribute with a joint overview of Hurston.

HAROLD BLOOM

Introduction

ZORA NEALE HURSTON (1891–1960)

I

Hurston was a vitalist, enormously alive. Sometimes I find myself thinking of her as a Shakespearean character, so much does she now belong to American literary legend. Of all major African-American writers, she appears to have possessed the most personal verve, a life-force wonderfully embodied in *Their Eyes Were Watching God* (surely one of the great titles).

Flamboyant writers—Lord Byron, Oscar Wilde, Hemingway—manifest a curious relationship of the work to the life, one that breaks down the wavering demarcation between art and reality. Hurston—novelist, anthropologist, folklorist—had a fierce dislike of racial politics, black *and* white, and loathed any attempt to subsume her individuality under any category whatsoever.

We all of us pay high prices for our freedom from cant, social dogma, and societal morality. Hurston, passionate and driven by a *daemon*, plunged into a terrible final decade, in which she alienated most of her friends, admirers, readers. She opposed desegregation, arguing that it would degrade black education. Rejected by the publishing world and by foundations, she died in a welfare home and was buried in an unmarked grave. Her mourners all have been retrospective.

Ralph Ellison, a great writer and a warm acquaintance, once at dinner together told me he could not understand my admiration for *Their Eyes Were Watching God*, a novel he found alternately overwritten and underwritten. I recall replying that the book's vitalism disarmed me: if the style was uneven, the abundant surge of outrageous will to live in the heroine Janie had a cosmic urgency, a persuasiveness I could not resist. Hurston is that rare

1

author who mothered herself into existence. She has a gusto that reminds me of Chaucer's the Wife of Bath and Shakespeare's Sir John Falstaff. It was probably inevitable that she would immerse herself in the destructive element, but she achieved one undying book, heroic and poignant.

II

Extra-literary factors have entered into the process of even secular canonization from Hellenistic Alexandria into the High Modernist Era of Eliot and Pound, so that it need not much dismay us if contemporary work by women and by minority writers becomes esteemed on grounds other than aesthetic. When the High Modernist critic Hugh Kenner assures us of the permanent eminence of the novelist and polemicist Wyndham Lewis, we can be persuaded, unless of course we actually read books like *Tarr* and *Hitler*. Reading Lewis is a rather painful experience, and makes me skeptical of Kenner's canonical assertions. In the matter of Zora Neale Hurston, I have had a contrary experience, starting with skepticism when I first encountered essays by her admirers, let alone by her idolators. Reading *Their Eyes Were Watching God* dispels all skepticism. *Moses: Man of the Mountain* is an impressive book in its mode and ambitions, but a mixed achievement, unable to resolve problems of diction and of rhetorical stance. Essentially, Hurston is the author of one superb and moving novel, unique not in its kind but in its isolated excellence among other stories of the kind.

The wistful opening of *Their Eyes Were Watching God* pragmatically affirms greater repression in women as opposed to men, by which I mean "repression" only in Freud's sense: unconscious yet purposeful forgetting:

> Now, women forget all those things they don't want to remember, and remember everything they don't want to forget. The dream is the truth. Then they act and do things accordingly.

Hurston's Janie is now necessarily a paradigm for women, of whatever race, heroically attempting to assert their own individuality in contexts that continue to resent and fear any consciousness that is not male. In a larger perspective, should the contexts modify, the representation of Janie will take its significant place in a long tradition of such representations in English and American fiction. This tradition extends from Samuel Richardson to Doris Lessing and other contemporaries, but only rarely has been able to visualize authentically strong women who begin with all the deprivations that circumstance assigns to Janie. It is a crucial aspect of Hurston's subtle sense of limits that the largest limitation is that imposed upon Janie by her grandmother, who loves her best, yet fears for her the most.

As a former slave, the grandmother, Nanny, is haunted by the compensatory dream of making first her daughter, and then her granddaughter, something other than "the mule of the world," customary fate of the black woman. The dream is both powerful enough, and sufficiently unitary, to have driven Janie's mother away, and to condemn Janie herself to a double disaster of marriages, before the tragic happiness of her third match completes as much of her story as Hurston desires to give us. As readers, we carry away with us what Janie never quite loses, the vivid pathos of her grandmother's superb and desperate displacement of hope:

> "And, Janie, maybe it wasn't much, but Ah done de best Ah kin by you. Ah raked and scraped and bought dis lil piece uh land so you wouldn't have to stay in de white folks' yard and tuck yo' head befo' other chillun at school. Dat was all right when you was little. But when you got big enough to understand things, Ah wanted you to look upon yo'self. Ah don't want yo' feathers always crumpled by folks throwin' up things in yo' face. And Ah can't die easy thinkin' maybe de menfolks white or black is makin' a spit cup outa you: Have some sympathy fuh me. Put me down easy, Janie, Ah'm a cracked plate."

III

Hurston's rhetorical strength, even in *Their Eyes Were Watching God*, is frequently too overt, and threatens an excess when contrasted with the painful simplicity of her narrative line and the reductive tendency at work in all her characters except for Janie and Nanny. Yet the excess works, partly because Hurston is so considerable and knowing a mythologist. Hovering in *Their Eyes Were Watching God* is the Mosaic myth of deliverance, the pattern of revolution and exodus that Hurston reimagines as her prime trope of power:

> But there are other concepts of Moses abroad in the world. Asia and all the Near East are sown with legends of this character. They are so numerous and so varied that some students have come to doubt if the Moses of the Christian concept is real. Then Africa has her mouth on Moses. All across the continent there are the legends of the greatness of Moses, but not because of his beard nor because he brought the laws down from Sinai. No, he is revered because he had the power to go up the mountain and to bring them down. Many men could climb mountains. Anyone could bring down laws that had been handed to them. But who can talk

with God face to face? Who has the power to command God to
go to a peak of a mountain and there demand of Him laws with
which to govern a nation? What other man has ever commanded
the wind and the hail? The light and darkness? That calls for
power, and that is what Africa sees in Moses to worship. For he is
worshipped as a god.

Power in Hurston is always *potentia*, the demand for life, for more
life. Despite the differences in temperament, Hurston has affinities both
with Dreiser and with Lawrence, heroic vitalists. Her art, like theirs, exalts
an exuberance that is beauty, a difficult beauty because it participates in
reality-testing. What is strongest in Janie is a persistence akin to Dreiser's
Carrie and Lawrence's Ursula and Gudrun, a drive to survive in one's own
fashion. Nietzsche's vitalistic injunction, that we must try to live as though
it were morning, is the implicit basis of Hurston's true religion, which in
its American formulation (Thoreau's), reminds us that only that day dawns
to which we are alive. Something of Lawrence's incessant sense of the sun
is paralleled by Hurston's trope of the solar trajectory, in a cosmos where:
"They sat on the boarding house porch and saw the sun plunge into the
same crack in the earth from which the night emerged" and where: "Every
morning the world flung itself over and exposed the town to the sun."
    Janie's perpetual sense of the possibilities of another day propels her
from Nanny's vision of safety first to the catastrophe of Joe Starks and then
to the love of Tea Cake, her true husband. But to live in a way that starts with
the sun is to become pragmatically doom-eager, since mere life is deprecated
in contrast to the possibility of glory, of life more abundant, rather than
Nanny's dream of a refuge from exploitation. Hurston's most effective irony
is that Janie's drive toward her own erotic potential should transcend her
grandmother's categories, since the marriage with Tea Cake is also Janie's
pragmatic liberation from bondage toward men. When he tells her, in all
truth, that she has the keys to the kingdom, he frees her from living in her
grandmother's way.
    A more pungent irony drove Hurston to end Janie's idyll with Tea Cake's
illness and the ferocity of his subsequent madness. The impulse of her own
vitalism compels Janie to kill him in self-defense, thus ending necessarily
life and love in the name of the possibility of more life again. The novel's
conclusion is at once an elegy and a vision of achieved peace, an intense
realization that indeed we are all asleep in the outer life:

> The day of the gun, and the bloody body, and the courthouse came
> and commenced to sing a sobbing sigh out of every corner in the
> room; out of each and every chair and thing. Commenced to sing,

commenced to sob and sigh, singing and sobbing. Then Tea Cake came prancing around her where she was and the song of the sigh flew out of the window and lit in the top of the pine trees. Tea Cake, with the sun for a shawl. Of course he wasn't dead. He could never be dead until she herself had finished feeling and thinking. The kiss of his memory made pictures of love and light against the wall. Here was peace. She pulled in her horizon like a great fish-net. Pulled it from around the waist of the world and draped it over her shoulder. So much of life in its meshes! She called in her soul to come and see.

IV

Hurston herself was refreshingly free of all the ideologies that currently obscure the reception of her best book. Her sense of power has nothing in common with politics of any persuasion, with contemporary modes of feminism, or even with those questers who search for a black aesthetic. As a vitalist, she was of the line of the Wife of Bath and Sir John Falstaff and Mynheer Peeperkorn. Like them, she was outrageous, heroically larger than life, witty in herself and the cause of wit in others. She belongs now to literary legend, which is as it should be. Her famous remark in response to Carl Van Vechten's photographs is truly the epigraph to her life and work: "I love myself when I am laughing. And then again when I am looking mean and impressive." Walt Whitman would have delighted in that as in her assertion: "When I set my hat at a certain angle and saunter down Seventh Avenue . . . the cosmic Zora emerges. . . . How can any deny themselves the pleasure of my company? It's beyond me." With Whitman, Hurston herself is now an image of American literary vitality, and a part also of the American mythology of exodus, of the power to choose the party of Eros, of more life.

DEBORAH G. PLANT

The Folk Preacher and Folk Sermon Form in Zora Neale Hurston's Dust Tracks on a Road

"I had been pitched head foremost into the Baptist Church when I was born. I had heard the singing the preaching and prayers. They were a part of me" (*Dust Tracks*, pp. 206–207).

No matter how much she rubbed her head against college walls or how cosmopolitan her perceptions became, Zora Neale Hurston remained a part of the religious folk tradition into which she was born. Her father a traveling Baptist minister, her mother the superintendent of the Sunday School, and her community a group of faithful church-goers, Hurston was indelibly impressed with the beliefs and practices of the Afro-American Southern Baptist religious tradition. Many of the characteristics of that tradition, particularly of the folk preacher and the folk sermon, are to be found not only in Hurston's fiction and in her nonfiction essays but also in her autobiography. The persona in *Dust Tracks on a Road* is akin to the folk preacher, and the narrative is comparable to the folk sermon. Hurston's knowledge and understanding of the sermon are perhaps to be expected. However, it is significant that her use of sermonic form and rhetoric was not restricted to her fiction or limited to academic discussions of the preacher but was also used to structure her own ideas and inform her own socio-political writings. For, as Larry Neale states in his profile on the author, Hurston had considered the folk preacher as Afro-America's "only true poet," an authoritative and forceful

Folklore Forum, Volume 21, Number 1 (1988): pp. 3–19. © 1988 Folklore Forum / CCC.

wielder of words (1974: 162). So it is utterly significant that Hurston's narrative voice is in many ways analogous to that of the folk preacher, a powerful
individual.

In general, the folk preacher, usually male, is part of the folk community
whose ethos he has internalized. He must possess oratorical abilities which are
derived from the community. But as Hurston points out in a letter to James
Weldon Johnson, oratorical skills are not enough. The preacher must have
and be able to effectively display histrionic skills.[1] Johnson echoes Hurston's
conclusions in his preface to *God's Trombones:* "The old-time Negro preacher
of parts was above all an orator, and in good measure an actor" (1927: 5).
Hurston's writings are infused with an oral quality which speaks to the reader.
In *Dust Tracks,* she makes use of various examples of oratory derived from
the community. Like the folk preacher, she tells stories, folktales, and jokes
and also gives renditions of prayers and sermons. More often than not, these
examples of oratory are dramatically cast; settings are described, characters
speak in dialogue, and the dialogue sets forth much of the action. Her renditions are nothing less than a "performance."

Hurston's use of folk materials is not only traditional, but it also serves
an important purpose. As Arna Bontemps points out in his introduction
to *The Book of Negro Folklore,* "The Negro preacher has had a vital role, not
the least important of which has been the awakening and encouragement
of folk expression" (Hughes and Bontemps 1958: xiii). As a collector of
Afro-American folklore, Hurston celebrated and encouraged the use of
Black folk expression. She also worked to see the songs and dances she
collected dramatized and concertized: for, like the preacher of God's word,
she "resolved to make them known to the world."

The lore Hurston presents in *Dust Tracks* is also characteristically humorous. She believes, as does the folk preacher, that humor is a vital part
of the folk community. And any representative of "the people" must have a
sense of humor. Bontemps writes that the preacher had to be entertaining
and "comic when comedy was needed" (xii). A good sense of humor made
the preacher "one of the folk," but he must also be authoritative. His role as
shepherd of the flock also required him to teach, inform, admonish, and lead
his congregation as well as inspire and uplift them. "What he gave, and what
they picked up was hope, confidence, a will to survive" (xiii).

The characteristics which are considered attributes of the folk preacher—
and of Hurston—could describe any leader within the folk community. Oratorical skills—a good straining voice, histrionics, and humor—are not exclusively ministerial attributes. The one important attribute which distinguishes
the folk preacher from the civic leader is that the folk preacher's authority to
lead is derived from God and is affirmed or denied by the church. He must
receive "the call," the divine summons. Like her characters, John Pearson in

Jonah's Gourd Vine, and Moses in *Moses, Man of the Mountain,* and like most folk preachers, the narrator in *Dust Tracks* also receives the divine call. Receiving the call is a complicated phenomenon. It entails visions and conversions, confusion and resistance to the call, suffering, and finally conviction and/or acceptance. We can better see Hurston's use of these conventions by comparing her story of visions and conversions to that of actual preachers in Bruce Rosenberg's *The Art of the American Folk Preacher* and in Langston Hughes' and Arna Bontemps' *The Book of Negro Folklore.*

Rosenberg interviewed several Baptist preachers and noted their response to "the call":

> According to the clergymen I interviewed, the calling to the church comes from God. There is no other way. In nearly all instances, as with [the Reverends] Lacy, Brown, and McDowell the calling comes against the will of the preacher. On one occasion Lacy said that he did not want to preach when he first felt the spirit of God come to him, and he resisted for many years.... He says a voice came to him then and said, "The next time it will be death...."
>
> Lacy tells another story about a friend who was deathly ill and who called out, "God if you spare me I'll do what you want, and become a preacher." God did and the man kept his promise. (1970: 22–3)

In *The Book of Negro Folklore,* one preacher testified that in seeking God he spent "seasons at fasting and praying." But it was only when God called him that he began to change. "God started on me when I was a little boy"; then God "began to show me things":

> Once while I was sick I saw in a vision three people and one was a woman. They looked at me and said, "He is sick." The woman said, "I can cure him." So speaking she took out a little silver vial, held it before me and vanished ... (1958: 258)

After his visions, God directed him to "Go preach my Gospel."

In *Dust Tracks,* Zora Neale Hurston attests to similar experiences. After running out of her yard to avoid punishment for a childish prank, Hurston writes that she came to a vacant house where she experienced her visions.

> I had not thought of stopping there when I ... set out, but I saw a big raisin lying on the porch and stopped to eat it. I sat and soon I was asleep in a strange way. Like clear stereopticon slides, I saw twelve scenes flash before me, each one held until I had seen it well

in every detail, and then be replaced by another. . . . I knew that they were all true, a preview of things to come, and my soul writhed in agony and shrunk away. . . . I did not wake up when the last one flickered and vanished, I merely sat up and saw the Methodist Church, the line of moss-draped oaks, and our strawberry patch stretching off to the left. (1984: 57)

Many of the motifs in Hurston's vision parallel those found in religious tradition: The eating of strange fruit, falling asleep, panoramic viewing of events, religiously symbolic numbers. The twelve scenes which flashed by may be symbolic of the twelve disciples or the twelve gates to the city. The assertion of the truth of the vision, the shrinking from it, and the return from extraordinary to ordinary scenes are part of religious tradition. As in the traditions of mystical literature, the call and the visions which accompany it come when the individual is alone, usually in some isolated environment. And these experiences usually begin in childhood. "I do not know when the visions began," Hurston writes. "Certainly I was not more than seven years old, but I remember the first coming very distinctly" (56). Her visions occurred for an extended period of time. And like the preacher, she resisted the "call" implicit in them.

> I was weighed down with a power I did not want. I had knowledge before its time. I knew my fate. . . . Often I was in some lonesome wilderness, suffering strange things and agonies . . .
> I asked myself why me? Why? Why? A cosmic loneliness was my shadow. Nothing and nobody around me really touched me. (57, 60)

Nevertheless, the author writes,

> Oh, how I cried to be just as everybody else! But the voice said No. I must go where I was sent. The weight of the Commandment laid heavy and made me moody at times. I would hope that the call would never come again. But even as I hoped I knew that the cup meant for my lips would not pass. I must drink the bitter drink. (59)

In the latter passage, the author acknowledges the voice and decides she must heed it. Like most Afro-American preachers and laypersons, she compares herself to Christ. Weighed down with the sins of the world and facing crucifixion Christ prays for deliverance, but at the same time accepts his fate, saying, "Father, if thou be willing, remove this cup from me: nevertheless not my will, but thine, be done" (Luke 22:42 King James version). Shortly thereafter, Jesus is tried and crucified, but arises to a new life. The author also considers all she had to suffer as trials. The end of her trials would bring the beginning of a new life for her. The anonymous preacher in *Negro Folklore* suggests that the trials or temptations of those who are called are an instance of God's way of purifying an individual and bringing her or him to conviction and conversion—to a new life in Christ (Hughes and Bontemps, 1958: 260).

Hurston's visions foretold both her trials and subsequent new life.

> I knew that I would be an orphan and homeless. I knew that while I was still helpless, that the comforting circle of my family would be broken, and that I would have to wander cold and friendless until I had served my time. . . . There was no turning back. . . . And last of all, I would come to a big house. Two women waited there for me. . . . When I had come to these women, then I would be at the end of my pilgrimage, but not the end of my life. Then I would know peace and love and what goes with these things and not before. (1984: 57–58)

The two women who would signify the author's "resurrection" are not unlike the women in the preacher's vision who said, "He is sick. . . . I can cure him."

This preacher's visions, however, did not prevent his continual participation in "worldly ways" before finally submitting himself to the call and God's directions. The Reverend Lacy likewise resisted complete submission until he was threatened by death. And in spite of Hurston's trials as accounted in *Dust Tracks*, she, too, did not completely submit to the call until she was threatened with death. And like Reverend Lacy's friend, she made a bet with God. Hurston writes that her illness of appendicitis required her to have an operation immediately.

> When I was taken up to the amphitheatre for the operation I went up there placing a bet with God. I did not fear death. . . . But I bet God that if I lived, I would try to find out the vague directions whispered in my ears and find the road it seemed that I must follow. How? When? Why? What? All those answers were hidden from me. . . .
>
> I scared the doctor and the nurses by not waking up until nine o'clock that night, but otherwise I was all right. I was alive, so I had to win my bet with God. (pp. 145–146)

This impending death Hurston describes served as a catalyst to recall her earlier experiences, renew her commitment to the call, and reconsider its portents. Her bet with God and her earlier determination to heed "the Commandment" and go where she was sent indicate her belief that God had some specific task for her. She was to suffer but not in vain. Her suffering would lead her not only to peace and love, but it would also strengthen her and lead her in directions which were not yet clear.

It is important to note that Hurston does not write that she sought her visions through "fasting and praying." They came to her unsought. In her essay titled "Conversions and Visions" in *The Sanctified Church*, she writes,

> The vision is a very definite part of Negro religion. It almost always accompanies conversion. It almost always accompanies the call to preach. In the conversion the vision is sought. The individual goes forth into waste places and by fasting and prayer induces the vision. . . . The call to preach is altogether external. The vision seeks the man. Punishment follows if he does not heed the call, or until he answers.
>
> In conversion, then, we have the cultural pattern of the person seeking the vision and inducing it by isolation and fasting. In the call to preach we have the involuntary vision—the call seeking the man. (1983: 85–87)

The visions in *Dust Tracks* do not seem to be intended to structure the work as Robert Hemenway suggests in his critical biography of Hurston (1977: 282–283). As the various uses of sermonic rhetoric in her works show, Hurston knew the forms and formulae, the why and wherefore of religious practices too well to use them totally unaware. Rather, the visions seem to serve to identify the author as a special individual who, in the latter part of the narrative sermon, realizes the destiny the visions portend. As a point of reference which serves to describe and explain the author and her "success," the visions never become "insignificant" as Hemenway suggests (282). For success in *Dust Tracks* has less to do with achievement in the Anglo-American sense of the term than it has to do with the Afro-American goal of equality and freedom. This the author achieves—if only in her autobiography. The visions, then, become a point of departure for the author, as folk preacher—a rite of passage into a less restricting and oppressive existence. As the last vision indicated, the author would have more positive experiences. She writes that the passing of the last vision brought the commencement of her professional career. It was one avenue to her goal of equality and freedom. The woman in the vision, declared to be Mrs. Osgood Mason, had "the key to certain phases of my life . . . in her hand" (1984: 309). The key was the financial support she needed to get her folklore collecting expedition and her career—her personal liberation—under way.

Hurston writes that she was not sure what the vague directions were that God whispered in her ear. Given the directions she took after her illness, it appears she interpreted the whispers as saying she must continue to struggle to formally educate herself and to go where those roads would lead her. One road seems to have been her career as anthropologist and folklorist; another, her career as an ethnographic writer. It is as a writer, specifically, that Hurston speaks again of the voice to which she responds. In the discussion of her writings in the chapter titled "Books and Things," she alludes to a mystical voice—"the force from somewhere in Space"— which commands her and again gives her no choice but to become a literary artist (pp. 212–213).

II

Zora Neale Hurston professes a divine inspiration which recalls the Biblical writers who are said to have been inspired by God. "You take up the pen when you are told, and write what is commanded" (213). *Dust Tracks* then, is a sacred text, a sermon. On this basis, any of Hurston's texts could be considered "sacred." However, *Dust Tracks* is a special case in that, first of all, it is not intended as fiction but as "truth," as are Biblical texts. And whatever the factual truths may be about the events in *Dust Tracks*, the narrative intentionally represents the author as one who was, like the Biblical prophets, called by God and whose experiences compare with those associated with the Biblical prophets.

As sacred text, *Dust Tracks* shares some of the same characteristics as the folk sermon. Bruce Rosenberg explains that the Biblical text of the sermon is read first and is followed by the context, a prosaic explanation of the text. Then the message the preacher derives from that text is preached and/ or chanted.[2] Hurston's title essay, "The Sanctified Church," demonstrates that she understood well the format of the chanted sermon. In "The Sermon," also in *The Sanctified Church,* she transcribes a sermon wherein the spoken part (text and context) is designated and the chanted part is noted by its metrical delineations (1983: 95–102). As with all oral performances which are written down, the sermon loses some of its distinguishing features which depend upon the dynamics between speaker and audience-folk preacher and congregation. Nevertheless, some aspects of those dynamics are noted or otherwise implied. For instance, the rhythm of the preacher's delivery is suggested by the poetic delineation, and the written "Ha!" of the preacher serves to indicate the audible breathing which is an integral part of the oral performance.

The sermonic structure and other characteristic features of the sermon, such as those discussed above, are found in the *Dust Tracks* narrative. As that of a chosen prophet, Hurston's life is itself an implied text, an actualization of God's work. The context, which explains and describes that life, is given in chapters one through eleven. The doctrine derived from those chapters and applied to everyday affairs is "preached" in chapters twelve through fifteen, the more controversial chapters in the autobiography. The final chapter serves as a cooling down from the fervor of the latter chapters and as a testimonial of personal salvation and fellowship. In comparing *Dust Tracks* to the folk sermon, I do not suggest that *Dust Tracks* follows in every respect the folk sermon form, nor that it was intended to. Some of the elements which characterize the folk sermon are intentionally introduced in the narrative, yet others seem to be more a consequence of psycholinguistic phenomena wherein internalized language structures are revealed in the speaker's performance. It is not obvious that Hurston intended to write a sermon, but because so many sermonic features characterize the narrative, it is obvious that the author's internalization of religious ritual, specifically that of the sermon, has in fact influenced the structure and tone of the autobiography.

Ecclesiastical and Biblical diction are some of the linguistic aspects of *Dust Tracks* which are indicative of ways in which the folk sermon influences the narrative. These aspects are most obvious in the chapter on religion, but they appear consistently throughout the narrative. "God," "Old Maker," the "Devil," "congregations," and "multitudes" are but a few examples of the ecclesiastical terminology which pervades the work. Phrases and sentences of Biblical diction and allusion are also abundant: "king of kings" (170); "Strange things must have looked out of my eyes like Lazarus after his resurrection" (117); "Just because my mouth opens up like a prayer book, it does not just have to flap like a Bible" (265); "He could not sing like Peter, and he could not preach like Paul" (276).

Although folk sermons are usually based on a Biblical text and sometimes rely on extended Biblical passages to support the preacher's explication or interpretation of the opening text, the complex syntax and grammar of the Bible is not characteristic of the sermon as a whole. In syntax, grammar, and vocabulary, the folk sermon is simple. *Dust Tracks*, too, is stylistically uncomplicated—on the surface. *Dust Tracks* is written in the language of the folk. Hurston addresses her audience in the vernacular. And the metaphors, similes, aphorisms, and proverbs which render folk expressions poetic and folk sermons dynamic are an integral and significant part of the narrative. They allow for the creation of such poetic passages as this one:

> The Master-Maker in His making had made Old Death. Made him with big feet and square toes. Made him with a face that reflects the face of all things, but neither changes itself, nor is mirrored anywhere. Made the body of Death out of infinite hunger. Made a weapon for his hand to satisfy his needs. This was the morning of the day of the beginning of things. (1984: 87)

This passage, cast in Biblical expression, imagery, allusion, and rhetoric, conjures up a picture of God, the creator, ironically creating death, as opposed to life, on the first day. The passage is also representative of narrative and dramatic exempla, which are important sermonic features (Rosenberg 1970: 47).[3] The two working together serve to intensify the poetic quality. The narrative exampla tell a story about the creation of death. The dramatic exempla enumerate death's descriptions and duties, thereby heightening the narrative and dramatic effect. Both the narrative and dramatic exempla create a rhetorical schema, which, on the one hand, allows the preacher flexibility in creating a story and buys him time to consider his next lines. And on the other, it allows the preacher to set up poetic structures, establishing a basic rhythm which leads him to chant his sermon.

The drama created by such sermonic stylistics is further intensified by the militant action of the Old Testament. As the Reverend John J. Jasper said in his sermon, "De Sun do Move," "de God of peace is also de man of war" (Hughes and Bontemps, 1958: 228). This affinity to Old Testament action and militancy is also seen in *Dust Tracks.* The author writes that she preferred the Old Testament to the New. In the Old Testament she found the kind of action she liked, and she admired the Biblical David, who was symbolic of that action. Locked in her mother's room after "a licking one afternoon," she turned her attention to the Bible—"the only thing in there for me to read."

> I happened to open to the place where David was doing some mighty smiting, and I got interested. David went here and he went there, and no matter where he went, he smote 'em hip and thigh. Then he sung songs to his harp awhile, and went out and smote some more. Not one time did David stop and preach about sins and things. All David wanted to know from God was who to kill and when. He took care of the other details himself. Never a quiet moment. I liked him a lot. (1984: 54–55)

The author portrays herself as a righteous militant akin to David. Inspired by the old White man of her childhood, who is depicted in the manner of an Old Testament prophet, to "tell the truth and then if you have to ... fight." She is always ready, like David, to "stand and give battle" (41, 21).

III

As Rosenberg's work shows and as Hurston's analyses of traditional church services in *The Sanctified Church* imply, the folk preacher's delivery is basically spontaneous and sometimes extemporaneous. But even with the varied rhetorical strategies at hand and sometimes because of them, the folk preacher generally moves from point to point in more of an associational pattern as opposed to a strict linear progression. This movement and attention to the audience account for the discursive nature of the sermon. Rosenberg writes that in the orally presented prose sermon, "logical development from sentence to sentence occurs more frequently than in chanted sermons . . ." (1970: 10). He writes that "it is in the nature of sermons to use examples, proverbs, parables, etc.," and that the "welding together [of] such illustrative materials with set passages and phrases" often defies a consistent "principle of organization" (33). In *Images of the Preacher in Afro-American Literature*, Walter C. Daniel suggests that it is this "irrational structure" of the sermon which authenticates it (1981: 50). But what appears to be illogical or irrational in the sermon is usually only superficially illogical or irrational. Rosenberg states that there is generally a specific theme, sometimes a single line of scripture, on which the sermon is based. "That single line may be expanded in many ways" (1970: 34). (In *Dust Tracks*, the main theme is self-empowerment, and the varied, seemingly contradictory ideas set forth in the narrative are instances of the author's expansion upon that theme.) The associational nature of the sermon allows for flexibility and for digression. But even the digressions are recognized sermonic features and are an integral part of the folk sermon. An apparent "principle of organization" is less important than the form and the effect of religious ceremony. Hurston explains in *The Sanctified Church* that "Beneath the seeming informality of religious worship there is a set formality. Sermons, prayers, moans and testimonies have their definite forms" (1983: 83).

James Weldon Johnson describes the sermon as "a progression of rhythmic words" (1927:5). Beginning in prose, it gradually progresses to chant and an emotional climax which frequently culminates in song, then recedes to a calm summary of message, testimonial, or extension of fellowship. The unfolding of the *Dust Tracks* narrative parallels the overall rhythmic pattern of the sermon as Johnson describes it. Chapters one through eleven are basically prosaic, though some passages are characteristic of the chant. Chapters twelve through fifteen have more of the emotional fervor which accompanies the chant, and chapter sixteen is the cooling down.

The rhythm of the chant depends on the talent and style of the preacher. In *Dust Tracks*, the rhythm is indicated by the author's diction, syntax, and sentence structure. Several passages are suggestive of the rhythm of the chanted sermon, but some more closely approximate the chant. For instance, note the rhythm of this passage and the characteristic sermonic expletive which punctuates it. Also, note the narrative and dramatic exempla and the characteristic sermonic "and." (This passage appears in traditional paragraph form in the narrative. Here, I have rendered it in suggestive metrical delineation):

The primeval in me leaped to life. Ha!
This was the very corn I wanted to grind. Fight!
Not having to put up with what she did to us through Papa!
Direct action and everything up to me.

. . .

I wanted her blood,
and plenty of it.
That is the way I went into the fight,
and that is the way I fought it. (1984: 101–102)

The following passage, also rendered in suggestive metrical delineation, is representative of an extended passage in "Research" (pp. 179–183) which is indicative of the fusion of chant and song, an essential aspect of the sermonic performance. It focuses on "Polk County," describing the work and work-songs, the play and pleasure of the women and men who work on the railroad or at the saw-mill and turpentine jobs in the day and who tell tales, sing songs, and dance, drink, and fight in the jooks at night. The songs of the workers and the mood of the place mingle and blend with the narrative voice to create a dramatic pastiche of chant and song. Often the preacher takes up the words and melody of a song and makes it an integral part of the performance, creating the antiphonal or call-and-response aspect of the sermon (Rosenberg 1970: 39). This is obviously the case as the narrative voice in this passage chants and/or sings lines which are influenced by folk songs collected in the text. The passage is punctuated with the sermonic expletives of "Polk County!" and "Hah!"; and the narrative passage tends to take on the fervor and tone of the songs recorded:

Polk County. The clang of nine-pound hammers on
railroad steel. The world must ride.
Hah! A rhythmic swing of the body, hammer falls,
and another spike driven to the head in the tie.
Oh, Mobile! Hank!
Oh, Alabama! Hank!
Oh, Fort Myers! Hank!
Oh, in Florida! Hank!
Oh, let's shake it! Hank!
Oh, let's break it! Hank!
Oh, just a hair! Hank!
The singing-liner cuts short his chant. The strawboss relaxes with a gesture of his hand. Another rail spike down. Another offering to the soul of civilization whose other name is travel. (Hurston 1984: 180–181)

The chants creates the rhythm of the sermon, and the rhythm is reinforced by repetition. "Repetition not only comforts, of course, but it adds to
the mounting emotional intensity nearly as much as does rhythm." Repetition
aids the folk preacher in formulating the next line. And because of the time
pressure, "he is more inclined to build his narrative in patterns of sequences,
known as the parallelism of oral style. . . . Idea builds upon idea. Image builds
upon image as a series of incremental repetitions increases in emotional pitch"
(Rosenberg 1970: 106). Parallelism is evident in the Polk County passage
cited above and is nicely illustrated in this passage, rendered in suggestive
metrical delineation:

> He predicted dire things for me . . . .
> I was going to be hung before I got grown
> Somebody was going to blow me down for my sassy tongue.
> Mama was going to suck sorrow for not beating
>   my temper out of me before it was too late.
> Posses with ropes and guns were going to drag me out
>   sooner or later
>   on account of that stiff neck I toted.
> I was going to tote a hungry belly
>   by reason of my forward ways. (Hurston 1984: 21)

These parallel clusters are what Rosenberg describes as formulaic systems which the preacher draws on to facilitate his delivery as well as to
illuminate and explicate his subject and create, by association, new clusters
or formulae (1970: 108–109). These formulaic systems are apparent in *Dust
Tracks;* so also are the formulae of stock phrases and themes, which are
largely memorized. They may or may not be original formulations. Some
may be borrowed from a text, from other preachers, or from tradition.
And they may also be frequently repeated—exactly or in near approximation—within a given sermon as well as in other sermons of the same
preacher (Rosenberg 1970: 51). This intertextual quality of stock formulae
is also prevalent in the *Dust Tracks* narrative. There are many narrative formulae which characterize oral art. But what distinguishes those peculiar
to folk sermons are their ecclesiastical and Biblical nature. For instance,
the phrase "from the earliest rocking of my cradle" is usually uttered in
traditional folk prayers, as this excerpt from a traditional prayer shows: ". . .
You have been with me from the earliest rocking of my cradle up until this
present moment. You know our hearts, our Father, And all de ranges of our
deceitful minds . . ." (Hurston 1935: 27). Though this phraseology and others like it are colloquial, it is the context in which these phrases are uttered
which make them of the church. Hurston uses this phrase, not only in the

Dust Tracks narrative, but in her other works as well. In the narrative, she writes, "From the earliest rocking of my cradle days, I have heard this cry [My People! My People!] go up from Negro lips" (1984: 215). "My heart beneath my knees and my knees in some lonesome valley" is also from traditional folk prayers. The narrator uses this phrase in *Dust Tracks* to describe her mood after her unfruitful folklore collecting trip: "Considering the mood of my going South, I went back to New York with my heart beneath my knees and my knees in some lonesome valley" (175). "Often I was in some lonesome wilderness" (60); "I had always thought I would be in some lone, arctic wasteland" (115); and "My knees dragged the basement of Hell" (323) are all variations of the same phrase and mood.

Such phrases are essentially rhetorical. Those which are more thematic are more consistent and prominent throughout the text and throughout Hurston's work as a whole. They subtly underscore and reinforce the major theme in the Dust Tracks sermon as well as in Hurston's other works: self-empowerment, a theme basic to the Afro-American (religious) tradition. "Zig-zag lightning and grumbling thunder," "with sword in hand," and "I stood on the mountain" are stock phrases symbolic of stock themes which figure significantly in Hurston's work and in folk sermons based on the Old Testament. They each suggest metaphors symbolic of strength and power. "Zig-zag lightning-thunder" phrases occur most frequently in *Dust Tracks,* and they also occur in contexts wherein power or strength is the subject. For example, "You, who play the zig-zag lightning of power over the world, with the grumbling thunder in your wake, think kindly of those who walk in the dust" (286). And, "Papa thundered, 'Get up and take dat young 'un outdoors! . . . If I hear one grumble, I'll . . . bust de hide on you!'" (pp. 98–99). Significantly, Hurston writes that during her initiation as hoodoo priestess, she had "strange exalted dreams": "In one, I strode across the heavens with lightning flashing from under my feet, and grumbling thunder following in my wake" (191). In this ceremony, she writes, "The symbol of lightning was painted on my back. This was to be mine forever" (192).[4]

Phrases featuring the sword also occur in contexts dealing with power and strength. Allusion is made to Constantine who started "out on his missionary journey with his sword" (275). More importantly, Hurston uses this symbolic phrase in reference to herself: "I am in the struggle with the sword in my hands"; and, "I am still in there tussling with the sword in my hand" (280). The sword is symbolic of battle and the spirit of struggle. The mountain is symbolic of strength and endurance. They both combine in this statement to signify the author's sense of self-empowerment: ". . . I have stood on the peaky mountain wrapped in rainbows, with a harp and a sword in my hands." The phrase imaging the mountain is most prominent in *Moses, Man of the Mountain*. In *Moses* and in the *Dust Tracks* passage, the mountain symbolizes

Moses' and Hurston's strength, power, and endurance. This image, along with the symbolic images of lightning and thunder, imply their likeness to God.

IV

The "message" in *Dust Tracks* is that individualism and achievement are the avenues to self-empowerment.[5] Each chapter in the narrative emphasizes these values, and the focus is on the individual. The author, as folk preacher, requires the individual to look to self, follow the "inner urge," and work for what one wants. She remonstrates against Afro-Americans for "crying" about their condition and praying about it when the "powers that need to be brought into exertion is within" them.[6] Hurston suggests that her people follow her example: "I do not pray. I accept the means at my disposal for working out my destiny" (278). The power for change is individual and internal. The author strongly argues these beliefs in the chapters "My People! My People!" and "Religion." Further, she argues that in order to achieve individual power, it is necessary for Afro-Americans to renounce the past of slavery and Reconstruction, as sinners had to renounce their worldly ways, and "settle for from now on" (284). Unencumbered by history, they, like she, could work, struggle, and direct their own destiny. They could be free and autonomous.

In the last chapter, "Looking Things Over," Hurston ends with a testimonial to the faith of individualism and an extension of fellowship to friend and foe. In the characteristic role of the preacher who chides the congregation for their pretension and hypocrisy, she warns her congregation against the vice of race prejudice while simultaneously offering them the salvation of individualism as she has experienced it. And she extends the hand of fellowship to both Blacks and Whites alike: "So I give you all my right hand of fellowship and love, and hope for the same from you. . . . Let us all be kissing-friends," she implores (286). This act of fellowship is another formality of the Afro-American religious folk tradition. Personal testimony and the extension of fellowship are typical folk sermon closures. It is also a ritual characteristic of the "Love Feast" or "Experience Meeting," a meeting held either the Friday night or the Sunday morning before Communion. Since no one is supposed to take communion unless he or she is in harmony with all other members, there are great protestations of love and friendship. It is an opportunity to reaffirm faith plus anything the imagination might dictate" (pp. 266–267).

The supplication that we all be "kissing-friends" may well be, in fact, only a protestation dictated by Hurston's imagination. Though she may play on her harp like David, she also stands on the mountain with a sword in hand. And like David, she is prepared for battle. Hurston, in this instance of unctuous peroration, is typical of early Afro-American folk preachers who disguised their radical ideologies and revolutionary tendencies with the cloak of peaceful religious contentment. Though their masked rage sometimes gave way to open rebellion, it more often found recourse in "the same subtle use of suggestion and innuendo as we find in spirituals. . . . Subterfuge, sabotage, fraud, trickery, foot-dragging and other behavior patterns of resistance were insinuated into the daily intercourse with white people in the guise of stupidity and obsequiousness, as a tactic of simple survival" (Wilmore 69, 73). Survival is necessary if struggle is to continue and freedom is to be won. In the *Dust Tracks* sermon, the author, as folk preacher, exhorts the values of individualism and achievement as essential to the struggle for freedom and equality.

Dust Tracks has been described as rambling, roving, erratic, confused, and chaotic—adjectives often used to describe folk sermons. Whether viewed as an autobiographical narrative or an autobiographical sermon, and regardless of the author's conscious and unconscious narrative choices, *Dust Tracks*, like the sermon, is a unified work with a unitary voice. It is a projection of the author's coherent point of view and her concerted intention to realize it: a point of view which advocates defiance, self-empowerment, and self-determination.

Notes

1. Larry Neale quotes from Hurston's letter in his article (162).

2. Rosenberg distinguishes the chanted sermon, the kind of sermon Afro-American folk preachers deliver, from the nonchanted one. In the former, the preacher abandons the text and is taken over by the spirit. The sermon at this point becomes chanted and poetic. In the latter, the sermon is basically "orally presented prose" and is characterized by its conversational oratory and conversational, non-chanted, speech (pp. 9–10).

3. In "Characteristics of Negro Expression," Hurston's discussion distinguishing characteristics of storytelling and religious expression suggests a stylistic difference between narrative and dramatic exempla. She writes, "In storytelling 'so' is universally the connective. It is used even as an introductory word, at the very beginning of a story. In religious expression 'and' is used. The trend in stories is to state conclusions; in religion, to enumerate" (68). (This article originally appeared in *Negro: An Anthology;* Nancy Cunard, editor. My source is *The Sanctified Church.*) Although the quoted passage has features of both exempla, it tends to be more characteristic of the dramatic exempla of religious expression. The omission of the connective "and's" in this instance is perhaps a consequence of the author's conforming to the stylistics of written composition.

4. Hurston's account of her induction into the hoodoo priesthood is most significant. It is not only another indication and actualization of her self-empowerment, but it also marks her as a religious leader. Gayraud Wilmore explains that the Afro-American folk preacher evolved from African priests who practiced conjure. "Actually, not a few of them were among the shipments of slaves from Dahomey and Togo, and it is they who must have formed the original cadres out of which the earliest Black preachers . . . began to emerge as the leaders of the slave society" (23). These Black preachers, as "conjure-men" or "Voodoo doctors," used their powers to inspire slaves to resistance and revolt. "Whenever we find [Voodoo] converging

with pneumatascopic elements in Black religion in America, as in the earliest days, we can expect to find a militant, religiously inspired rejection of white values and white control" (29). Wilmore's ideas are evident in *Dust Tracks* and even more so in *Moses* where the author has cast Moses in the role of the greatest conjure man who ever lived.

   5. These ideas are based in part on Marion Kilson's essay, "The Transformation of Eatonville's Ethnographer." She writes: "Despite alterations in literary form and perspective, two fundamental value orientations underlay all Hurston's writing: an emphasis on individualism and an orientation towards achievement" (112).

   6. From Reference C.L. Franklin's sermon, "Moses at the Red Sea," in Rosenberg (pp. 107–108).

WORKS CITED

Daniel, Walter C. *Images of the Preacher in Afro-American Literature*. Washington, D.C.: University Press of America, 1981.

Hemenway, Robert E. *Zora Neale Hurston, a Literary Biography*. Urbana: University of Illinois Press, 1977.

Hughes, Langston and Arna Bontemps. *The Book of Negro Folklore*. New York: Dodd, Mead & Co., 1958 [1983].

Hurston, Zora Neale. *Jonah's Gourd Vine*. Philadelphia: Lippincott, 1934.

———. *Mules and Men*. Bloomington: Indiana University Press, 1978 [1935].

———. *The Sanctified Church*. Berkeley: Turtle Island, 1983.

———. *Moses, Man of the Mountain*. Urbana: University of Illinois Press, 1984 [1939].

———. *Dust Tracks on a Road, An Autobiography*, edited by Robert E. Hemenway. 2nd edition. Urbana: University of Illinois Press, 1984 [1942].

Johnson, James Weldon. *God's Trombones, Seven Negro Sermons in Verse*. New York: Viking, 1927.

Kilson, Marion. "The Transformation of Eatonville's Ethnographer." *Phylon* 33 (1972): 112–119.

Neale, Larry. "A Profile: *Zora Neale Hurston*." *Southern Exposure* 1 (1974): 160–168.

Rosenberg, Bruce. *The Art of the American Folk Preacher*. New York: Oxford University Press, 1970.

Wilmore, Gayraud S. *Black Religion and Black Radicalism*. Garden City, New York: Doubleday, 1972.

DANIEL J. SUNDAHL

Zora Neale Hurston: A Voice of Her Own/ An Entertainment In Herself

But our humanity is our burden, our life; we need not battle for it; we need only to do what is infinitely more difficult—that is, accept it. The failure of the protest novel lies in its rejection of life, the human being, the denial of his beauty, dread, power, in its insistence that it is his categorization alone which is real and which cannot be transcended.

—James Baldwin, "Everybody's Protest Novel"

A word, first of all, needs to be said about this title. When Zora Neale Hurston wrote her introduction to her collection of Negro folklore, *Mules and Men,* she rejected the proletarian motives of most black writers of her time. The theory behind her tactics: "If I had exalted myself . . . somebody would have sent me word in a match-box that I had been up North there and had rubbed the hair off of my head against some college wall, and then come back there with a lot of form and fashion, and outside show to the world. But they'd stand flat-footed and tell me that they didn't have me, neither my sham-polish to study 'bout. And that would have been that."[1]

Hurston suggests that her literary proving ground was formed from standards other than the "sham-polish" standards of social propaganda writers. Looking at the sparse range of misdirected responses to her work, one cannot fail to notice that the criticism was determined by an insufficient understanding of Hurston's own motives.

Southern Studies: An Interdisciplinary Journal of the South, Volume 1, Number 3 (Fall 1990): pp. 243–255. © 1990 Southern Studies / Northwestern.

In 1936 Hurston's *Mules and Men* aroused the attention of Sterling Brown, who was less than certain about the book's value as a portrait of black life in the South. It was authentically done, but the picture of the South was incomplete; missing were the acts of terrorism, the misery and exploitation. Brown objected to Hurston's "socially unconscious" characters, whose lives were "made to appear easy-going and carefree."[2] Where was the smoldering resentment, more characteristic of Southern black life? He concluded that *Mules and Men* should have been more bitter; it would portray a more truthful picture and serve a more beneficial purpose.

Hurston's South, though, was vastly different than the South demanded by Brown. Her Southern landscape was not characterized by the psychological, existential, bitter ramifications of racial oppression and a black response to it; neither was her South a Faulknerian distillate of disharmony, disunity and despair over the black man's history, a history portraying black men and women as alien presences living on an absurd landscape. Hurston held a different point of view.

Her fiction, despite its lack of a deep, dark, racial wound, was an attempt to portray black, rural folk in such a way as to picture poetically a different category of Black Southern Literature. This different category was also the result of a different racial perspective, although it still required the expression of a genuine ethos for an ethnic culture that had been caricatured, as Larry Neal has suggested, "by the white minstrel tradition, made hokey and sentimental by the nineteenth-century local colorists, debased by the dialect poets, and finally made a 'primitive' aphrodisiac"[3] by the social anthropology of the twenties. Overall, her more human themes suggest that multi-ethnic literature must go beyond weeping, social documentary to laughter and tears.

> I was born in a Negro town. I do not mean by that the black-back-side of an average town. Eatonville, Florida is, and was at the time of my birth, a pure Negro town—charter, mayor, council, town marshall, and all. It was not the first Negro community in America, but it was the first attempt at organized self-government on the part of Negroes in America.
>
> Eatonville is what you might call hitting a straight lick with a crooked stick. The town was not in the original plan. It is a by-product of something else.[4]

This passage occurs early in the first chapter of her autobiography *Dust Tracks on a Road*, and is worth contemplating. The passage illustrates Hurston's awareness of the uniqueness of her experience, her oeuvre and the manner by which it placed her apart from the experiences of other black writers. She was free in a more personal way, and she took different liberties. In the chapter "Books and Things" she described that freedom and liberty thematically:

What I wanted to tell was the story about a man, and from what I had read and heard, Negroes were supposed to write about the Race Problem. I was and am thoroughly sick of the subject. My interest lies in what makes a man or a woman do such-and-so, regardless of his color. It seemed to me that human beings I met reacted pretty much to the same stimuli. Different idioms, yes. Circumstances and conditions having the power to influence, yes. Inherent difference, no.[5]

Hurston was also willing to allow the black, and in that sense, peculiar, character of her race to influence her work. In the chapter "My People! My People!" Hurston catalogs the class-consciousness of her race and the Negro's evaluation of himself:

Race Prejudice, I was instructed, was something bad that white people used on us. It seemed that white people felt superior to black ones and would not give Negroes justice for that reason. Race Pride was something that, if we had it, we would feel ourselves superior to whites. A black skin was the greatest honor that could be blessed on any man. . . . *Race Consciousness* is a plea to Negroes to bear their color in mind at all times. It was just a phrase to me when I was a child. I knew it was supposed to mean something, deep. By the time I got grown I saw that it was only an imposing line of syllables, for no Negro in America is apt to forget his race. . . . What fell into my ears from time to time tended more to confuse than to clarify. . . . It was the genius of the Negro which had invented the steam engine, the cotton gin, the airbrake, and numerous other things—but conniving white men had seen the Negro's inventions and run off and put them into practice before the Negro had a chance to do anything about it . . . but let some member of the community do or say something underhand; the verdict would be "Dat's just like a nigger!" or "Nigger from nigger leave nigger." It was not said in either admiration or pity. Utter scorn was in the saying. "Old Cuffy got to cut de fool, you know. Monkey see, monkey do. Nigger see de white man do something, he jump in and try to do like de white man, and make a great big old mess. My People! My People!"[6]

It is this connection with a consummate folk sensibility that gives Hurston's work a broader range of cultural vision, colloquial language and idiom. Hurston shies away from a depiction that takes its form by whittling and lopping human creatures down to what Baldwin terms "categorizations, life neatly fitted into pegs . . . moral, neatly framed, and incontestable like those improving mottoes sometimes found hanging on the walls of furnished rooms."[7]

There are ethnic American writers whose avowed aims are to bring greater freedom to the oppressed, the goal of society coming before the niceties of style and characterization. That does not mean the fiction is moribund or without merit, but with racial considerations motivating most of their work, they write chiefly about a segregated, ridiculed and exploited minority. Thus the fictional mosaic of Negro life in America is most frequently influenced by a racial temperament and minority group emphasis. The result often is, as Baldwin says again, that "we find ourselves bound, first without, then within, by the nature of our categorization. And escape is not effected through a bitter railing against this trap; it is as though this very striving were the only motion needed to spring the trap upon us."[8]

The great vitality in Hurston is the lack of categorization and bitter railing. Consequently, Hurston reinforces the unique sense of her black experience not only through characterization but through the niceties of style, while avoiding "life neatly fitted into pegs:" Perhaps naively, she ends *Dust Tracks on a Road* by saying "I have no race prejudice of any kind." She reduces the degree and manner of the problem by describing her own individual temper:

> My kinfolks and my "skin-folks" are dearly loved. My own circumference of everyday life is there. But I see the same virtues and vices everywhere I look. So I give you all my right hand of fellowship and love, and hope for the same from you. In my eyesight you lose nothing by not looking just like me. . . . Consider that with tolerance and patience, we godly demons may breed a noble world in a few hundred generations or so.[9]

Langston Hughes has said of Hurston's temperament: "Zora Neale Hurston was certainly the most amusing. . . . She was full of side-splitting anecdotes, humorous tales and tragi-comic stories, remembered out of her life in the South as a daughter of a travelling minister of God. She could make you laugh one minute and cry the next. To many of her white friends, no doubt, she was a perfect 'darkie,' in the nice meaning they give the term—that is a naive, childlike, sweet, and highly colored Negro."[10] Aside from Hurston's autobiographical uniqueness, she is still in decided contrast to the bulk of Southern and Harlem Renaissance artists, stopping at the point of renunciation, disillusion and self-exile from America. All of which might suggest that Hurston was more of an establishment writer with simplistic notions about race.

But Hurston's attitude toward race was simply nonpolemic, and running counter to the fervent attitudes of the 1930s. In the same chapter "My People! My People!" she writes: "This irritated me until I got to the place where I could analyze. The thing they were trying to do went wrong because it lacked reason. It lacked reason because they were trying to stand equal with the best in America without having the tools to work with. They were attempting a flight away from Negrodom because they felt that there was so much scorn for black skin in the nation that their only security was in flight. They lacked the happy carelessness of a class beneath them and the understanding of the top-flight Negro above them."[11]

Hurston's argument does not evade the ambiguity, hunger and disquieting complexity of the human self, a unique self that expresses itself as the explication of a character finding his way to an enlightened understanding. Where this human self is concerned, it is both the mortification of the flesh, and the unpredictable and indefinable human heart that lies at the center of Hurston's argument. Her narrative focus is on the process of a character's becoming rather than solely on the character's being. As for the characters themselves, she presents them without apology, and does not distinguish between "us" and "them." *Jonah's Gourd Vine*, for example, sets the standard for the bright stories that follow.

The plot of this first novel concerns the rise of an untutored, mulatto sharecropper-preacher, John "Buddy" Pearson, who marries the intelligent good woman, Lucy Potts, and begins his rise from the plantation in Macon County, Georgia to the church in Sanford, Florida. At crucial steps along the way, John Pearson backslides as a result of his susceptibility to feminine charms. Lucy suffers. After John moves the family to Sanford, he becomes the controversial pastor of Zion Hope. Lucy dies after bearing John many children. John is beaten down, loses his church as the result of a scandal and, in a most conclusive scene, is killed by absent-mindedly running a car into a train on his way back from yet one more liaison. At the funeral service his friends beat upon an ancient drum: "Not Kata-Kumba, the drum of triumph, that speaks of great ancestors and glorious wars. Not the little drum of kid-skin, for that is to dance with joy and to call to mind birth and creation, but O-go-doe, the voice of Death—that promises nothing, that speaks with tears only, and of the past." The final eulogy is spoken: "So at last the preacher wiped his mouth in the final way and said, 'He wuz uh man, and nobody knowed 'im but God; and it was ended in rhythm. With the mournful drumming of feet, and the mournful dance of the heads in rhythm, it was ended."[12]

Much of *Jonah's Gourd Vine* is devoted to Hurston's folk philosophy. There is a frequently repeated phrase: "Ah ain't got to do but two things—stay black and die." The relationship between blacks and whites is also explicit, as in this exchange:

> "What the news?"
> "Oh the white folks is still in the lead."[13]

Hurston also lets the social consciousness pass; her concern is still with the no-less-desperate struggle among the members of her own race, with envy impelling minor characters in *Jonah's Gourd Vine* to destroy John, the man on top.

Interest is also focused on the recreation of a particular and specified dialect and through that the particular and realized life of a Southern black man, removed from the world of overt racism, but struggling against the weaknesses of his nature—and losing. One *New York Times* reviewer praised the dialect which "does not seem to be merely the speech of a white man with the spelling distorted. Its essence lies rather in the rhythm and balance of the sentences, in the warm artlessness of the phrasing."[14]

Many of the superstitions, games, songs and cultural practices of the Florida Negro folks are also repeated in *Jonah's Gourd Vine*. Such customs as feeding sheep shadney (a tea made from sheep droppings) to infants, who somehow seem to survive, are recounted which seems only a little more horrifying than putting woodlice around the infants' necks to help them cut their first teeth, a practice mentioned in *Dust Tracks on a Road*.

Character, not anthropological custom, life-style or superstition, is of primary importance in the novel. While criticism of *Jonah's Gourd Vine* has been sparse, there has been some comment on character stereotypes. Nancy Tischler in *Black Masks: Negro Characters in Modern Southern Fiction* discusses the preacher John as a folk-type—"mindless, selfish, over-sexed, preaching hell-fire and the golden streets of Glory Land, categorizing sin and salvation, neatly and superficially reveling in the applause of the crowds, shrewdly soliciting money from supporters, and at times seducing females in the congregation."[15]

On the other hand, Hurston's folk are not simply folk-stereotypes, part of a cultural anthropology remarkable for their superstitions. Neither are they folk-objects, who should be studied for their anthropological value, nor simply good story-tellers with the regional humor of local-color fiction. Skillful narration, idiom and imagery, and strong characterization combine with the folk experience to produce a fictional picture of Hurston's Eatonville life experiences but with deeper social overtones. In *Jonah's Gourd Vine* the overtones are between John and Lucy over the inequality of their love and constancy. The profligate is pitted against the martyr. Here the double standard is unabashedly upheld:

> The next day John called Lucy to him.
> "Lucy."
> "Yeah, John."
> "Dey done told you 'bout Big 'Oman and me?"
> "Yeah, John, and some uh yo' moves Ah seen mahself, and if you

loves her de bes; John, you gimme our chillun and you go where yo' love lie."

"Lucy, don't tell me nothin' 'bout leavin' you, 'cause if you do dat, you'll make two winters come in one year."

There was a feeling silence.

"Lucy, Ah loves you and you alone. Ah swear Ah do. If Ah don't love you, God's gone tuh Dothan."

"What makes yuh fool wid scrubs lak Big 'Oman and de rest of 'em?"

"Dat's de brute-beast in me, but Ah sho aim tuh live clean from dis on if you 'low me one mo' chance. Don't tonguelash me—jes' try me and see. Here you done had three younguns fuh me and fixin' have uh 'nother. Try me Lucy."[16]

John Buddy never willfully takes advantage of people, but he seems inadvertently to find himself in dubious situations. As a result, his is a life of temptation and torment, of begging forgiveness and flaunting sin, of nobility and degradation. Lucy is hurt repeatedly by his exuberance. She suffers and endures; he kneels and rises to sin once again. His ambivalence is emphasized by his personal conflict with his own lustful sin. Unable to resolve his conflict, John loses the battle and dies in disgrace, a victim of his own roguery.

In *Their Eyes Were Watching God*, Hurston continues to write with a different racial perspective. The tension here is between the character Janie and her coming of age: the initiation furnishes the backdrop for the working out of her private harmony with man and with God's nature. Individual growth is the key.

The novel's action begins with a flashback. Janie, back in Eatonville as an "odd" forty-year-old woman with long hair and muddy overalls, first tells her tragic story to a friend. Thus, we first see Janie when at sixteen she is forced by her granny to marry an old farmer with sixty acres, prostituting her youth and beauty for Brother Logan Killicks's wealth and position in the community. Janie learns the initial lesson in her coming of age: "She knew now that marriage did not make love. Janie's first dream was dead, so she became a woman."[17] Then Joe Starks, "a citified, stylish dressed man with his hat set at an angle," a "shirt with silk sleeve holders . . . dazzling enough for the world," who "was a seal-brown color," comes along, charms Janie, marries her and takes her away with him to Eatonville.[18] Bigamy never becomes an issue worthy of mention. As Joe rises from store owner to landowner to mayor, Janie grows increasingly disillusioned with her social status, attained at the expense of her husband's absence from her. Starks crushes her identity. Money and position, social class and, finally, disillusionment combine to destroy the happiness of her marriage. Thus, when Starks dies, Janie burns her head rags in a gesture of defiance. She realizes consequently that she "hated her grandmother and had hidden it from herself all these years under a cloak of pity. She had been getting ready for her great journey to the horizons in search of *people;* it was important to all the world that she should find them and they find her. But she had been whipped like a cur dog, and run off down a back road after things."[19]

Janie is ready for the remarkable Tea Cake, a genuine good-time kind of fellow, who comes along to teach Janie how to fish, play checkers, pick beans and make love. By this time a wider meaning begins to emerge in the novel. Nancy Tischler explains the significance of this meaning:

> Janie's soul needs freedom and experience, not security and power and wealth. But significantly her search for real values comes after the acquisition of material wealth proves unsatisfying.[20]

Tea Cake takes Janie to the Everglades and they earn a living in the groves. In this section of the novel Hurston also probes (in a minor chord) the consciousness of racial oppression. For example, a hurricane destroys the area, and Tea Cake is forcibly recruited to dig graves for the dead. The dead whites are given pine coffins; the blacks are thrown into ditches. Furthermore, racial conflict is introduced by the "colorstruck" Mrs. Turner, who disapproves of Janie's love for the very dark Tea Cake. "Ah can't stand black niggers. Ah don't blame de white folks for hatin'em 'cause Ah can't stand em mahself. Nother thing, Ah hates to see folks lak me and you mixed up wid 'em. Us oughta class off."[21] Hurston makes a strong case against this attitude:

> Mrs. Turner, like all other believers had built an altar to the unattainable—Caucasian characteristics for all. Her god would smite her, would hurl her from pinnacles and lose her in deserts. But she would not forsake his altars. Behind her crude words was a belief that somehow she and others through worship could attain her paradise—a heaven of straight-haired, thin-lipped, high-nose boned white seraphs. The physical limitations in no way injured faith. That was the mystery and mysteries are the chords of gods. Beyond her faith was a fanaticism to defend the altars of her god. It was distressing to emerge from her inner temple and find these black desecrators howling with laughter before the door. Oh, for an army, terrible with banners *and swords!*"[2]

Both of these race conflicts contribute to the bitter irony and dark horror of the climax. When the hurricane occurs, Tea Cake is bitten by a rabid dog in a scuffle to save Janie's life. Some weeks later, suffering horribly, he loses his senses and attacks Janie when she refuses to give him a drink of water. Janie kills Tea Cake in self-defense, his teeth in her arm:

> It was the meanest moment of eternity. A minute before she was just a scared human being fighting for its life. Now she was sacrificing self with Tea Cake's head in her lap. She had wanted him to live so much and he was dead. No hour is ever eternity, but it has its right to weep.[23]

Structurally, *Their Eyes Were Watching God* is a simple story. Hurston has a way of allowing catastrophe to descend upon characters at precisely the moment when they have achieved some insight into the fundamental nature of their lives. She introduces disruptive forces into essentially harmonious situations. The moral fiber of her characters is always being tested. This testing quality of Hurston's fiction leads Roger Rosenblatt to say in *Black Fiction*, "nothing in Janie's accomplishment is simple or easy. Indeed, the enormous effort she must make in order to feel human only serves to demonstrate how strong the opposition to her humanity is."[24]

In true Hurston spirit, it is the folk culture which provides the means for Janie's spiritual fulfillment. Janie and Tea Cake shared the hard play and hard work of the folk, laughing at the "dickety" Negroes who think that "us oughta class off." As Robert Bone says, "in this milieu of . . . 'blues made and used right on the spot' . . . Janie at last finds true happiness."[25] The simple values, disregard for money and social position with corresponding love and unselfishness found in the folk experience are praised, making *Their Eyes Were Watching God* a novel of carpe diem, zest for life.

Like all lovers of the simple life, Janie and Tea Cake become aware that there is a world outside waiting and able to destroy them. As for Janie, her happiness entails tragedy. Her reflective view sheds light on the supremely wise, supremely passionate folk spirit. Through Tea Cake's death, Janie experiences an understanding and an emotion that can only be described as poetic and divine:

> Love is lak de sea. It's uh movin' thing, but still and all, it takes its shape from de shore it meets, and it's different with every shore.[26]

That is basically the story Janie tells. There is no moralizing; neither is there a moral implicit in the story. This is simply the road of life; it begins when it begins and ends when it ends. One does one's best while travelling it, but do not try to get a lesson out of it; do not search for a meaning where there is none. To Janie's folk mind, the gods dispense suffering without reason. As Tea Cake is dying Janie ponders:

Tea Cake, the son of the Evening sun had to die for loving her. She looked hard at the sky for a long time. Somewhere up there beyond blue ether's bosom sat He. Was He noticing what was going on around here? Did He *mean* to do this thing to Tea Cake and her? It wasn't anything she could fight. She could only ache and wait. Maybe it was some big tease and when He saw it had gone far enough He'd give her a sign. . . . The sky stayed hard looking and quiet so she went inside the house. God would do less than He had in His heart.[27]

While this questioning view is clearly dark, the world the gods have made is also all too clearly fragrant:

The wind through the open windows had broomed out all the fetid feeling of absence and nothingness. She closed in and sat down. Combing road dust out of her hair. Thinking.

The day of the gun, and the bloody body, and the courthouse came and commenced to sing a sobbing sigh out of every corner in the room; out of each and every chair and thing. Commenced to sing, and commenced to sob and sigh, singing and sobbing. Then Tea Cake came prancing around where she was and the song of the sigh flew out of the window and lit in the top of the pine trees. Tea Cake, with the sun for a shawl. Of course he wasn't dead. He could never be dead until she herself had finished feeling and thinking. The kiss of his memory made pictures of love and light against the wall. Here was peace. She pulled in her horizon like a great fish-net. Pulled it from around the waste of the world and draped it over her shoulder. So much of life in its meshes! She called in her soul to see.[28]

Thus at the risk of understatement and cliché, Hurston's themes arise from the human heart in conflict with itself and its pendulum orbit of laughter and tears. Hugh Gloster in *Negro Voices in American Fiction* has called those themes examples of "folk realism" from the "rural south," and an "intimate transcript of folk life." Hurston has an "unusual capacity for appropriating folklore to the purposes of fiction." On the other hand, like most Hurston critics, Gloster sees equal validity in Andrew Burris's comment that Hurston uses "her characters and the various situations created as mere pegs upon which to hang their dialect and folkways." This leads Gloster to praise, then criticize: "The peculiar idiom of folk speech and the 'big old lies' of folk characters are competently handled. Less convincing is the development of character and the analysis of social problems."[29] Therefore the critical attitude toward what Hurston was doing is simultaneously laudatory and censorious and, in the main, suggests that all fiction by black writers has to dwell on serious racial conflict.

Hurston herself substantiated her argument that the portrayal of individual characters was her major concern. She says in *Dust Tracks on a Road:*

> Light came to me when I realized that I did not have to consider any racial group as a whole. God made them duck by duck and that was the only way I could see them. I learned that skins were no measure of what was inside people. So none of the race cliches meant anything any more. I began to laugh at both white and black who claimed special blessings on the basis of race. Therefore I saw no curse in being black, no extra flavor by being white. . . . You can consider me Old Tar Brush in person if you want to.[30]

Hurston's vision in this framework is realistic: folk-lore is life. Judging from her own original and unique vantage point, Hurston succeeds brilliantly. She deals with matters of the heart and soul rather than political, economic or social matters. Her genuine gifts penetrate the yearning human heart to portray the pendulum orbit of laughter and tears. If there is a final image that expresses both the longing and serenity that Hurston worked to find in that pendulum orbit, a serenity and longing which she believed lay at the heart of all folk experience, it is the image of the sea in the first few lines of *Their Eyes Were Watching God.* That image, furthermore, expresses the folk spirit and the uniqueness that was Zora Neale Hurston:

> Ships at a distance have every man's wish on board. For some they come in with the tide. For others they sail forever on the horizon, never landing until the Watcher turns his eyes away in resignation, his dreams mocked to death by Time. That is the life of men.[31]

NOTES

1. Zora Neale Hurston, *Mules and Men* (New York, 1970), 18.
2. Noted in Robert Hemenway, *Zora Neale Hurston* (Chicago, 1977), 219.
3. Larry Neal, "A Profile: Zora Neale Hurston," *Southern Exposure* 1 (Winter, 1974): 162.
4. Zora Neale Hurston, *Dust Tracks on a Road* (New York, 1969), 11.
5. Ibid., 214.
6. Ibid., 225, 226, 228–29.
7. James Baldwin, "Everybody's Protest Novel," *The Black Novelist*, ed. Robert Hemenway (Columbus, Ohio, 1970), 223.
8. Ibid., 224.
9. *Dust Tracks on a Road*, 293–94.
10. Langston Hughes, *The Big Sea* (New York, 1940), 238–39.

11. *Dust Tracks on a Road,* p. 241. When Hurston refers to the "topflight Negro" there is no connotation of snobbishness. It is the understanding that was Hurston's concern. Baldwin's understanding paraphrases in more detail Hurston's attitude toward race: "It is the peculiar triumph of society—and its loss—that it is able to convince those people to whom it has given inferior status of the reality of this decree; it has the force and the weapons to translate dictum into fact, so that the allegedly inferior are actually made so, insofar as the societal realities are concerned. This is a more hidden phenomenon now than it was in the days of serfdom, but it is no less implacable. Now, as then, we find ourselves bound, first without, then through a bitter railing against this trap; it is as though this very striving were the only motion needed to spring the trap upon us. We take our shape, it is true, within and against that cage of reality bequeathed us at our birth; and yet it is precisely through our dependence on this reality that we are most endlessly betrayed. Society is held together by our need; we bind it together with legend, myth, coercion, fearing that without it we will be hurled into that void, within which, like the earth before the Word was spoke, the foundations of society are hidden. From this void—ourselves—it is the function of society to protect us; but it is only this void, our unknown selves, demanding forever, a new act of creation, which can save us—'from this evil that is in the world.' With the same motion, at the same time, it is this toward which we endlessly struggle and from which, endlessly, we struggle to escape." "Everybody's Protest Novel," *The Black Novelist,* 224.

12. Zora Neale Hurston, *Jonah's Gourd Vine* (Philadelphia, 1934), 213.

13. Ibid., 109.

14. Margaret Wallace, "Real Negro People," *New York Times Book Review,* 6 May 1934.

15. Nancy M. Tischler, *Black Masks: Negro Characters in Southern Fiction* (Pennsylvania State University Press, 1969), p. 158. Tischler also calls *Their Eyes Were Watching God* an especially effective attack on black Babbittry. "This remarkable novel is the chronical of Janie . . . (whose) acquisition of material wealth proves unsatisfying." Tischler also makes the point that this cannot "become a paradigm for Negro-centered novels until more Negroes have known and rejected affluence."

16. *Jonah's Gourd Vine,* 144.

17. Zora Neale Hurston, *Their Eyes Were Watching God* (New York, 1969), 44.

18. Ibid., 47

19. Ibid., 137–38.

20. Tischler, 143.

21. *Their Eyes Were Watching God,* 210.

22. Ibid., 216.

23. Ibid., 273.

24. Roger Rosenblatt, *Black Fiction* (Cambridge, Massachusetts, 1974), 219.

25. Robert Bone, *The Negro Novel in America* (New Haven, 1958), 131.

26. *Their Eyes Were Watching God,* 284.

27. Ibid., 264.

28. Ibid., 285–86.

29. Hugh M. Gloster, *Negro Voices in American Fiction* (Chapel Hill, 1948), 235–36.

30. *Dust Tracks on a Road,* 243.

31. *Their Eyes Were Watching God,* 243.

DOLAN HUBBARD

"'...Ah said Ah'd save de text for you'": Recontextualizing the Sermon to Tell (Her)story in Zora Neale Hurston's Their Eyes Were Watching God

If you want to find Jesus, go in de wilderness
Go in de wilderness, go in de wilderness.
Mournin' brudder, go in de wilderness
I wait upon de Lord. (qtd. in Dixon 13)

Zora Neale Hurston writes in *Their Eyes Were Watching God* (1937) from the interiority of black culture. The fact that she sees religion as a mode of making sense of the experiences of a black tradition makes *Their Eyes Were Watching God* a strong, assertive statement. In contrast, many of the novels of the 1920s and '30s view blackness as a pathology. Van Vechten's *Nigger Heaven* and McKay's *Home to Harlem*, for example, emphasize the exotic primitive, while Fauset's *There Is Confusion* and Larsen's *Passing* emphasize assimilation. For this reason, *Their Eyes Were Watching God,* along with Hurston's work as an anthropologist and folklorist, bears witness to the desire of black people to argue, live, love, and die in a place of their own creation and to center themselves in a universe independent of the tyranny of manmade states of oppression. That she set her novel of romantic love in Eatonville, Florida, one of the first all-black towns in the United States, is itself a religious expression. Hurston, thus, challenges black writers to enter the mainstream of American society on their own terms, which means to accept and promote the integrity

African American Review, Volume 27, Number 2 (Summer 1993): pp. 167–178. © 1993 Dolan Hubbard.

35

of black culture. To the extent that she externalizes through language the values of black culture, Hurston saves the text.

The power of Hurston in *Their Eyes Were Watching God* centers on her ability to fix extant cultural values in language and in the work of art. Like the preacher, Hurston's artistic gift "consists in discovering the not-yet-discovered subsistent values and meanings that make up [her text's] object in the creative act which is the revelation of that object in and through the language" (Vivas 1073–1074; Fontenot 38–41). In other words, *Their Eyes Were Watching God* brings the meanings and values of the culture to its participants' attention. The narrative performs a normative function, since the participants espouse the values and meanings which the narrative reveals.

The end product of Hurston's vision is to create a new black woman, through a critique of the past. In looking back, Janie also looks forward to the day when American women of African descent will no longer be the mules of the world. Using familiar Bible-based tropes and metaphors, Hurston drives to the heart of a series of related questions: What does it mean to be black and female in America? What are the terms of definition for women outside the traditional hierarchies? Is female status negated without a male defining principle? And she raises these questions to reveal to the black community the one face it can never see—its own.

Although Hurston's narrative focuses on the emergence of a female self in a male-dominated world, she tells her magnificent story of romantic love against the background of church and extrachurch modes of expression. Understanding this fact helps to explain those sections of the narrative that have been said to have no meaning beyond their entertainment value (Hemenway 218). Hurston knew that the religious life of Americans of African descent manifests itself in all spheres of this life. The extrachurch modes of expression possess great critical and creative powers that have often touched deeper religious issues regarding the true situation of black communities than those of the institutional black church. These church and extrachurch modes of expressions may be seen in the novel's narrative structure, in the texture of Hurston's language and imagery, and in the manner in which her language itself is alive with history and historical struggle in order to convey the story of the emergence of a female self in a male-dominated world.

Divided into three sections that correspond roughly to modes of religious expression, *Their Eyes Were Watching God* celebrates the art of the community in such a manner that "the harsh edges of life in a Jim Crow South seldom come into view" (Hemenway 218). Section one has a spiritual orientation and covers the time of Janie's marriage to Logan Killicks (which sets in motion the initial tension in the novel—that between Janie and her grandmother over what a woman ought to be and do); section two focuses on the richness and diversity of the styles of life in the black community (black peoples' will to adorn and our sense of drama are daily put on display on Joe Starks's storefront porch); and section three, which focuses on the blues impulse, covers Janie's life with Tea Cake in the Everglades (and provides movement toward the resolution of the tension that has sent Janie to the horizon and back). Given Janie's history, an overarching question that unifies these sections is: What rescues Janie from becoming a full-fledged blues figure—and is Hurston ambivalent about this?

Their Eyes Were Watching God is a story within a story, deeply influenced by the power of language and myth in and out of the homiletical mode. The received language "dictates" that *Their Eyes Were Watching God*, though set in Florida, must occur outside of a specific time and place. (This strategy receives its fullest deployment in James Baldwin's *Go Tell It on the Mountain*.) By placing her narrative in the context of the Christian journey, itself a romance, Hurston overrides reader expectation that the protagonist should marry her black prince charming and live happily ever after. Having returned from the horizon, Janie Crawford represents the mature voice of experience and wisdom as she retrospectively tells her story to one who is, from an experiential point of view, a novice. Janie intends to convert Pheoby and the reader/participant. Her first move in her conversion narrative is to revise the patriarchal vision of seeing the world through a male dialectic.

Janie's story, as sermon and testimony, merges the material with the spiritual world. This constitutes the "unsaid" in the novel's arrestingly powerful opening scene:

> Ships at a distance have every man's wish on board. For some they come in with the tide. For others they sail forever on the horizon, never out of sight, never landing until the Watcher turns his eyes away in resignation, his dreams mocked to death by Time. That is the life of men.
>
> Now, women forget all those things they don't want to remember, and remember everything they don't want to forget. The dream is the truth. Then they act and do things accordingly. (1)

Hurston presents us with the classical Biblical picture of the looker standing before the horizon and wondering if she and the horizon shall ever meet. The looker sees a picture that is both in time and timeless, finite and infinite. The ships on the horizon are emblematic of the dreams of the person standing on shore. This timeless picture speaks of a person's desire to be related to God, the ultimate Other—"a need in the moment of existence to belong, to be related to a beginning and to an end" (Kermode 4).

As her story unfolds, we come to realize that the naïve, sixteen-year-old Janie, as the Looker, stands before the horizon (the pear tree in bloom) as one whose spiritual loyalties are "completely divided, as [i]s, without question, her mind" (Walker 236). Her spiritual loyalties are divided because she has not yet earned the unspeakable intimacy that binds the community of faith. In contrast to her grandmother, Janie lacks the faith-knowledge that comes from a firsthand experience with the Holy Spirit.

Faith-knowledge does not rely on the evidence of the senses but is, in the scriptural phrase, "the evidence of things not seen"—that is, not presented to sense-perception—and it would lose its essential nature and be transformed into a mere sorry empirical knowledge if it relied on any other evidence than "the witness of the Holy Spirit" (Otto 228), which is not that of sense-experience.

Sustained by her faith-knowledge born in the midnight of despair of the slave experience, Nanny, a recognizable figure in the black community, breaks the pervasive silence of her sixteen-year "silent worship," as she passionately tells Janie of her dream. Her sermonic monologue, one of the most moving scenes in all of black American literature, serves to order experience. Janie's life is the sermon, as Nanny makes clear:

> "Ah wanted to preach a great sermon about colored women sittin' on high, but they wasn't no pulpit for me. Freedom found me wid a baby daughter in mah arms, so [on my knees] Ah said [to my God] Ah'd take a broom and a cook-pot and throw up a highway through de wilderness for her. She would expound what Ah felt. But somehow she got lost offa de highway and next thing Ah knowed here you was in de world. So whilst Ah was tendin' you of nights Ah said Ah'd save de text for you." (15–16)

The text that Nanny saves is the cultural genealogy of black America in general and the black woman in particular. This believable, manageable fiction centers on an interpretation of history that is consistent with a JudeoChristian view that emphasizes patience, humility, and good nature. Created by blacks in the face of limited options, this interpretation of history makes it possible for many in the oppressed corporate community to interpret their behavior as being Christlike. In fact, the posture adopted by Nanny is necessary for the maintenance of self-esteem, rather than as the realization of the Christian ideal. With each of her three marriages, Janie challenges this externally imposed stereotype, which served in slave days as the ideal self-image for the corporate community (Fullinwider, 27–28).

Janie's application of the text, her reinterpretation of history, provides her with the impetus to break free of gendered silence and inferior status. In her movement from passive looker to active participant, Janie discovers that, to change one's way of thinking, the individual must change her perceptions of the world. Whereas Nanny and Janie share the same mythic belief system, each differs in her choice of an end to reach the goal, the dream.

In many respects, the tension to be resolved in the Nanny-Janie argument involves the route to freedom and respectability for the black woman. This tension is presented in the novel as two competing perspectives on reality: Janie's romantic vision, and her grandmother's pragmatic grounding in reality. They, however, have different interpretations and applications of the dream of "'whut a woman oughta be and to do'" (15), which is to say, they have different interpretations of history. Whereas Nanny, whose brooding presence dominates the narrative, sees the dream as protection and security, Janie sees Nanny's dream as restrictive; it circumscribed existence. The grandmother's dream has no room for an idyllic view of nature. For Nanny the pressure of history is a pressure in favor of remembering and not forgetting, whereas for Janie the pressure of history is in favor of forgetting and against remembering (Fish 6).

The tension between Nanny and Janie as presented in the opening paragraphs centers on the highly charged word *truth*, meaning 'to be free from other people's fictions.' What is the truth as socially constructed: (1) security and respect (Logan Killicks); (2) excessive competition and overcompensation as a result of marginalization (Joe Starks); or (3) the sensualization of pain and pleasure (Tea Cake and life on the Everglades)? These versions of the truth, presented from the perspective of black males, confront the female Looker as she stands before the horizon: "Now women forget all those things they don't want to remember and remember everything they don't want to forget. The dream is the truth. Then they act and do things accordingly."

This enigmatic paragraph begins to make sense in the wake of Jody's death, when Janie allows her suppressed emotions to surface: "She had an inside and an outside now and suddenly she knew how not to mix them" (68). Janie has come to an awareness that her grandmother had pointed her in the wrong direction—the realization that her grandmother's best of intentions had contributed to her divided self:

> She had been getting ready for her great journey to the horizons in search of *people;* it was important to all the world that she should find them and they find her. But she had been whipped like a cur dog, and run off down a back road after *things.* It was all according to the way you see things. Some people could look at a mud-puddle and see an ocean with ships. But Nanny belonged to that other kind that loved to deal in scraps. Here Nanny had taken the biggest thing God ever made, the horizon—for no matter how far a person can go the horizon is still way beyond you—and pinched

it in to such a little bit of a thing that she could tie it about her
granddaughter's neck tight enough to choke her. (85)

In the wake of this realization, Janie begins earnestly the process of her
search for self and form, the process of finding a voice and creating a woman.
The process of healing her divided mind includes the rejection of protection
and security, which Nanny, Logan, and Jody sought to provide, and entering
into a relationship with a man regarded as her social inferior. Coming to see
her grandmother's well-intended actions as a fiction, Janie, in her search for
self and form, turns her world upside down in order to make it rightside up.
The break from gendered silence—exemplified by the negative community
of gossiping women who sit on the front porch—involves the reconnection
of subject (Janie) and object (pear tree) on the same imaginative plane; that
is, Janie, in her quest, unknowingly sets out to smash a fiction that has out-
lived its usefulness—black women as the mules of the world.

The polarities represented by Nanny and Janie in her movement toward
the horizon stem from Janie's desire to seek an authentic place for an expression of the autonomy and independence of her consciousness:

> The desire for an authentic place for the expression of this reality
> is the source of the revolutionary tendencies in [black religion]. But
> on the level of human consciousness, religions of the oppressed
> create in another manner. The hegemony of the oppressors is
> understood as a myth—a myth in the two major senses, as true
> and as fictive. It is true as a structure with which one must deal in
> a day-to-day manner if one is to persevere, but it is fictive as far as
> any ontological significance is concerned. (Long, 169–170)

It is in their day-to-day existence as laborers that members of the oppressed
community challenge the oppressors' definition of them. Their autonomy
arises from their labor, but paradoxically their autonomy takes on a fictive
character. The principal figures in Janie's life respond to the contradictory
nature of myth as true in a variety of ways. Nanny's intimate knowledge of
the violence perpetuated upon the corporate community dictates her determination to have Janie marry in order to protect her granddaughter from such
a history. Joe Starks's response to history is to overcompensate by lording his
accomplishments over those of his fellow citizens. Tea Cake's response is to
seek freedom and release through his music and style of life; the perpetual
mobility of this blues figure is indicative of his not becoming "institutionally"
dependent on a system over which he exercises no control. Tea Cake remains
outside the system. Though the blues as a "religious" counterstatement against
the fictive character of the autonomy of the corporate community stands

outside the sway of the institutional church, the community of faith (Nanny) understands its anarchic personality. In her movement toward the horizon, the sheltered Janie will come to understand the fugitive element that makes the music swing jump, and cry.

Crayon Enlargements

In the Eatonville section of the novel, Hurston focuses on the style of life in a vibrant and dynamic community. From her perspective, best-foot forward presentations of the folk represent the triumph of the human spirit over oppression, meaning that black enjoyment of life "is not solely a product of defensive reactions" to the dominant white culture.[1] Hurston believes that the distinguishing feature, the corporate signature, of the African imagination to America is creativity—the ability to invest the Other's linguistic structure with new meanings. In "Characteristics of Negro Expression," she refers to this irrepressible quality as "the will to adorn" (50). That which permeates the soul of the black community is drama. Hurston comments:

> Every phase of Negro life is highly dramatized. No matter how joyful or how sad the case there is sufficient poise for drama. Everything is acted out. Unconsciously for the most part of course. There is an impromptu ceremony always ready for every hour of life. No little moment passes unadorned. ("Characteristics" 49)

Hurston implicitly presents blacks as offering an image of vitality to a civilization dimly aware of its lack of both vitality and color (Bennett 149).

In terms of narrative tension, Hurston contrasts this vitality with the increasingly withdrawn Janie, who is excluded from participating in the storytelling sessions, the "crayon enlargements of life" (48) on the store front porch. She has become a prisoner of the pretty picture of "'whut a woman oughta be and to do'" as outlined by Joe when he courted her: "'A pretty doll-baby lak you is made to sit on de front porch and rock and fan yo'self and eat p'taters dat other folks plant just special for you'" (28).

The imaginative freedom that the big-picture talkers have on the front porch contrasts with Janie's despair inside the store, where she silently listens with the dumb obedience of a mule. Forced to become a passive observer, Janie longs to participate in these spirited storytelling sessions, the male community in unison enjoying release from the day's work. "Janie loved the conversation and sometimes she thought up good stories on the mule, but Joe had forbidden her to indulge" (50). The restricted space gnaws away at her soul. Squeezed out of the big picture, an appendage that derives her identity through her husband, Mrs. Mayor Starks finds herself ensnared in a choking kind of love; this is not what she envisioned under the pear tree.

Reserved for the big-picture talkers, the porch of Joe Starks's store is treated as a sacred space wherein secular performances take place. Within this space, the storytellers exhibit the creative capacities of black people defining themselves in the order of things. Like their preacher counterparts, the personae the storytellers employ in performance sanction these men as guardians of the word, of the text—of the aesthetic values of the community. The performance, with its dynamic give-and-take that one associates with the black church, runs through all segments of black life.

Matt Bonner's decrepit mule is the focal point of the daily drama played out in the ritual space of Joe's storefront porch. Sam and Lige and Walter take the lead in creating the "pictures" the male members pass around, which an envious Janie rightly divines as "crayon enlargements of life" (48):

> "Dat mule uh yourn, Matt. You better go see 'bout him. He's bad off."
>
> "Where 'bouts? Did he wade in de lake and uh alligator ketch him?"
>
> "Worser'n dat. De womenfolks got yo' mule. When Ah come round de lake 'bout noontime mah wife and some others had 'im flat on de ground usin' his sides fuh uh wash board."
>
> The great clap of laughter that they have been holding in, bursts out. Sam never cracks a smile. "Yeah, Matt, dat mule so skinny till de women is usin' his rib bones fuh uh rub-board, and hangin' things out on his hock-bones tuh dry." (49)

As a mode of religious expression, these good-natured stories show that the creative capacities of blacks are not dependent on living in trembling and fear of the white man—nor do the tales use white oppression as a point of departure. Coexisting with the laughter, banter, and humor of the jokes about Matt Bonner's mule are references to poverty and marginality, as well as the life-and-death struggle for survival, especially when the buzzards swoop down to eat the dead mule. The humor, however, takes the edge off the tale tellers' poverty and marginality (the sides of the mule are so flat as to be used as wash boards).

The stories told on Joe Starks's porch appear to have significance beyond their immediate entertainment value. The people who make fun of Matt Bonner's tired mule can identify with this beast of burden, that works in dumb obedience and silence much as they have been trained—and more, *pronounced*—to do, and as Joe has trained Janie to do. But unlike the mule, Janie rebels rather than going silently to her grave.

Imagistically, the humor inherent in the mock funeral for the mule may be read on two levels. First, the parody of mule heaven crystallizes the people's desire for a better world—plenty of food and no work. Second, it echoes Nanny's desire not to have Janie work with little or no tangible reward for self. The frustrated Janie is isolated from the imaginative life of the community where "... the people [specifically, the *men*] sat around on the porch and passed around the pictures of their thoughts for the others to look at and see ..." (48).

Overall the stories in this section are not so much documents for understanding black life as they are representations of Hurston's attempt to capture the vibrancy and drama that are part of the creative soul of black America. As Hemenway notes, Hurston's efforts "are intended to show rather than tell, the assumption being that both behavior and art will become self-evident as the tale texts (performance events) accrued during the reading" (168).

To know how people view the world around them is to understand how they evaluate life; and people's temporal and nontemporal evaluations of life provide them with a "charter" of action, a guide to behavior. In this regard, Hurston makes it explicit that Christian explanations have never proved fully adequate for blacks, whose sensibilities are deeply rooted in folk traditions. In chapter 8, for example, the reader/spectator is more inclined to rejoice in Janie's confronting Joe on his deathbed about the woman she has become—declaring her independence—than to note the extent in which the extrachurch (remnants of African traditional religion) informs this pivotal scene. Hurston, in a statement radical for its time, brings to the surface these submerged values, beliefs, and practices in the root doctor and Janie's description of Joe's death. Though Hurston does not give an exegetical explanation of the religious values which underlie Joe's calling on the root doctor, she makes it clear that his apparent act of desperation is interrelated with Janie's description of her husband's death. In making these extrachurch forms of expressions central to our understanding of Joe and Janie Starks, the town's most venerated citizens, Hurston perceptively reveals the epic complexity of black life.

As he nears death, the status-conscious Joe engages the assistance of a conjure man to ward off the spell he believes Janie, his wife of twenty years, has had put on him. Hurston suggests that, though African traditional religion and medicine, which the root doctor represents, have been forced underground, these once-viable traditional values and outlooks continue to exist and to exercise an influence among segments of the corporate community, as Pheoby indicates in her all-knowing, sympathetic response to the shocked Janie: "'Janie, Ah thought maybe de thing would die down and you never would know nothin' 'bout it, but it's been singin' round here ever since de big fuss in de store dat Joe was 'fixed' and you wuz de one dat did it'" (78).

As a representative of a once-proud living tradition, the root doctor has been forced underground and divested of an essential dimension of his *raison d'être*. Known in Africa as medicine men, herbalists, traditional doctors, or *wagangas;* knowledgeable in religious matters, these influential African men and women are expected "to be trustworthy, upright morally, friendly, willing and ready to serve, able to discern people's needs and not be exorbitant in their charges" (Mbiti 218). But in the face of an uncompromising and indifferent Christianity, Hurston's root doctor, as a remnant of African traditional religion and medicine on the North American continent, is forced to stand outside the dominant Christian culture as something foreign and alien (Shorter, 1–2). The root doctor in America, as the public face of a submerged religion, is reduced to a caricature of his or her former self. Operating at the edge of American society, the root doctor is more likely to be a charlatan or hustler than "the friend of the community [who] comes into the picture at many points in individual and community life" (Mbiti 218).

Hurston demonstrates her understanding of the complexity of the black experience with its discontinuity-within-continuity in the stressful departure scene between Joe and Janie. That this scene is filled with subtle juxtaposition of thought and idea becomes apparent when Janie begins to think of Death,

> that strange being with the huge square toes who lived way in the West. The great one who lived in the straight house like a platform without sides to it, and without a roof. What need has Death for a cover, and what winds can blow against him? He stands in his high house that overlooks the world. Stands watchful and motionless all day with his sword drawn back, waiting for the messenger to bid him come. Been standing there before there was a where or a when or a then. (79–80)

Janie's conception of death reveals the manner in which language itself is alive with history and the historical to tell of the emergence of a black ethos in a Eurocentric world. Like her African American ancestors before her, Janie uses the language and imagery of the Christian Bible because it was readily available. Nevertheless, her aesthetic orientation differed from those in the dominant community, as is evident in her conceptualization of death. Hurston presents a well-developed religious consciousness that has penetrated the universe in ways the dominant culture has not. The attitude toward death and dying Janie expresses displays a certain intimacy. Her conceptualization is not predicated on fear and stands in sharp contrast to the conventional Western attitude toward death. Death is not final; God has not died in Africa. Physical death is a passage from one realm of existence to another. As long as there is God, man or woman will never be a *finite* being.

In conjoining the root doctor and death, Hurston is not attempting to depict one woman's knee-jerk rejection based on submerged religious belief. While one might argue that, as a matter of historical genesis, the association might have been awakened in Janie's mind during a moment of stress, the inward and lasting character of these interlocking passages is to make the connection that, in the United States, the root doctor has become separated from his divine calling. Hurston would have us understand that African traditional medicine is a part of African traditional religion (Mbiti, 217–252; Shorter, 1–19).[2]

What Hurston, in effect, is evoking is the historical genesis of the blues—the reconstitution of self out of a religion that has come to be viewed as foreign and alien. She is talking about black people's ability to squeeze out a song, story, or sermon from the near-lyric, near-tragic situation of their lives as a result of their inability to texturize the world. Ultimately, the text for Hurston is not a fixed object, but a dialectical process in which contradictory elements coexist, in which parts and wholes depend upon each other, and in which negation and affirmation are closely joined. It is in this sense that we can speak of Hurston as showing how an African continuum is maintained. In spite of the fragmentation that has occurred, the corporate community maintains continuity in the face of discontinuity, and discontinuity in the face of continuity.

The Blues Impluse

If Hurston's intent in the first two sections of *Their Eyes Were Watching God* is to screen out white antipathy, then the last section shows the response of the community to this oppression and to black society's assigned marginality. Hurston does not view the blues so much as the failure of religion as it is the intensification of religious expression in the absence of fundamental checks and balances of the strong against the weak. While the perpetrators of the oppression remain essentially in the background, the effects of their oppression manifest themselves in the hedonistic lifestyle of many in the black community. Not surprisingly, Janie discovers her voice among the socially downcast segment of society, who sensualize pain and pleasure. After twenty years of marriage, Jody dies and Janie falls in love with Vergible "Tea Cake" Woods, a man twelve years younger than she and, by most people's estimations, her social inferior. In a reversal of the romantic moment that we associate with fairy tales such as the Cinderella story, Janie and Tea Cake go to live in the Everglades, rejecting the finery and status of the mayor's house because of their desire to know and love each other.

Janie's life with Tea Cake, a cultural archetype, represents the third and final movement in her march toward the horizon, toward self-definition. Tea Cake, as the blues-made-flesh, is the objectification of Janie's desire. In spite of his sexism, Tea Cake, a rounder, drifter, and day laborer, is the embodiment of the freedom which Janie's divided mind has long sought. And unlike the traditional bluesman, Tea Cake does not love Janie and then leave her.

Tea Cake's life style expresses a practical, existential response to the world, and stands in direct opposition to the values Nanny had attempted to instill in Janie. A hedonistic howl replaces silent worship; a desire for security and stability yields to comfort with flux. Whereas Nanny's life is dedicated to the patient forbearance of Protestant Christian worship, Tea Cake's life—with its roots in the slave seculars—represents another dimension of the day-to-day secular expression of the community. Tea Cake's irrepressible laughter embodies the tough-minded spirit of the blues. It stands as a reminder that there is more to the everyday than the struggle for material subsistence.

The tradition which Tea Cake embodies recognizes no dichotomy between a spiritual and a blues mystique. The blues are the spirituals, good is bad, God is the devil, and every day is Saturday. The essence of the tradition is the extraordinary tension between the poles of pain and joy, agony and ecstasy, good and bad, Sunday and Saturday (Bennett 50). Unlike the spiritual vision, the blues vision "deals with a world where the inability to solve a problem does not necessarily mean that one can, or ought, to transcend it" (Williams, 74–75). Tea Cake, who stands outside the influence of the institutional church, responds to his circumscribed existence by squeezing as much pleasure out of the moment as possible. Needless to say, his life style, in contrast to Nanny's patient forbearance, is tantamount to paganism.

Tea Cake, who appears to live only for the moment, comes from "an environment filled with heroic violence, flashing knives, Saturday night liquor fights, and the magnificent turbulence of a blues-filled weekend of pleasure and joy" (Barksdale, 110–111). This child of the morning star makes Janie feel alive, vital, needed, loved, unlimited—and she gives of herself freely. Janie's blissful "marriage" with Tea Cake lasts for about two years; then a storm hits the Everglades, and God takes His glance away.

During the raging storm, God seems to be speaking. Janie and Tea Cake wait for God to make His move, and when destruction appears imminent, Janie and Tea Cake strike out for the high ground. In a heroic struggle against the raw power of nature, they make it, but not before Tea Cake is bitten by a rabid dog in an effort to save Janie. Several weeks later, Janie is forced to kill the man she loves. As "a glance from God" (102), Tea Cake has been temporary "The Lord giveth, and the Lord taketh away" (Howard, 105–106).

Janie's response to the flood is not simply intellectual; it is experiential and total. It is a religious response born out of her having come to terms with the impenetrable majesty of the divine. For Janie, the experience of *mysterium tremendum* is brought to bear when she is suspended between life and death:

"If you kin see de light at daybreak, you don't keer if you die at dusk. It's so many people never seen de light at all. Ah wuz fumblin' round and God opened de door." ...

The wind came back with triple fury, and put out the light for the last time. They sat in company with the others in other shanties, their eyes straining against crude walls and their souls asking if He meant to measure their puny might against His. They seemed to be staring at the dark, but their eyes were watching God. (151)

The storm in this, Janie's last movement toward the horizon, symbolizes the struggle the corporate black community has to come to terms with in the oppressor's negation of its image. Out of this negation, the mythic consciousness seeks a *new* beginning in the future by imagining an *original* beginning. The social implications of this religious experience enable the oppressed community to dehistoricize the oppressor's hegemonic dominance. Metaphorically, the phrase *their eyes were watching God* means the creation of a new form of humanity—one that is no longer based on the master-slave dialectic. The utopian and eschatological dimensions of the religions of the oppressed stem from this modality—which Hurston arrests by concluding her moving story of romantic love with a flourish of Christian iconography (Long, 158–172).

With the spellbound Pheoby at her side, Janie struggles to find her voice and, equally important, an audience that will give assent to her testimony. Janie taps into the responsive mythology of the black sermon as she assigns meaning to her experience. She exercises autonomy in making her world through language. However, while the language of the black church provides her one means of translating her experience into a medium which can be comprehended easily by a member of her aesthetic community, Hurston keeps before us the inescapable fact that the community acts upon Janie, and Janie upon the community. She differs from her community in that her action represents a break from gendered silence.

The logical conclusion to Janie's female-centered discourse occurs when Pheoby, who aspires "'to sit on de front porch'" (28), undergoes a transformation. With the exhilaration that only the newly converted can know, Pheoby enthusiastically becomes Janie's disciple:

"Lawd!" Pheoby breathed out heavily, "Ah done growed ten feet higher from jus' listenin' tuh you, Janie. Ah ain't satisfied wid mahseff no mo'. Ah means tuh make Sam take me fishin' wid him after this. Nobody [i.e., the negative community of women and the signifying men] better not criticize yuh in mah hearin'." (182–183)

Pheoby responds excitedly to Janie's call to break with hierarchies of representation and to stop seeing herself as a silent subject. It is significant that Janie comes to Pheoby, religiously speaking, from a point of strength, not coping. She knows who her God is. She does not seek confirmation for her actions, but affirmation of her voice. The religious imagination of the community enters into Janie's verbal consciousness and shapes her response to historical pressures.

The language of the black church is a communal language invested with authority. Not only does this communal language give Janie voice and legitimacy, but it also sustains her. Through it, she can prevent the memory of Tea Cake from dying. The connection to romance—a vertical language— becomes apparent to the mesmerized Pheoby, as well as the reader/spectator. Janie's ritual retelling of her journey toward the horizon enables her to suspend the rules of time and space as she moves toward the climatic moment in her sermon—the tragic death of her beloved Tea Cake. Each time Janie tells of their short but intense life together, she relives the experience, much as Christians do when they participate in the Eucharist. In fact *Their Eyes Were Watching God* may be viewed as a series of revelations leading toward ultimate revelation—Janie's being reunited in the spirit with Tea Cake.

The novel ends where it began, with the perceptual field of the narrator, who releases it from the temporal world. In this way, Janie and Tea Cake achieve a greater freedom in the world tomorrow, and Janie triumphs over her critics, the negative community of gossiping women to whom the reader is introduced in the book's opening sequence. With her spiritual loyalties no longer divided, Janie, in a picture at least as arresting as the novel's opening scene, draws the various strands of her sermon together:

> She pulled in her horizon like a great fish-net. Pulled it from around the waist of the world and draped it over her shoulder. So much of life in its meshes! She called in her soul to come and see. (184)

In pulling the fish net around her shoulders, Janie arrests the "eschatological despair" she has experienced (Kermode 9). An optimist and romantic, Janie seeks a larger space for herself and her life's story; her quest involves woman's timeless search for freedom and wholeness. Her charge to her new convert is "'. . . you got to go there tuh *know* there'" (183). Janie, in her movement toward the horizon (i.e., in the successful execution of her performance via the sermon), is transformed from blues figure to prophet. In so doing, she both achieves personal fulfillment and assumes a communal role traditionally reserved for males. She appropriates tropes of creation ("She had given away everything in their little house except a package of garden seed that

Tea Cake had bought to plant" [182]) and reunion ("She pulled in her horizon like a great fish-net") in order to insert her voice into history.[3]

In the end, Janie's sermon becomes a poetry of affirmation—with self, community, and loved ones. Janie and Pheoby are uplifted through the preached word. Operating from a position of strength within the ethos of her community, Janie achieves an unspeakable intimacy that bonds her community of faith.

Notes

1. My comments in this section are informed by the observations of Hurston's biographer Robert Hemenway (221). Part of Hazel Carby's project is to demystify the idealization of the folk.

2. I have written at greater length about voodoo as a submerged religion in "Society and Self."

3. For a critique of the "prophetic moment as a distinctly male enterprise, see Krasner 113.

Works Cited

Barksdale, Richard. "Margaret Walker: Folk Orature and Historical Prophecy," in *Black American Poets Between Worlds, 1940–1960,* edited by R. Baxter Miller. Knoxville: University of Tennessee Press, 1986, pp. 104–117.

Bennett, Lerone, Jr. *The Negro Mood.* Chicago: Johnson, 1964.

Carby, Hazel. "Ideologies of Black Folk: The Historical Novel of Slavery," in *Slavery and the Literary Imagination,* edited by Deborah E. McDowell and Arnold Rampersad. Baltimore: John Hopkins University Press, 1989, pp. 125–143.

Dixon, Melvin. *Ride Out the Wilderness: Geography and Identity in Afro-American Literature.* Urbana: University of Illinois Press, 1987.

Fish, Stanley E. *Self-Consuming Artifacts.* Berkeley: University of California Press, 1972.

Fontenot, Chester J., Jr., Rev. of *The Craft of Ralph Ellison,* by Robert G. O'Meally. *Black American Literature Forum,* 15.2 (1981): 79–80.

Fullinwider, S. P. *The Mind and Mood of Black America.* Homewood: Dorsey, 1969.

Hemenway, Robert. *Zora Neale Hurston: A literary Biography.* Urbana: University of Illinois Press, 1977.

Howard, Lillie P. *Zora Neale Hurston.* Boston: Twayne, 1980.

Hubbard, Dolan. "Society and Self in Alice Walker's *In Love and Trouble.*" *Obsidian II,* 6.2 (1991): 50–75.

Hurston, Zora Neale. *Characteristics of Negro Expression.* 1935. *The Sanctified Church.* Berkeley: Turtle Island, 1983, pp. 49–68.

———. *Their Eyes Were Watching God.* 1937. New York: Harper, 1990.

Kermode, Frank. *The Sense of an Ending.* Oxford: Oxford University Press, 1966.

Krasner, James. "Zora Neale Hurston and Female Autobiography." *Black American Literature Forum,* 23 (1989): 113–126.

Long, Charles H. "The Oppressive Elements in Religion and the Religions of the Oppressed," in *Significations: Signs, Symbols, and Images in the Interpretation of Religion.* Philadelphia: Fortress, 1986, pp. 158–172.

Mbiti, John S. *African Religions and Philosophy.* London: Heinemann, 1969.

Otto, Rudolf. *The Idea of the Holy,* translated by John W. Harvey. Rev. ed. London: Oxford University Press, 1936.

Shorter, Aylward. *African Christian Theology.* Maryknoll: Orbis, 1977.

Vivas, Eliseo. "The Object of the Poem," in *Critical Theory since Plato,* edited by Hazard Adams. New York: Harcourt, 1971, pp. 1069–1077.

Walker, Alice. "In Search of Our Mothers' Gardens." 1974. *In Search of Our Mothers' Gardens: Womanist Prose.* San Diego: Harcourt, 1983, pp. 231–243.

Williams, Sherley Anne. "The Blues Roots of Contemporary Afro-American Poetry," in *Afro-American Literature: The Reconstruction of Instruction,* edited by Dexter Fisher and Robert B. Stepto. New York: MLA, 1979, pp. 73–87.

WILLIAM M. RAMSEY

The Compelling Ambivalence of Zora Neale Hurston's
Their Eyes Were Watching God

"I wrote 'Their Eyes Were Watching God' in Haiti. It was dammed up in
me, and I wrote it under internal pressure in seven weeks. I wish that I
could write it again."

Long out of the literary mainstream, Zora Neale Hurston's *Their Eyes Were
Watching God* (1937) is now a popular text in college studies, and Hurston her
self the subject of a growing industry. Yet eager to establish canonical status
for *Their Eyes,* that industry tends to gloss over, evade, or ingeniously explain
away the novel's most troubling problems, while it is sharply divided on related
interpretive issues. Increasingly, as one turns from Hurston's text to the subtle
theoretical stratagems in its critical praise, one feels a discrepancy between
that initial reading experience and current worship of Hurston's achievement.
In the classroom, moreover, students are quick to note evident problems in the
text, and are suspicious of strained elaborations and ideological agendas where
more candid explanations might better suffice. As Joseph R. Urgo warns:
"The need to explain, especially when the explicator is not quite convinced,
only emphasizes the assumption of textual weakness. In this way the novel is
allowed into the canon with a wink" (42).

Their Eyes is an inventive, original, and provocatively compelling novel;
nonetheless, it is not a fully finished or conceptually realized text. On this

Southern Literary Journal, Volume 27, Number 1 (Fall 1994): pp. 36–50. © 1994 Southern Literary Journal / UNC Press.

51

issue the circumstances of its inception are of crucial relevance, as Hurston's own words in her autobiography *Dust Tracks on a Road* (1942) might suggest. "I wrote 'Their Eyes Were Watching God' in Haiti. It was dammed up in me, and I wrote it under internal pressure in seven weeks. I wish that I could write it again. In fact, I regret all of my books."[1] Those productive seven weeks are more incredible in light of her other activities, for she was on an anthropological research trip funded by a Guggenheim Fellowship. Her biographer, Robert Hemenway, notes she arrived in Haiti in late September, 1936, and it was concurrent with anthropological collecting that she poured out her novel, dating the finished manuscript December 19, 1936 (244, n. 24). During this time, explains Hemenway, "she perfected her Creole, acquired a working knowledge of voodoo gods, attended a number of ceremonies presided over by a voodoo priest," and was "sometimes writing late at night after a day of collecting" (230).

    Moreover, it is well known that her creative motives were enmeshed in the emotions of a failed love relationship. In *Dust Tracks,* she explains how an aborted affair with a man she identifies as A.W.P. (Arthur Price) gave rise to the novel. He was from New York, and they were in love when both were doing Master's work at Columbia University. In her words, "I did not just fall in love. I made a parachute jump" (252). Though it was, as she said, "the real love affair of my life" (255), his wish that she give up her career for him began an "agonizing tug of war" (256). It was partly to escape the "exquisite torture" (259) of this relationship that she accepted the research fellowship in the Caribbean. There, she explains, "I pitched in to work hard on my research to smother my feelings. But the thing would not down. The plot was far from the circumstances, but I tried to embalm all the tenderness of my passion for him in 'Their Eyes Were Watching God'"(260).

    In short, *Their Eyes* was conceived in conditions certain to compromise even a far lesser novel's gestation. It was written in a hasty seven weeks, with little time for the ripening process of multiple drafting; it involved difficult emotional sortings out of a failed affair; and, presumably because of Hurston's marginal race and gender status, the J. B. Lippincott Company took her manuscript without requiring the rigorous redrafting of a conscientious editorial process.[2] The result is a text tantalizing in excellent promise, fertilely ambivalent thinking, technical uncertainties, and latent self-contradictions. Had she let her novel mature more slowly, had she an opportunity to have it back, and had Lippincott asked for more substantive finishing, its final shape might have been quite different.

    The text we now have is roughly equivalent to Herman Melville's *Billy Budd,* which was unfinished at his death but published, received, and assessed practically as if it were a finished novel. Some of that text's famed interpretive issues (is it a testament of resistance or acceptance?) might never have arisen if Melville had lived to give it full gestation. As it is, one can see Melville's brilliantly tentative probings of Billy, Claggart, and then Vere in that fascinating creative flux preceding final design, and therefore final coherence. Likewise, Hurston's text displays probings, discoveries, and tentative—even contradicting—critiques that resist shapely, formalist interpretive decodings. The current fashion is to fault formalist and patriarchal interpretive assumptions;[3] yet while we now appreciate much in Hurston's project that we did not once see, significant technical and interpretive issues remain, and critics read *Their Eyes* in dramatically opposing ways.

At the heart of the text's self-contradictions, at the bedrock of Hurston's personality, was her extraordinary individualism, her self-reliant, at times adversarial, drive toward autonomy. This will toward independent self-realization illuminates why her love story is rooted in rejection of love, and why her romantic, racial folk immersion is at odds with the idea of personal happiness. In *Their Eyes,* the consequence of Hurston's personal individualism is that her thoughts unfold in polarities, through bedrock oppositions of self to community, and of female self to male control. As each gravitational pole tugs against the other, negating the opposite attraction even as the opposite negates it, her text is creatively enriched and complicated.

But for critics, one pole or the other tends to exert the stronger attraction. The result, as Jennifer Jordan astutely explains, is that "critics often view the text through ideological prisms that color their conclusions." In particular, Jordan cites black feminist critics who advocate "the unsupportable notion that the novel is an appropriate fictional representation of the concerns and attitudes of modern black feminism" (107). The text is in fact ambivalent, both a precursor to the modern feminist agenda yet also a reactionary tale embalming Hurston's tender passions for a very traditional male. Such tensions, born of Hurston's fast yet fertile creative process, give the novel considerable provocative power.

The issue of self and community arises in the novel's much discussed opening pages, as the heroine Janie returns home to Eatonville, Florida, much as Hurston returned to Eatonville, her birthplace, to gather folklore. Unlike Hurston, coming from New York to do elitist professional work, Janie returns in laborer's overalls, having previously wandered off with the gambling, drinking, fighting migrant laborer Tea Cake. Janie, formerly the staid, bourgeois wife of the town mayor, feels the community's eyes scrutinizing her in that prelude before their judgmental gossip. Thus both Ivy League Hurston and renegade Janie stand in ambiguous relationship to community, partly in it, yet partly outside and at odds with its provincial temperament.

How one interprets this homecoming depends on the critical strategems applied to the whole text. Molly Hite argues this is the "triumphal return" of a woman liberated from the heterosexual romantic model. In her view, Janie's maturing into her storytelling voice shows Hurston's intention to subvert and displace Janie and Tea Cake's love paradigm as a preliminary, transformative step toward a reconstituted social order empowering women. In a contrary view, Jennifer Jordan argues that Janie fails to achieve "an independent, self-fulfilled womanhood," never overcoming her passionate dependence on Tea Cake. So this cannot be a liberated heroine's triumphal return, in that Janie "has demonstrated no ability to survive alone" (113). Yet another view, advanced by Cyrena N. Pondrom, is that Tea Cake is modeled on mythic male gods of regeneration like Adonis and Osiris, which Hurston studied under Franz Boas at Columbia. Accordingly, when Janie says, "So Ah'm back home again and Ah'm satisfied tuh be heah,"[4] she will reintegrate the community not along feminist lines but by transmitting Tea Cake's "personal, unpossessive, mutually-affirming love" (197).

Clearly the novel's opening pages are crucial. They are part of the narrative's frame, occupying primarily the first and final chapters, in which Janie returns to her home after Tea Cake's tragic death and recounts her experiences to her friend Pheoby Watson, who in turn will relate them to the community. Here, if anywhere, the novel's coherence should reveal itself, as Janie's relationship to the community is reestablished, and the significance of her experiences is clarified. Instead, the text inspires remarkably diverse and antithetical readings. The problem, I have suggested, is that toward both Tea Cake and the Eatonville community Hurston is profoundly ambivalent because the privileging of her own autonomy undercuts some of the values the novel means to promote.

To be sure, *Their Eyes* was written to celebrate rural black folkways, which Hurston's anthropology training showed her had great cultural significance. As Hemenway explains, "Zora had come to think of herself as a woman with a mission: she would demonstrate that 'the greatest cultural wealth of the continent' lay in the Eatonvilles ... of the black South" (113). Moreover, a chief tenet of the Harlem Renaissance was to speak for the folk masses, as Hurston learned when studying at Howard University under Alain Locke, who advocated that young black writers speak for the masses. Above all, *Their Eyes* was a return to Hurston's roots, because Boas and anthropology had prompted her to seek, in Hemenway's words, "a scientific explanation for why her own experience in the black rural South, despite all her education, remained the most vital part of her life, and why the black folk experience generally was the primary impetus for her imagination" (62–63).

Nonetheless, Hurston's personal ambition had taken her long ago from Eatonville to a wider, cosmopolitan, more educated world. At fourteen she left home alone, unhappy with her new stepmother. Then, with uncanny and resilient resourcefulness, she obtained college scholarships, wealthy Northern patrons, publications, and a Guggenheim Fellowship. In this significant respect she parallels Janie, who tells Pheoby in Chapter 1, referring to Eatonville's townspeople: "Ah could . . . sit down and tell'em things. Ah been a delegate to de big 'ssociation of life. Yessuh! De Grand Lodge, de big convention of livin' is just where Ah been dis year and a half y'all ain't seen me" (6). Because they have never left, Janie implies, the folk of Eatonville haven't fully lived.

With her travels and training at Howard, Barnard, and Columbia, Hurston illustrates Thomas Wolfe's awareness that even if you look homeward, you can't entirely go home again. In *Dust Tracks* she humorously notes her alienation from the rural South when she first tried to collect folklore there, and failed: "The glamor of Barnard College was still upon me" (174). No longer a child of the South, she confesses: "I went about asking, in carefully accented Barnardese, 'Pardon me, but do you know any folk-tales or folk-songs?' The men and women who had whole treasuries of material just seeping through their pores looked at me and shook their heads," some of them suggesting evasively, "Maybe it was over in the next county" (175).

Various commentators have noted Hurston's ambivalent relationship to Eatonville. John D. Kalb aptly describes her status as that of anthropological participant-observer, which required her "to separate and disassociate herself from her community and culture" in order to comprehend it scientifically.[5] Diane F. Sadoff, very perceptively examining Hurston's ambivalent "double perspective," states, "Hurston's record of return south covertly exposes her distance from her home" (19). Perhaps Hurston's own words, in *Mules and Men* (1935), best define her situation: "It was only when I was off in college, away from my native surroundings, that I could see myself like somebody else and stand off and look at my garment. Then I had to have the spy-glass of Anthropology to look through at that" (3). In sum, Hurston stood with one foot in the folk community and the other in the wider world without, paralleling the very tension Janie feels in the frame chapters.

The novel's opening words, comparing people's dreams to "ships at a distance" that "sail forever on the horizon" (1), establish Janie as someone who has sailed to the horizon (much as Hurston had sailed to the Caribbean just before writing this narrative). The theme recurs in the closing chapter when Janie concludes, "Ah done been tuh de horizon and back now. Ah kin set heah in my house and live by comparisons." The enlargement of Janie's mind is now clear: "Dis house ain't so absent of things lak it used tuh be befo' Tea Cake come along. It's full uh thoughts . . ." (182). If Janie implies her mind once was empty of the thoughts coming with growth experiences, Pheoby's response validates that: "Ah done growed ten feet higher from jus' listenin' tuh you, Janie. Ah ain't satisfied wid mahself no mo'" (182–183). Not so with the untraveled folk, who are disposed first to condemn rather than praise. Knowing this, Pheoby asserts, "Nobody better not criticize yuh in mah hearin'"(183).

As they are described in Chapter 1, the town gossips reflect the obverse side of that rural folk spirit Hurston wants to preserve in anthropology and art. Insignificant toilers by day, at dusk "They became lords of sounds and lesser things. They passed nations through their mouths. They sat in judgment" (1–2). Reflecting Hurston's ambivalence, they may be regal speakers in a dynamically oral folk culture, but their petty narrowness can be cruel with the "envy . . . they had stored up," so that now "they chewed up the back parts of their minds and swallowed with relish. They made burning statements with questions, and killing tools out of laughs. It was mass cruelty" (2).

Their remarks are withering, all the more depersonalized in that Hurston does not attach to them speaker attributions. "What she doin' coming back here in dem overhalls? Can't she find no dress to put on?" says one anonymous person. Another adds, "what dat ole forty year ole 'oman doin' wid her hair swingin' down her back lak some young gal?" Another asks, "why she don't stay in her class?—" (2). This class issue, reflecting a rigid belief that social definition is grounded in class status, is soon repeated: "She sits high, but she looks low. Dat's what Ah say 'bout dese ole women runnin' after young boys" (3). At the very least there is ambivalence here, if not a latent contradiction. On the positive side, the Eatonville folk are fiercely equalitarian, assuming that since the lowest individual has worth equal to the socially privileged, anyone may stand on Jody Starks's store porch to speak his mind in lies, jokes, and verbal contests. This is indeed a significant element in the novel's antibourgeois argument. But more negatively, that individual aspiring to go too far above or beyond the communal circle is suspect.

Hurston's ambivalence is embedded in gender as well as class concerns.[6] The envy of these women toward Janie clearly is as sexual as it is provincially social. Moreover, though the novel depicts the love between Janie and Tea Cake in highly lyrical terms, Hurston is well aware that if men can be gods they are also simply men: "The men noticed her firm buttocks like she had grape fruits in her hip pockets; the great rope of black hair swinging to her waist and unraveling in the wind like a plume; then her pugnacious breasts trying to bore holes in her shirt. They . . . were saving with the mind what they lost with the eye" (2).

In this social context, no wonder Tea Cake prompts such disparate critical views. Putting behind her two disastrous marriages to possessively patriarchal men, Janie finds romantic love in Tea Cake because, in her view, "He was a glance from God" (102), a declaration at odds with anti-patriarchal criticisms of his character. Indeed, if separated from the frame chapters, the core love romance might seem less ambiguous than the whole text. But here in a very probing, ambivalent frame, men notice Janie's buttocks, hair, and breasts—her parts rather than her person. Later, it is difficult to reconcile the regenerative side of Tea Cake with what the author already has shown she knows of men.

This awkward yoking of frame to core narrative is both a flaw, in consequence of seven hasty weeks of composing, and partly a saving strength. As a flaw, it gives rise to the technical clumsiness of Janie's narrating her tale directly to Pheoby in the frame, the narration then shifting to third person in the core. It also manifests some of the text's unresolved contradictions, because in the frame Hurston's wavering between realistic and lyrical impulses is more pronounced than in the core.

Fortunately, Hurston's ambivalence checks her from excessive idealizing and gives the novel a significant and saving criticality. As Janie strides provocatively back into Eatonville, her hips and breasts so evident through her overalls, her hair swinging freely, she surely feels the strain of men's eyes boring at her in possessive desire and mounting resentment at her unavailability. "Yes," she would seem to say, "just as Zora I return to my roots, and here I will stay." "However," she would add, "my individual personhood is something that I now proudly assert." In the polar sexual and social tensions of Janie's situation lie much of the novel's complexity and provocative power. Nothing, not even Janie's romantic love, eludes Hurston's ambivalent impulses.

Latently, in Janie's love of Tea Cake are the same seeds of contradiction that Hurston describes in her love of Arthur Price. The crippling issue was not their age difference, she like Janie being the older, but that he, studying for the ministry, wanted her to be a supporting wife instead of independent career woman. So the relationship's problematic nature was, as Hemenway surmises, "its sense of ultimate impossibility" (231), which Hurston replicates in Tea Cake's fictionally arbitrary infection by rabies. Much as Hurston finally broke away from Price with her Caribbean fellowship, herself ending the love affair of her life, Janie shoots Tea Cake to death as he rabidly attacks and bites her. The plotting here is melodramatically gratuitous, much as the hurricane is that blows onto the Everglades to destroy Janie's happiness. That is because Hurston meant to embalm in Tea Cake only the "tenderness" of her passion for Price. If, presumably, she reserved her criticisms of him for husbands Logan Killicks and Jody Starks, then Tea Cake must die a Romeo-like innocent, destroyed by star-crossed natural forces rather than by character limitations. Yet, as commentators like to note, Tea Cake's murder suggests there is a snake in Janie's pastoral Eden, and the snake is man.

"He was the master kind. All, or nothing, for him," says Hurston of A.W.P. in *Dust Tracks* (257). In demanding she give up her career, he took a patriarchal protector's role that, curiously, she refused to criticize no matter the pain it produced. Once, when he resented her offer of a quarter for his fare home, his argument was: "He was a *man!* No woman on earth could either lend him or give him a cent. . . . Please let him be a *man!*" To which Hurston acquiesced in both principle and deed: "He had done a beautiful thing and I was killing it. . . . he wanted to do all the doing, and keep me on the receiving end. He soared in my respect from that moment on. Nor did he ever change. He meant to be the head, *so help him over the fence!*" Amazingly, though "That very manliness, sweet as it was, made us both suffer," she also loved him for it (253).

Similar qualities are evident in Tea Cake, despite the conspicuously egalitarian aspects of their relationship. When Janie jokes about his flattery of women, he responds biblically, "Ah'm de Apostle Paul tuh de Gentiles. Ah tells 'em and then agin Ah shows 'em" (100). He is quasi-divine, a "glance from God" who "seemed to be crushing scent out of the world with his footsteps"; and "Spices hung about him" (101–102). If, as Janie asserts, "Dis is uh love game" (108), Tea Cake's role is at times traditionally very masculine. In an act of astounding male prerogative, he takes Janie's hidden two hundred dollars as she sleeps, leaves her in the hotel for a day and a night, blowing all but twelve dollars on a guitar and a party, at which "he stood in the door and paid all the ugly women two dollars not to come in" (117).

The next day, toting switch-blade and cards, he leaves again to win back Janie's money by gambling. For her part, Janie defends him rather than criticize: "She found herself angry at imaginary people who might try to criticize," because "Tea Cake had more good nature under his toe-nails than they had in their so-called Christian hearts" (120). When he returns with his winnings and two razor slashes, he closely echoes Arthur Price's sentiments: "Ah no need no assistance tuh help me feed mah woman." Janie's reply is, "Dat's all right wid me." When he drifts into sleep, after she has tenderly nursed his wounds, she feels such a "self-crushing love" that "her soul crawled out from its hiding place" (122).

With such incidents Hurston deliberately provokes the bourgeois reader, and her defense of Tea Cake here would be along class rather than feminist gender lines. Her point is that as Janie descends the socioeconomic ladder with a man who "ain't got doodly squat" (98), she is progressively liberated from the empty values of her earlier middle-class life. To borrow Hurston's phrase from *Dust Tracks,* the idyllic interlude with Tea Cake is Harlem Renaissance praise of the "raucous sayings and doings of the Negro farthest down" (177).

On the other hand, for all his machismo Tea Cake exhibits some protofeminist qualities. In teaching Janie checkers and rifle shooting, in fishing with her, and allowing her out of the kitchen to be in the fields with him, he cuts the oppressive shackles that her first two husbands put on her. In sum, Tea Cake is a self-contradiction, partly a man's man, partly a women's advocate. He presents the same contradictions in love that Arthur Price did, who accepted and loved Hurston's intellectual parity,[7] but who insisted on being her bread-winning protector.

These opposing polarities in Tea Cake's characterization remain unresolved. Only an arbitrary death by Janie's rifle ends them, and the reader is left pondering what his significance precisely is. One cannot know. In contrast to Killicks and Starks, he would seem unequivocally to be Janie's regenerative liberator. But in contrast with Janie's emerging independence, and with Hurston's own deepest needs for self-fulfillment, Tea Cake presents problems. Just as her own affair with Price was an ambivalent "exquisite torture," Janie's love of Tea Cake keeps her on tenterhooks: "She adored him and hated him at the same time. How could he make her suffer so and then come grinning like that with that darling way he had?" (103). Would Janie remain happy if tied to the seasonal cycles of grinding migrant work? Would she have money of her own that she could expect not to be taken? The novel ends conveniently before such issues arise to require resolution.

Hurston's characterization of Tea Cake is its most strained in the handling of his violence toward Janie. Irrationally fearful that Janie will be wooed away from him by Mrs. Turner's light skinned brother, Tea Cake gratuitously beats her, "Not because her behavior justified his jealousy, it relieved that awful fear inside him. Being able to whip her reassured him in possession." No matter that he "just slapped her around a bit to show he was boss," his possessive jealousy is flatly incompatible with Janie's concurrent liberation (100). Earlier she rejected Logan and Jody for exactly such patriarchal prerogative. The chief difference here is that it is Tea Cake who controls her, and on the pedestal of their exclusive love this violence seems acceptable.

Hurston's confusion here stems in large part from an ideological shift from the feminist theme to the anti-bourgeois class critique. Tea Cake, an antibourgeois folk hero representing the raucous "Negro farthest down," has given Janie a marriage that is a medium of growth and mutuality. With his slapping Janie around, Hurston means to flaunt the stuffy elitism of her genteel middle-class readers. Indeed she very carefully precedes this episode with Janie's beating of Tea Cake first, because of her jealousy over Nunkie's interest in him; thus Janie exerts a sexual control equal to Tea Cake's. Likewise, Janie learns rifle shooting from Tea Cake and soon surpasses his skill. In the rough and tumble, give and take of this love, the reader is intended to focus foremost on Janie's developing self-reliance and egalitarian autonomy, even in conflictual moments.

But Hurston's folk romanticism founders here on the conflicting premises of her ideologies. Tea Cake's polarities—regenerative lover but slap-her-around plebeian—undermine plausibility even as they enrich the narrative with ambivalence. Further, Hurston's critiques are too hastily doctrinaire. For instance, in most male-on-female marital violence, women lack the power that Hurston gives to Janie. Richard Wright, who negatively reviewed the book, accused Hurston of a "facile sensuality" in which her depiction of "the

Negro folk mind" is characterized by "pure simplicity" (25).[8] His own writings present a completer picture of the racial, economic, and psychological determinants of male frustration and violence. *Their Eyes,* however, is "uh love game," and the text won't treat Tea Cake as it did Logan and Jody, as controlling men who enforced their wife's submission. Rather, in fellow migrant workers the beating of Janie "aroused a sort of envy in both men and women." In fact, Tea Cake's subsequent petting and pampering of her "made the women see visions and the helpless way she hung on him made men dream dreams" (140).

In this episode, Janie's growing individualism fails to counterbalance grimmer American social realities, making life on the egalitarian Florida muck implausibly Edenesque. In the closing frame chapter, Pheoby declares, "Ah means tuh make Sam take me fishin' wid him after this" (183). Pheoby's new autonomy is a response quite at odds with those admirers of Janie's helpless hanging on to Tea Cake. Indeed, Hurston herself finally refused to hang onto Arthur Price. She left for the Caribbean and the gains, both monetary and intellectual, of a self-fulfilling career. But she must have felt as if she had shot her man. In that respect, Janie's killing of Tea Cake is no more arbitrary than Hurston's painful, necessary insistence on her self-realization. Tea Cake's death is Hurston's vicarious revenge on Arthur Price, a concealed recognition of the snake in Hurston's southern folk Eden.[9] At the end of the novel, her covert rage is displaced onto the fury of the hurricane, which brings with it a rabid dog and Tea Cake's inevitable doom.

Their Eyes is neither an evasively nostalgic, pastoral folk romance, nor is it wholly a feminist text. It is an ambivalent and contradictory text reflecting tensions Hurston felt both in love and in her rural South. Above all, it is powerfully provocative, as its admirers well know despite discomfort with its problems. To dismiss it out of hand, with formalist charges that it has evident flaws, is to deny its exciting and informing values. If *Their Eyes* were simply an unambiguous tragic romance, it would have only the power of a love lament for Arthur Price. If it were only an uncritical folk idealization of Eatonville, it would be romantic ethnography wedded to a Harlem Renaissance taste for fashionably exotic primitives.

What the novel does, while immersing one first in a woman's patriarchal oppression and then her lyrical love, as well as the richly felt life of a dynamic folk culture, is to probe these worlds with instinctively keen acumen. For Janie, Tea Cake is undeniably attractive and liberating, but beneath her love lurks a troubling unease. His polarities, rooted in Hurston's experience with men, give his idealized characterization a curious complexity, a submerged criticality that finds vent in his death. Neither anger alone nor love alone is Hurston's narrating motive. The anger is there, covertly, Sadoff perceptively states, as "the subterranean theme in Hurston's *Eyes* that women most truly become themselves without men" (22). But the love equally is there, the recognition in Tea Cake's loss that to privilege personal autonomy over heterosexual love is to suffer a stinging sacrifice.[10] The contradictions of Eatonville, too, carry Hurston deeper than the cosmetics of nostalgia. Eatonville may be a world of racial and cultural vibrancy, but it can be mean to Janie once she has become an outsider. Hurston may have intended to celebrate Eatonville's richness, but from her probing comes an emergent, tentative critique of it as a paradise flawed and needing reconstruction.

Hurston is, then, an example of the Southerner who leaves the South and returns with ambivalent perspective, which in *Their Eyes* pulls in two contradictory directions, folk praise and criticism. In a word, Hurston's feet stood in two quite different soils. As Eatonville's representative to the North and the Harlem Renaissance, Hurston kept one foot planted proudly in the South. In this posture she was uncritical of her roots, her motive being to explain her culture—or flamboyantly to brag about it—to outsiders who were unaware of its values.

In this stance, she backdrops Eatonville's folkloric wealth in a luxuriant Southern Eden, which is presided over by tutelary god Vergible Tea Cake Woods. Tea Cake offers regenerative force. His first name is clearly vegetal in suggestion, and his last realizes the promise of Janie's teenage pear tree vision of organic harmony. In the end, a liberated Janie brings back his seeds to the village for its own regeneration in love. Eatonville, from Hurston's proud stance within her indigenous culture, is an implicit critique of a modern civilization that has lost important frontier, village, and folk values, and which has ignored the African-American cultural legacy. Indeed *Their Eyes* should have made Hurston's mentor Boas happy, for his anthropological efforts contained a similar, implied culture critique.

Surely, as Janie informs Pheoby of the stories, humor, signifying, and wisdom of the black village—things Pheoby need not be taught since she is immersed within them—Hurston is looking past Pheoby to the wider, Northern audience. Richard Wright astutely sensed this, accusing her of writing "to a white audience" for their mere entertainment (25). He feared the white response would be condescension toward—as he saw it—the story's simplistic pathos and laughter. He was correct in part, for the more celebratory, uncritical stance of *Their Eyes* is to convey an idyllic picture of racial wholeness to outsiders ignorant of it.

Yet this novel hardly whitewashes the South. That is because Hurston's other foot was in the North, and from this more alienated viewpoint Janie's arduous maturation seems threatened by snakes newly found in the garden. As Hemenway perceptively argues, Hurston discovered "one of the flaws in her early memories of the village: there had usually been only men telling lies on the front porch of Joe Clarke's store" (232). Logan Killicks, his first name suggesting low worth and a gun's violence, kills Janie's pear tree dream. Because his farm is like "a stump in the middle of the woods" (20), he is a truncation of love (and an antithesis to Tea Cake "Woods"). Subsequently, bourgeois Joe Starks brings only more anti-vegetal starkness to Janie's life. Finally, if there is blight in the garden, it would be expected that the liberating Tea Cake live; his death suggests Hurston instinctively sensed blight in him as well.

His contradictory characterization emerges from the conflicting feminist and class ideologies discussed earlier, as well as Hurston's divided rhetorical stance. In her more alienated posture, Hurston's critical aim is directed against her home, for most definitely she, a staunch individualist, had discontents with a culture blighted by patriarchal oppression and, behind that, racism. This theme is announced memorably by Janie's Nanny:

> Honey, de white man is de ruler of everything as fur as Ah been able tuh find out. Maybe it's some place way off in de ocean where de black man is in power, but we don't know nothin' but what we see. So de white man throw down de load and tell de nigger man tuh pick it up. He pick it up because he have to, but he don't tote it. He hand it to his womenfolks. De nigger woman is de mule uh de world so fur as Ah can see. (19)

In this mode of address, illustrated by Janie's confiding only to Pheoby what the hostile villagers would resist accepting, Hurston cannot be wholly celebratory. From the alienation in this critical posture comes a destructive hurricane and Tea Cake's violent death, a recognition that personal happiness cannot be found in the garden. As Janie loves then shoots him, Hurston both loves and objects to her fallen, unregenerated paradise. Hastily composed and published, *Their Eyes* is a text of unfolding, unresolved ambivalences, a narrative begun perhaps as pastoral romance yet veering toward feminist resistance, a celebration of the low-down folk but a prickly critique of provincial mentality, a novel whose unresolved tensions reflect its remarkable creative intelligence. Hurston's ambivalent pull between praise and critique, while not always yielding a fully coherent text, should continue to compel with its inventive vigor, to cast its widening net around new readers.

Notes

1. Zora Neale Hurston, *Dust Tracks on a Road: An Autobiography* (Urbana: University of Illinois Press, 1984), p. 212. All subsequent references are to this edition.

2. As Hemenway notes, "the editors had found little need for revisions" (231). Part of the marginality problem was that Lippincott's lacked enough racial knowledge to work constructively with her manuscript. Carby cites a Hurston letter

to James Weldon Johnson, January 22, 1934, complaining that the firm was "not familiar with Negroes" (92, n. 25).

3. An anti-formalist example is Michael Awkward's argument that "Hurston's narrative strategies demonstrate not a failure of the novelist's art, but her stunning success in *denigrating* the genre of the novel" (17). A notoriously masculinist critique is Darwin Turner's, which now is universally and rightfully condemned, despite his perceptions of technical flaws in *Their Eyes*.

4. Zora Neale Hurston, *Their Eyes Were Watching God* (New York: Harper and Row, 1990), p. 182. All subsequent references are to this edition.

5. Carby also treats this issue, brilliantly questioning the current cultural privileging of Hurston who, as autonomous intellectual, was not embedded in the folk community she presumed to represent. Carby argues that Pheoby must mediate for Hurston the gap between Janie and Eatonville. My own argument focuses more on the power of the text, which I perceive Hurston's authorial ambivalence as enhancing.

6. A brilliant feminist demonstration of gender, class, and racial determinants, especially in her reading of Janie's courtroom trial, is given by Rachel Blau DuPlessis. She also shows how the whole narrative is a community trial of Janie, arguing that one must read the text "multifocally, conflictuality" (99).

7. Hemenway notes the attraction was intellectual as well as physical, that "the two of them held long conversations about religious issues," and she was attracted to his "quick intelligence and considerable learning" (231).

8. Even Alain Locke regards the book as an "oversimplification" lacking the social weight of "motive fiction and social document fiction" (10).

9. Sadoff argues, when linking Janie's resentment to Jody: "Janie's desire . . . to tell stories and to achieve verbal power in the face of Jody's denial are figures for Hurston's drive to write novels and essays in the face of Price's insecure demand that she give up her career for their relationship" (20). Regarding Tea Cake's death she argues, "Hurston has motivated her narrative, perhaps unconsciously, to act out her rage against mate domination" (22).

10. Various commentators note this contradiction, including Shirley Anne Williams, who suggests, "Zora was evidently unable to satisfactorily define herself in a continuing relationship with a man, whereas such definition is the essence of Janie's romantic vision" (x). See also Donald R. Marks's perceptive examination of Hurston's ideological contradictions.

WORKS CITED

Awkward, Michael. *Inspiriting Influences: Tradition, Revision, and Afro-American Women's Novels*. New York: Columbia University Press, 1989.

Carby, Hazel V. "The Politics of Fiction, Anthropology, and Folk," in *New Essays on "Their Eyes Were Watching God,"* edited by Michael Awkward. New York: Cambridge University Press, 1990, pp. 71–93.

DuPlessis, Rachel Blau. "Power, Judgement, and Narrative in a Work of Zora Neale Hurston: Feminist Cultural Studies," in *New Essays on "Their Eyes Were Watching God,"* edited by Michael Awkward. New York: Cambridge University Press, 1990, pp. 95–123.

Hemenway, Robert E. *Zora Neale Hurston: A Literary Biography*. Urbana: University of Illinois Press, 1977.

Hice, Molly. "Romance, Marginality, Matrilineage: Alice Walker's *The Color Purple* and
    Zora Neale Hurston's *Their Eyes Were Watching God.*" *Novel*, 22 (1989): 257–273.

Hurston, Zora Neale. *Dust Tracks on a Road: An Autobiography*. Urbana: University of Illinois
    Press, 1984.

———. *Mules and Men*. Bloomington: Indiana University Press, 1978.

———. *Their Eyes Were Watching God*. New York: Harper & Row, 1990.

Jordan, Jennifer. "Feminist Fantasies: Zora Neale Hurston's *Their Eyes Were Watching God.*"
    Tulsa Studies in Women's Literature, 7 (1988): 105–117.

Kalb, John D. "The Anthropological Narrator of Hurston's *Their Eyes Were Watching God.*"
    Studies in American Fiction, 16 (1988): 169–180.

Locke, Alain. "Jingo, Counter-Jingo, and Us." *Opportunity*, 16 (Jan. 1938): 7–12.

Marks, Donald R. "Sex, Violence, and Organic Consciousness in Zora Neale Hurston's *Their
    Eyes Were Watching God.*" *Black American Literature Forum*, 19.4 (1985): 152–157.

Pondrom, Cyrena N. "The Role of Myth in Hurston's *Their Eyes Were Watching God.*"
    American Literature, 58 (1986): 181–202.

Sadoff, Diane F. "Black Matrilineage: The Case of Alice Walker and Zora Neale Hurston."
    Signs, 11 (1985): 4–26.

Turner, Darwin. *In a Minor Chord*. Carbondale: Southern Illinois University Press, 1971.

Urgo, Joseph R. "'The Tune is the Unity of the Thing': Power and Vulnerability in Zora
    Neale Hurston's *Their Eyes Were Watching God.*" *Southern Literary Journal*, 23.2 (1991):
    40–54.

Williams, Shirley Anne. "Foreword." *Their Eyes Were Watching God*. Urbana: University of
    Illinois Press, 1978.

Wright, Richard. "Between Laughter and Tears." *New Masses*, 5 (Oct. 1937): 23, 25.

GORDON E. THOMPSON

Projecting Gender: Personification in the Works of Zora Neale Hurston

Concerning voice in Zora Neale Hurston's *Their Eyes Were Watching God,* Robert Stepto declares: "Hurston's curious insistence on having Janie's tale—her personal history in and as a literary form—told by an omniscient third person, rather than by a first-person narrator, implies that Janie has not really won her voice and self after all—that her author (who is, quite likely, the omniscient narrating voice) cannot see her way clear to giving Janie her voice outright."[1] Stepto concludes that "control of the tale remains, no matter how unintended, with the author alone" (Stepto, 166).

Henry Louis Gates Jr., in his discussion of free indirect discourse, has summed up much of the scholarship associated with the problem of voice in *Their Eyes Were Watching God.*[2] Rather than attempt to establish that either Janie's or Hurston's voice ultimately controls the text, Gates and others have noted a rather high degree of cooperation and intimacy between the two voices. This literary convention so greatly illuminates the novel's inner workings that the issue of control as originally framed by Stepto has been eclipsed.

Although the approach of Gates and others has proven valuable, I nevertheless agree with Stepto's position that Hurston is ultimately in control of her text. Yet as Stepto says, "Hurston is genuinely caught in the dilemma of

American Literature, Volume 66, Number 4 (December 1994): pp. 737–763. © 1994 Duke University Press.

how she might both govern and exploit the autobiographical impulses that partially direct her creation of Janie" (Stepto, 166).

I hope to indicate here how readers may resolve the "dilemma" with which Stepto says Hurston is burdened. As I see it, Hurston "governs" and "exploits" her "autobiographical impulses" not only in the creation of Janie, but also, and more important, in the creation of most of her fiction. By taking Hurston's oeuvre and examining the persistent recurrence of a single rhetorical convention, personification, I hope to present an advance on past readings of Hurston's fictions—readings which were unable to situate Hurston comfortably in a tradition of African Americanist or feminist rhetoric and were thus never able to successfully resolve the dilemma Stepto originally posited. More to the point, my reading involves exploring the connections made throughout Hurston's work between the literary convention of personification and the psychology of projection.

The following discussion will attempt to make clear how Hurston's use of projection and personification functions to reflect her attainment of a literary voice. This leads us to how Hurston projected her gender upon a male storytelling tradition as well as how her ideas concerning a folktale genre are characterized chiefly by their reliance upon personified images. Her philosophical investigation of issues related to gender and storytelling remains submerged, however, beneath more colorful and dynamic narrative episodes, such as those associated with travel. A trope that can be easily reinterpreted as a species of social projection, metaphors of the journey reveal another dimension of Hurston's method—namely, the nondidactic means of depicting gender differences vis-à-vis the inner self. She uses travel to contrast the negatives of domesticity with the benefits of exploration and its self-affirming powers, be such exploration fanciful and psychological or literary and geographical. Consequently, throughout her works, but particularly when using metaphors of travel, Hurston uses personification as a device to make new locales appear strange and wonderful and therefore desirable, or contrarily, she makes various places appear uncanny, frightening, and undesirable. When the personification is negative, Hurston is setting up a problematic or conflict—often related to gender or the storytelling tradition—that she intends to resolve.

But while gender and its intraracial component are critical issues in the black community and a major theme with which many African American women's texts are identified,[3] Hurston handles neither issue in a conventionally literary or orthodox, party-line fashion.[4] Rather, Hurston's privileging of black folkloric materials represents the key to her championing of black and black female "self-determination."[5] Racial conflict in Hurston, hence, remains muted and indirect and her handling of gender concerns somewhat problematic, especially in light of contemporary feminist ideology.[6]

While many scholars have examined Hurston's *Dust Tracks on a Road* with a view toward extracting from it the intimate details of her life that could serve to reinforce our reading of her fictions and deepen our understanding of Hurston herself, few have been satisfied with what this autobiography has had to offer.[7] In Robert Hemenway's view, for example, Zora Neale Hurston was incapable of creating a coherent vision of her life in *Dust Tracks on a Road*. Though impressed with Hurston's work, Hemenway expresses some major reservations in his introduction to the latest edition of Hurston's autobiography: "Hurston avoided any exploration of the private motives that led to her public success. Where is the author of *Their Eyes Were Watching God?* One is never sure in *Dust Tracks*, even as we know that the mystery behind the question—who is Zora Neale Hurston?—continually sends us back to the *Dust Tracks* text for whatever clues might be wrestled from its enigmatic author" (*DTOAR*, pp. xxxv–xxxix). Even as he appears mystified by Hurston's style, Hemenway is nevertheless on target. We are, indeed, continually led back to *Dust Tracks on a Road* for clues to Hurston's talent, where she does paint, as is her style, a vision within which one might discover those "private motives" that helped to create her literary style.

"I am so visual minded that all the other senses induce pictures in me," Hurston once stated. So for Hemenway, "one *sees* Hurston's prose." Her style, explains Hemenway, is a "natural by-product of her attempt to represent the oral voice in written narrative . . . a process," Hemenway declares, "that marks the only times that public and private personae come together." Her "expressive language . . . is really a complex product of an author who sees through two sets of eyes simultaneously" (*DTOAR*, xxxvi).

Hemenway suggests, nevertheless, that "Hurston never found a voice that could unify the dualistic vision of *Dust Tracks*" (*DTOAR*, xxxv). Her style "becomes a kind of camouflage," he says, "an escape from articulating the paradoxes of her personality" (*DTOAR*, xxxviii). This style of writing does not make her a "serious painter" of visual imagery, he concludes; and so, in the end, *Dust Tracks* fails as a literary statement because it is "deliberately less than its author's talents" (*DTOAR*, xxxix). To some degree, Nellie McKay appears to concur, pointing out that the autobiography "does not reveal intimate details" of Hurston's life; and neither is the text "a polemic on racial injustice."[8]

But McKay explains these absences brilliantly, thereby turning Hemenway's argument on its head. She suggests that "in attempting to cope with the powerlessness and vulnerability of the racial self, blacks have employed language strategies, particularly artifice and concealment, in their relation with white America." She concludes that Hurston, in a similar act of concealment, rooted her autobiographical identity in "the collective self of Eatonville" (McKay, 176). Thus, in a strategy aimed at combating the negatives of the racial and/or sexual gaze, Hemenway's aesthetic or stylistic "camouflage" becomes McKay's "concealment."

It seems, however, that if Hurston employed the language of concealment, it was, paradoxically, a language of revelation as well; for Hurston was not a typically bookish introvert: she was extraordinarily extroverted. And while she certainly spoke in a voice rooted in the "collective self of Eatonville," it is perhaps more accurate to say this collective self offers Hurston a transparent vehicle for the conveyance of her creative impulses.

Elizabeth Fox-Genovese bolsters this theory considerably: Hurston, according to Fox-Genovese, set "her sights on an ideal beyond the horizon of everyday life [and] . . . beyond the boundaries of her gender."[9] Hurston, she adds, "unmistakably identifies the problematic relation between her private self and her self-representation: 'I did not know then,'" Fox-Genovese quotes Hurston, "as I know now, that people are prone to build a statue of the kind of person that it pleases them to be" (176). McKay would agree with this elaboration, especially when she describes the image Hurston presents of herself in *Dust Tracks* as the creation of a "black female self." One must ask, finally, what were the tools and what media did Hurston employ in her construction of a private self for public consumption?[10]

In the best moments of her autobiography, Hurston's presence is clearly pronounced. Though she may have a dualistic vision, and one which is all about camouflage or concealment, her vision is in fact reflected in a literary style perfectly suited to expressing her deepest desires.[11] In *Dust Tracks*, Hurston's act of concealment serves as a metaphor not only for the representation of her historical persona, but also as she might interpret the character of her black folk community. The literary convention and the rhetorical technique best suited to represent Hurston's "camouflaged" style and rhetoric of concealment are, respectively, personification and prosopopoeia. Thus, if one examines the many manifestations of personification or prosopopoeia in *Dust Tracks,* one will notice that Hurston paints, as is her custom, a vision within which one might discover those "private motives" that helped to create her literary style and, albeit submerged, ideological rhetoric.

In fact, personification appears to be a major component of Hurston's literary style as witnessed by its presence and function in her four novels, short fictions, autobiography, and anthropological treatises.[12] An examination of the connection between how Hurston uses personification in these fictions and in her autobiography informs us not only about the politics of folktale telling in the black community but also about the reciprocal effect these folk tales then had on Hurston's own tales and her autobiographical posture. Such an approach, I believe, is eminently reasonable since, as it becomes more and more obvious, "the distinction between fiction and autobiography is not an either/or polarity," but, as Paul de Man observes, very likely "undecidable."[13]

• • •

Hurston's second novel, *Their Eyes Were Watching God*—which can be thought of as a "fictionalized autobiography"—can serve as an example of how Hurston utilized the vagaries of the convention of personification and the rhetoric of prosopopoeia in her fictions. The text opens with metaphors of judgment and retribution: "So the beginning of this was a woman and she had come back from burying the dead. Not the dead of sick and ailing with friends at the pillow and the feet. She had come back from the sodden and the bloated; the sudden dead, their eyes flung wide open in judgment" (*TEWWG*, 9). A clear reference is made here to the storm and subsequent flood which, over two-hundred pages later, is quite traditionally anthropomorphized or personified—a storm that changes the course of the heroine's psychic life: "'De lake is comin'!' and the pursuing waters growled and shouted ahead, 'Yes, Ah'm comin'!', and those who could fled on" (*TEWWG*, 240). In this episode, personification is manifested when a personality or "face" is given to a nonsentient object and to an "absent power." Superimposing a second "face" over the face or personality of certain characters (or characteristics) comes into focus as an identifying feature of Hurston's work.

At the commencement of her first novel, *Jonah's Gourd Vine* (1934),[14] for instance, Hurston's handling of personification as projection is fascinatingly complex. The narrator announces that "God was grumbling his thunder and playing the zig-zag lighting thru his fingers" (*JGV*, 9). The narrator's statement represents a classic Hurston image which Hurston herself describes as "crayon enlargements of life," or "thought pictures," "mind-pictures" that bring feelings that drag "out dramas from the hollows" of her characters' hearts.

Immediately following the narrator's observations about God's grumbling, Amy Crittenden decides "Ole Massa gwinter scrub floors tuhday." Her expression—another personified image—is exceedingly close to that of the narrator's, with the main exception that Amy's speech is represented in "dialect." As a result of this similarity in their "modes" of imagining the world, a certain intimacy is established between the narrator and Amy.[15] One might also detect Amy's need to bring the world closer to her, to make it more intelligible and less awesome. "Ole Massa," for example, is going to scrub floors just like Amy. More pointedly, here is a powerful instance of psychological projection presented in the form of a personified *visual* image, providing us with a "mind-picture" of, or glimpse into, Amy's heart.[16] Though it is the approach of rain to which Amy refers, her projection of a new image onto the world also reveals the power of personification, like metaphor, to "remake" reality.[17] Amy's behavior becomes a prototype for many of Hurston's characters who also project their designs, fears, or desires upon inanimate objects or even other characters to transform the world into a more manipulable and manageable environment.

Moreover, when linked with the "zig-zag" lighting and the grumbling thunder introduced by the narrator, "Ole Massa's" scrubbing—or cleansing as Amy sees it—takes on a wrathful, vengeful tone. Amy's act of projection thus reveals her deeply felt need for judgment and retribution—a notion reinforced, in fact, by the entire tenor of *Jonah's Gourd Vine;* indeed, if the pathos of its wayward hero's tragic and sudden death at the end of the text does not demonstrate as much, nothing else will. Personification is used here to express Amy's need for justice and retribution and perhaps, more conventionally, a longing for escape, be it physical or mental.[18]

Amy's novel image, in its collapsing of two instances of personification, reveals the indeterminacy of the distinction between psychological projection, a cognitive term associated with personality, and personification, an artistic convention. For psychologists, personification is also a projected image "an individual has of himself or of another person. It is a complex of feelings, attitudes, and conceptions that grows out of experiences with need-satisfaction and anxiety."[19] But Quintillian's definition of prosopopoeia, from whence our current notions of personification are derived, includes rhetorical figures by which an "inanimate or abstract thing is represented as a person with personal characteristics," or "a person or thing in which some quality or abstraction is as it were embodied" [*OED*]. In the context of personification, certainly "embodied" would be synonymous with projected.[20]

Thus in Hurston one ought not to emphasize the literary aspect of personification without noting its psychological, projective aspect; the converse should also be noted. The common ground between the two lies in the superimposition and thus projection of the subject's needs or desires onto the world—the result would be a personified image. By focusing on the subject's needs and desires, by locating and analyzing them, the reader is able to discover the correlation between strategies hidden in rhetorical patterns, tropes, and metaphors and more overt narrative units, plots, themes, and narrative structures.[21]

In this regard, the following episode from *Their Eyes* is particularly revealing: "Through the pollinated air she [Janie] saw a glorious being coming up the road. In her former blindness she had known him as shiftless Johnny Taylor, tall and lean. That was before the golden dust of pollen had beglamored his rags and her eyes" (25). Projection here is created by taking a given image, the ragged, shiftless Johnny Taylor, and attaching to him a second image—here, a beglamored and glorious one which represents the erotic projection of the heroine. The difference between the given object and the additional superimposed image serves to highlight the displaced and deferred aspects of the original object. "Clearly," says Michael Awkward, "Janie's 'pollinated' perception of Johnny Taylor is faulty." It is her "intense desire for a mate" that forces her to see him as she wishes rather than as her community believes she should. "She views him," in short, "in [a historical] manner," says Awkward, "that is inconsistent with her knowledge of his character."[22] Janie's act of projection exemplifies the sharp discrepancy between what actually exists and what Janie thinks she sees. Psychologists recognize this phenomenon as a form of projection, explained as the "tendency on the part of the subject to perceive or understand his environment in such a manner as to make it congruent with or justify his needs, affects, and impulses . . . [in short] his own emotional state" (Hall and Lindzey, 195). The strange guises that this mercurial allegorical convention takes in Hurston's work are understandably multiple.[23]

To take another example, when Janie goes off with her lover, Tea Cake, she rejects the community's judgments and restrictions, for the community believes that Tea Cake is neither old enough for the mature Janie, nor rich enough for the relatively wealthy widow she has become, nor light enough for the light-complexioned beauty with long flowing hair that she continues to be despite her age. By running off with Tea Cake, however, Janie appears to have discovered her perfect lover. As she might see it, having turned against both her grandmother's and the community's wishes, she finally finds love. She feels very little guilt, and, consequently, appears to have "conquered"—in a manner of speaking—her superego. But later, her personification of the lake or "sea" in the flood and storm episode, in fact, suggests otherwise.

For it appears Janie has internalized, to some extent, the community's taboos or laws; as I have argued elsewhere,[24] if she has, she is in great part a representative of her community—a "model per-sona."[25] Consequently, Janie may not be able to escape the community's wishes because she carries them with her, inside her psyche. Hence the following episode is blatant, exceptional, and rather telling directly as the result of the presence of personified images:[26] "The monstropolous beast had left his bed. The two hundred miles an hour wind had loosed his chains. He seized hold of his dikes and ran forward until he met the quarters; uprooted them like grass and rushed on after his supposed-to-be conquerors, rolling the dikes, rolling the houses, rolling the people in the houses along with other timbers. The sea was walking the earth with a heavy heel" (*TEWWG*, 239).

Because she personifies the storm and gives it vindictive intentions, one might wonder if Janie implicitly accepts the storm as an act of divine retribution. In fact, to the extent that the flood is responsible—though indirectly—for the death of her Tea Cake, a man the community in its fears and jealousies rejects, the superego was not slain but had only lain dormant. Such would be true if Janie has projected the "face" of her restrictive community upon the lake, turned it wrathful and retributive so that its actions appear to do the community's bidding, its face reflecting the heroine's superego or bad conscience—in short, guilt. Once the dictates of the superego reappear in the guise of the flooding lake, she is unmasked as being at best a "supposed-to-be conqueror." As a manifestation of Janie's deeper fears, the personified lake proves a stronger force than the community, whose taboos she believes she has conquered. It is no wonder, then, that Janie's shooting of Tea Cake is his most immediate cause of death; for she has, as I say, internalized these very taboos. The trope of personification is unpacked and we discover the text's private symbolism, which otherwise comes to us highly disguised and displaced.

In Hurston's last work, *Seraph on the Suwanee* (1948), her ideas concerning projection and personification are rendered in a highly naturalistic medium.[27] When Arvay, the protagonist, is first introduced to the swamp, her "eyes flew open in terror." She makes it clear that she doesn't "want no parts of that awful place. It's dark and haunted-looking and too big and strong to overcome. It's frightening!" (71). In her youth, Arvay demonstrated an aversion to men after having been spurned. The novel is exclusively concerned with Arvay's unusual fear of men, a fear that colors her relationship with her husband and poisons her family life, for she resides in a marriage to which she does not reconcile herself until text's end. It is not difficult to see that in her aversion to men, Arvay may see them rather than the swamp as being "dark and haunted-looking and too big and strong to overcome"—indeed, based on how Arvay treats her husband, this image comes close to describing how Arvay must also regard him. Arvay's fear of the swamp, one could say, is a reflection of some personified image (of men) that she projects upon this natural, nonsentient phenomenon. Such a vision is in line with the psychology of *projection*, a "mechanism by which neurotic or moral anxiety is converted into an objective fear" (Hall and Lindzey, 50). Though Arvay may be afraid of the swamp, she is afraid of something else besides—namely, sexuality. For deep psychological reasons related to her rigid formulation of sexual motives, Arvay finds lovemaking with her husband difficult and almost intolerable. While Arvay believes she is passing judgment on this swamp, Hurston sets up Arvay so that the reader may pass judgment on Arvay's personality or character and psychological stability.

From a psychological perspective, projection conversion is "easily made because the original source of both neurotic and moral anxiety is fear of punishment from an external agent." But projection also "reduces anxiety by substituting a lesser danger for a greater one" (Hall and Lindzey, 50). Here we see that it is not "objective reality which serves as a determinant of behavior but rather objective reality as it is *perceived* or assigned meaning by the individual" (Hall and Lindzey, 25).

In "Sweat" (from a collection of Hurston's short stories entitled *Spunk*, 1985),[28] personification takes still another form, that of symbolic tool. Delia, the heroine of "Sweat," has been beaten and abused by her husband, Sykes.

When he terrorizes her with a snake, the snake—especially in Sykes's absence—serves as a substitute for and reflection of Sykes, further defining the nature of his character. Delia's attitude towards the snake resembles her attitude towards Sykes; Sykes's manipulation of the snake and his bravado suggest—in the context of the story—that handling snakes is a male privilege. This social maxim is upset, however, when Sykes is killed by this same snake, allowing Delia to triumph in the end. In one of the earliest moments in Hurston's oeuvre, an independent woman is thus partially responsible for her husband's death, thus signaling Hurston's move towards depicting women who change their lives by seeing their world anew.

Similar symbolism confronts us in *Their Eyes* when Janie uses a shotgun to kill her crazed lover, Tea Cake. Sykes and Tea Cake are killed only after they come to personify certain animals: Sykes, the lowly snake that bites him; the rabies-infected Tea Cake, with his loping walk and his mad need to bite Janie, a rabid dog that must be shot. But the disposing of Tea Cake has greater symbolic significance: Tea Cake's essential personality is not truly slain, since for all intents and purposes when she shoots Tea Cake, Janie is shooting the mad dog Tea Cake in his madness now impersonates. The privileged personality of Tea Cake—as the incarnation of positive male behavior—is actually preserved. As Awkward says, but from a slightly different perspective: "The fact that Tea Cake ultimately fails to achieve the status of ideal male as delineated by late-twentieth-century literary critics does not detract from the effectiveness of his gifts" (52).

By text's end, with Tea Cake gone, Janie begins—but not so miraculously—to impersonate (or personify) the image of the independent male. And here personification takes on still another guise: that of the mask. She inherits all the trappings the text had hitherto ascribed to men (notably, most were almost exclusively traits and behavior exemplified by Tea Cake): she is, relative to the other members of her community, independently wealthy, and she wears overalls, knows how to fish, but more important, how to shoot a rifle—all gifts (except the wealth) she inherits from living with Tea Cake. She also remains free enough to choose any man she wishes. In this way, Janie is elevated to a position in which she may tell her own tales of anthropomorphized creatures and personified beings, as indicated by the tale of the talking buzzards that Janie imagines, but which is articulated by the narrator in free indirect discourse.

In great part, Janie appropriates through various forms of impersonation the arbitrary signs or "signifiers" of manhood without appropriating the thing or "signified" itself—that is, maleness. Interestingly, Hurston's transfer of privileges associated with men onto women such as Janie, is sustained, though in a somewhat complex manner, throughout Hurston's oeuvre.

Janie's battle with the law, with forces that judge and condemn, finally must also be taken into account. It is no wonder circumstances arise that force

Janie into an actual court of law where she must await the judgment of white men—another manifestation of power to which Janie and her black community are subject. But the very fact that she is accused of coldblooded murder, not only by white law but by black people as well, further aligns the black community with the flood that terrifies the dog, which, in turn, bites and transmits rabies to Tea Cake. Perhaps, while we are alerted to Janie's thirst for justice and her tremendous struggle to ward off the effects of communal and social persecution, we are also alerted to Hurston's more private concerns in this regard. For, when understood as a form of psychological projection, personified images in Hurston's texts may not only reveal her characters' hidden motivations, they might also reveal, like an actor's mask, Hurston's own private concerns or motives, though serving, initially, as a form of distancing that acts to shield the author from direct scrutiny, as in any successful fictional enterprise.

• • •

Perhaps Hurston's need to conceal was as much a literary impulse as it was an internal directive whose origins may be found in her personal past. When we turn to Hurston's life, for instance, we find that she cannot say exactly when she "began to make up stories," but "Little things that people did or said," as she reveals in her autobiography, "grew into fantastic stories" (*DTOAR*, 78). She speaks of trees and lakes as if they were men, and of men who turn into alligators—no more at first than the usual fantasies of children, but neither her father nor her grandmother would stand for it. Once she ran out of the house to escape a whipping from her father. But her grandmother's fury was worse. After Zora related a tale to her mother, her grandmother glared at her like "open-faced hell and snorted," demanding that the mother "Wring [Zora's] coat tails over her head and wear out a handful of peach hickories on her back-side! Stomp her guts out! Ruin her!" (*DTOAR*, pp. 71–72). Hurston never explains her grandmother's or her father's fury except to say that they were responding to her stories as simple lies: "My phantasies were still fighting against the facts," Hurston rationalizes, thus laying the foundation for her later literary exploits (*DTOAR*, 83).

For black women, as black feminist bell hooks suggests, "the urge to construct a writer-identity" is generated by a need to "challenge and subdue all impulses" that lead "away from speech into silence."[29] hooks's commentary offers timely insight into Hurston's response to her grandmother's outrage and her father's ire. Only partially daunted, Zora continues, for instance, to quench her imaginative needs by clandestinely personifying discarded household objects, thereby creating a world of her own. In a chapter entitled "Figure and Fancy," Zora picked up an ear of corn and crawled under the side of the house to love it all by myself. In a few minutes, it had become Miss Corn-Shuck, and of course needed some hair. So I went back and picked up some cornsilk and tied it to the pointed end. We had a lovely time together then Miss Corn-Shuck got lonesome for some company.

> I do not think that her lonesomeness would have come down on her as it did, if I had not found a cake of sweet soap in Mama's dresser drawer. . . . So Miss Corn-Shuck fell in love with Mr. Sweet Smell. (*DTOAR*, 73)

The deepest, most cherished aspect of Zora Neale Hurston's personality—the one of which she was most aware—was her desire to paint the world in crayon enlargements of life because this would be not only how she saw it, but also a vivid style of representation that permeated her very being. In Hurston's mind, her fantasies and personifications are closely associated with the tales the townsfolk related on the store porch. She says that the reason "the store porch was the most interesting place I could think of" is that there she could hear the "menfolk holding a 'lying' session," an activity on which she loved to eavesdrop. These men told tales about "God, the Devil, animals and natural elements," many of which "stirred up fancies in men. It did not surprise me at all to hear that the animals talked" (*DTOAR*, 69). Of course, this phenomenon does not surprise little Zora, for as *Dust Tracks* demonstrates, Zora's relationship to storytelling was not only a preconscious formation, since she was unable to say exactly when she "began to make up stories"; it was also a very personal activity, in light of her clandestine storymaking sessions alone behind the house, as well as a communal, though highly restricted activity, as represented in her eavesdropping on the store porch's "lying" sessions. Without a doubt, for Hurston, these animal fables, with their anthropomorphic, personified creatures, continued to hold deep cultural implications; she would naturally find it supremely unjust that anyone would want to prevent her from indulging in these fantasies.

Hurston offers several hints as to what she appreciated about the tales she heard as a child on her family's front porch and on the store porch. "I picked up glints and gleams out of what I heard and stored it away to turn it to my own uses," she says. Her own tales, it appears, were formed through a process of accretion, by "adding detail" to the tales she heard on the porch. In this way, by expanding on tales and anecdotes from her daily experiences, "Life took on," she says, "a bigger perimeter" (*DTOAR*, 69)—"bigger perimeter" referring as much to her imaginative life as it does to her enlarging sense of the physical world. In short, tale-telling was connected in Hurston's mind with reenvisioning worlds—the fantastic or personified character of which imaginatively transported these worlds to her or brought her closer to them.[30]

It becomes increasingly obvious that by earning the license to tell tall tales, Hurston's writing career represents her attempt to achieve what she was not allowed to indulge in when she was a child. Hurston's decision to write was additionally complicated by her identification of storytelling with men and male privileges—a concept impressed on her by her family and neighbors in the all-black town of Eatonville, Florida, during the early decades of the twentieth century. Having internalized and thus accepted this traditional precept, Hurston found it necessary to come to terms with this gender-based prescription even in her fictions. "Hurston," Fox-Genovese concurs, "should be understood as a woman who was, in terms of self-representation, concerned primarily with a 'self' unconstrained by gender in particular and condition in general" (Fox-Genovese, 193).[31]

Consequently, by creating tales governed by personified images, Hurston "literarily" impersonates the men who told fantastic stories. She transforms the male perspective of the world by superimposing upon their tall tales a presence of her own—a presence manifested by her fictional narrators. It is possible, then, that by uncovering the meanings behind Hurston's use of personification, we may discover what McKay calls Hurston's "created fictional self," a self, in short, that would be permitted to tell tall tales.[32] Perhaps Hurston's personified images hide or mask, as with psychological projection, her "private motives"—one of which might be her need to attack traditional notions of the storyteller and the socially determined requisite gender of that storyteller.

From the very start of her writing career, Hurston looked for ways to express her concerns about the politics of storytelling in her all black community. We need take only one example to acknowledge Hurston's struggle with presenting herself, and therefore women, as storytellers. In her earliest published piece, for instance, in order to camouflage her private (female) concerns with telling tall tales and travel, Hurston purposely uses a male rather than a female character to dramatize these concerns and their interrelatedness in Hurston's universe.

In "John Redding Goes to Sea" (1926), written long before *Dust Tracks*, Hurston recounts the life and tragic death of one John Redding, a boy whose inner life is strangely reminiscent of the girl, Zora.[33] Here a comparison of an episode from the autobiography and one from the tale may be illustrative, for a link can be drawn between the imaginative life of Hurston as a young girl and of the boy, John. First, examine Zora's description of a pine tree in her yard: "It was just another pine tree about a hundred feet tall then, standing head and shoulders above a grove. But let the dusk begin to fall, and it would put the crown on its skull and creep in close" (*DTOAR*, 70). Notice the contribution of the sun and shadow to Zora's personification of the tree and the fear she feels as a consequence of her insight. Similarly, John Redding and his father are taking a walk when John notices a peculiar looking tree; notice that John is as fearful of his own perceptions as is Zora in the previous excerpt:

> "See dat tallest pine tree ovah dere how it looks like a skull wid a crown on?"
>
> "Yes, indeed!" said the father looking toward the tree designated. "It do look lak a skull since you call mah 'tention to it. You 'magine lotser things nobody else evah did, son!"
>
> "Sometimes, Pa dat ole tree waves at me just aftah th' sun goes down, an' makes me sad an' skeered, too." ("John Redding," 16)

As mentioned earlier, Hurston's peculiar inner life was highly restricted by communal and familial prohibitions—prohibitions John Redding also encounters. Back at home, John's mother clearly distrusts her son's personi-fication of his environment. In *Dust Tracks*, it was both Hurston's father and her father's mother who distrusted Zora's personification of her surround-ings. We may find that the father's pride in his son, John Redding, fulfills an emotional need Hurston's father only occasionally fulfilled for her, one which her mother more frequently met. And yet, John's father happily real-izes that his son can "imagine lotser things nobody else evah did" ("John Redding," 16). To an extent, then, one can see that John Redding "imper-sonates"—though with a notable change in gender—the figure of Hurston as we have seen her describe herself in *Dust Tracks*.

Autobiography as a creative or imaginative act takes on great urgency here. For it is worth keeping in mind that Hurston's autobiography was writ-ten many years after this short story—a fact which might cause one to ponder the age-old problem of life imitating art (and the reverse), especially when that life, represented and displaced into and by language, then follows rather than precedes an earlier artistic representation of the same.

Two points must be emphasized: "John Redding Goes to Sea" serves as an entrée into the literary world for Hurston. This is quite appropriate, for by first changing the gender, Hurston proceeds to endow/invest her (male) hero with desires it has been shown Hurston herself had, but which were not recorded until well after the short story was written. The fact that the change in gender serves to mask as well as distance the author from her literary production should now be evident. But Hurston appears to have continued to apply this technique which actually turns out to be a form of personifica-tion, since such a mask is nothing else if it is not the creation of a version of the author in disguise.[34] When Hurston changes the gender of a character, furthermore—though this act may occur prior to or outside of the text—she employs a structure or mechanism not unlike that associated with the conven-tion of personification or prosopopoeia, which is the creation of face through defacement, a trope, quintessentially autobiographical, that shuttles between autobiographical rhetoric and that of fiction. It thus provides a method of reading that transcends the limitations of traditional methods of biographical exegesis. As such, the projection of individualized, personal characteristics onto other objects would constitute the most definitive attribute of personified images.[35]

•••

For Hurston, telling tall tales about personified figures, travel, and sexual infidelities are not only related to one another but are also linked with men. Travel, for instance, appears to be closely linked with sexual promiscuity, as when Hurston identifies her father by his "meanderings" from Alabama to Florida and also with his possible infidelities, as suggested in her comment: "looking back, I take it that Papa and Mama, in spite of his meanderings, were really in love" (*DTOAR*, 18). These travel and sexual pursuits are certainly privileges coveted by the men in Hurston's life; given that men—at least traditionally and conventionally—are allowed somewhat greater leeway in respect to sexually illicit relationships, the ability to be open about such relationships—at least among men—is a privilege men are allowed to exercise with less social opprobrium than women. Yet preventing their men from "wandering" would represent a considerable burden to the women in Hurston's life and fiction, as is noted in the attitude of John Redding's mother.

Hurston dates the beginnings of her own travels with the occasion of her mother's death as represented in a chapter of *Dust Tracks* entitled "Wandering." The previous chapter, "Figure and Fancy," contains much of the information about her imaginative activities. Hence, it is not surprising that "Wandering" should follow, for here Hurston's association of travel with death is (re)configured. As her many titles suggest, travel also resides at the center of her literary concerns, not only in *Dust Tracks on A Road* and "John Redding Goes to Sea" but in all of her fictions. When John Redding reaches manhood, for instance, he too, like his father John, has a great desire to travel. It is no wonder that the perceived perversity of John Redding's imagination would entice him to do something his mother simply cannot tolerate, such as travel, especially travel by sea. By expanding the "perimeters" of his world, so to speak,[36] travel offers John a physical extension or projection of what he feels when personifying objects in his immediate environment. John's mother and later John's wife fear John's need to travel, creating a strong familial prohibition with which John must contend. John's father tries to explain John's desire to his befuddled wife: "Matty, a man doan need no travel dust tuh make 'im wanter hit de road. It jes' comes natcheral fuh er man tuh travel," he says in response to Matty's belief that a witch has sprinkled her son with travel "dust" ("John Redding," 18). Pointedly, travel is an inner force inexplicable to women like Matty. To the extent John's acts of personification are at all responsible for his fate, in Hurston's texts, personification, like travel, comes to signify escape from communities perceived as small and confining.

So it is quite provocative that, as described in *Dust Tracks*, Hurston's mother believes that when Zora was quite young she was likely to continue to walk in the direction of the horizon until someone came for her: "This alarmed my mother a great deal. She used to say that she believed a woman who was an enemy of hers sprinkled 'travel dust' around the doorstep the day I was born. . . . I don't know why it never occurred to her to connect my tendency with my father, who didn't have a thing on his mind but this town and the next one. That should have given her a sort of hint. Some children are just bound to take after their fathers in spite of women's prayers" (*DTOAR*, 32). Personification, then, especially as found in Hurston's tales, also symbolizes travel or voyaging as a projection of the mind at play. Often the urge to personify is associated with the exploration of new worlds by *projecting* oneself physically or mentally. Travel serves as the physical form of this projection, personification proper the psychological and/or imaginative equivalent. In this construction, Hurston's private preoccupations or motives become highly transparent. The relationship between personification and the tall tale, projection and travel—as a desire for movement, of flux even, of shifting ground—can bring with it a sense of groundlessness, of existing in a no-man's-land. While the traveler may be lauded for seeking to enlarge her cultural experience, she may also find that escaping the strictures of her cultural community is both difficult and painful; as depicted in Hurston's fictions, it is very likely deadly.[37]

Before John Redding can make his escape, for example, he is killed in a flood; Tea Cake, Janie's lover, is bitten during a flood, forcing Janie in the end—after shooting Tea Cake—to find her way back to her old home alone; and John Crittenden, from *Jonah's Gourd Vine*, is killed in a double irony, in his car by a train while in the process of rejecting his past life of sexual promiscuity. To the extent that the communal consciousness has been internalized, the traveling hero or heroine in Hurston's fictions is forced to conform.

If travel in Hurston is depicted as a specific male need, as a privilege even, Janie in *Their Eyes Were Watching God* is a masterful exception. Storytelling, too, especially when dominated by instances of personification, is associated in Hurston's world with the life of men and boys more than it is with that of women. But storytelling and travel, as any Hurston reader would know, are also quintessential Hurston traits. Yet it is almost as if Hurston, being female, felt that storytelling was a taboo and decided to allow a male character to represent this aspect of herself. Even in the short excerpt from "John Redding," one notes the displacement of Zora's preoccupations with travel and notable imaginative abilities onto the boy, John Redding. In a manner of speaking, this displaced version of Zora allows Hurston to represent a private concern in a boy who now represents a "virtual self" of the child Zora and her flights of fancy.[38] Hurston appropriates by and in her writings selected male privileges conventionally denied to women but ironically intrinsic to the private world of Zora Neale Hurston, which she then transfers back onto her male characters, as exemplified by her creation of John Redding.

While it could be said that John Redding is a literary impersonation of Zora, it could also be said that certain aspects of Hurston's autobiography might actually be reprisals, paradoxically, of ideas she collected from "John Redding" and other early short stories. Whatever the case, Hurston's travel and creative interests, however much her own, were thought of by herself and others as activities from which women were strictly forbidden because they were considered to be strictly male privileges, not only because the community so stipulated, but also because Hurston may have, in fact, associated such privileges with a particular man, her father John. If so, it becomes more difficult, now, to determine whether certain motifs found in Hurston's fictions were patterned after her own life experiences or after those of her father.

Whatever Hurston's problems with her father, she certainly sought to emulate him, particularly where storytelling and travel were concerned. The repetition of his name throughout her work is no accident. It is also no wonder that, like the "meanderings" of John Hurston, who was something of a folk minister, John Crittenden of *Jonah's Gourd Vine* is also a folk minister who loves to travel; Moses, from *Moses, Man of the Mountain,* is also a man who travels in search of and at the command of God, becoming the object of the obsessions of three different women. Though it also appears that John Redding, John Crittenden, Moses, and other male characters are initially taken from the same, but highly flexible template, this template appears to have been molded, again ironically, as much on the desires, wishes, and activities of Hurston's father as on Hurston herself—Hurston's own travels and multiple relationships being, of course, almost common knowledge. So then, to what degree, one might ask, was Hurston's life merely an unconscious mimicking of her father's? As I see it, most of the heroes in Hurston's texts are male because they represent the privileged elite who are empowered to engage in activities Hurston covets; while she practiced these privileges in her actual life, she also adopts these privileges—perhaps secondhand—mostly through her male characters, though interestingly enough also through Janie.

Consequently, the feminist perspective of *Their Eyes Were Watching God* must be reexamined; for even though Janie, the novel's protagonist, in her travels from locale to locale in search of love, appears to be a reflection of Hurston's own travels and concomitant multiple marriages or matings, Janie may also appear to be a converted projection of Hurston's father. James Krasner points

out that, "as it stands, Janie's life story is built on the male model." He demonstrates that in the language used by many feminist critics, "Janie's story"
is directly tied "to the paradigm for male autobiography established at the
beginning of" the novel.[39] How feminist, then, can such a text be, if the heroine is only acting out male privileges? The answer in part is that Janie is not
simply impersonating men by remaining single and independent, or when
she travels in a pair of overalls, as noted in the opening scene of the book, or
when she actually has the will to use a hunting rifle on her lover—Janie is
merely adopting privileges that Hurston regards, finally, as gender neutral. As
Fox-Genovese noticed, "Once the gaps between sexuality and gender begin
to appear, men and women can begin to question whether gender flows naturally from sexuality, whether social demands on the individual are biologically
determined . . . Neither masculinity nor femininity exists as an absolute"
(Fox-Genovese, 187). And this is a conclusion at which Hurston also appears
to have arrived.

It is no wonder, then, that Hurston wrote stories generated in great part
by personified images—images which lie at the heart of her attempt to remake in her own image the sexual/social traditions she encountered during
her youth. But the roles and privileges of the sexes in the all-black town
where Hurston was raised restricted her, since she was a girl, from making
up tall tales or "lies," as they were called. That Hurston goes on to become
a major writer of the tall tale flies in the face of these earlier prohibitions.
The very act of writing, then, represents for Hurston a rebellious moment of
great social and literary significance, the indications or markings of which
are figured as much in the structure and theme of her many texts as in their
linguistic patterns.

If only intuitively, it appears that Hurston was aware that storytelling in her black community—whatever other purposes such tales might
serve—was a means of projecting human desires and passing judgment
against a terribly unjust sociopolitical system. The black community "had
been tongueless, earless, eyeless conveniences" for the "bossman." But there
comes a time, we learn in *Their Eyes Were Watching God,* "to hear things and
talk." So when the bossman was gone, they became "lords of sound" and
"sat in judgment" (*TEWWG,* pp. 9–10). Storytelling, when understood as
"lies" or "lying," to use Hurston's language, is a mythopoeic activity that
can "expand the perimeters" of one's life. Such an expansion may take place
if "lying" is a means of "projecting" oneself both upon other sensibilities
or into other worlds. At bottom, "lying" allows the actor to toss his/her
desires out upon the world. The world can be either threatening or indifferent, against which the act of projection may serve as a defense mechanism.
One may, in addition, seek to control the world far more aggressively by
superimposing on it one's desires: the result could be a form of personification

expressed in images as beautiful and as tenuous as "A mood come alive. Words walking without masters" (*TEWWG*, 10).

Storytelling thus creates desirable conditions and gives one a sense of control. Perhaps this is also why men in Hurston's texts attempt to prohibit women from participating in this form of self-empowerment and self-assertion, which appears to be at the bottom of the struggle between Moses and Miriam in Hurston's third novel, *Moses Man of the Mountain*. But since storytelling in Hurston's community was dominated by "menfolk," with women tacitly prohibited from participating as equals among men, little Zora was not authorized to listen to or relate any animal tales. hooks explains how, just as children "were meant to be seen and not heard . . . Madness, not just physical abuse, was the punishment for too much talk if you were female" (hooks, 7). It is no wonder, then, that in her earliest published short story, Hurston projects her youthful preoccupations with personification upon a boy—John Redding.

But there are exceptions: in her anthropological treatise, *Mules and Men*,[40] Hurston introduces "Big Sweet," a powerfully built woman with plenty of character and stories of her own. She is an exception to the male rule, for with her verbal and physical sorties, she challenges the black male world. Her decision to tell "lies" and other tales is carried out with a tremendous amount of self-assertive willpower. This anecdote sets the stage for Hurston's occult political concerns—namely, to subvert the notion that storytelling is essentially a male activity. Storytelling, whatever traditional notions may be, can be appropriated by men or women. Consequently, "for us [black women]," as hooks says, "true speaking is not solely an expression of creative power; it is an act of resistance, a political gesture that challenges [the *gender*] politics of domination that would render us nameless and voiceless" (hooks, 8).[41]

Yet Hurston does not intend to feminize the storytelling process. Her "communal self" would prohibit so radical a turn; instead, she offers a more splendid compromise. She uses personification to bypass society's taboos so that she may appropriate the honors and privileges of the storyteller, which include the projection, or the enactment, of "virtual selves": in other words, "By insisting on being a self independent of history, race, and gender," as Fox-Genovese says, "she comes close to insisting on being a self independent of body" (Fox-Genovese, 197).

Such a compromise represents perhaps one of the most significant literary devices at work in Hurston's texts. That this transfer of Hurston's face or personality onto the other gender (or generic other) resembles the logic of personification—namely, the superimposition of one face over another—leads me to think that Hurston used personification in order to realize in some form her desire to act out privileges customarily associated with men, especially those concerned with telling tall tales, as well as her love of the fantastic and the highly imaginary images associated with personification. Such are the impulses that led her to retain this personifying convention in all its various guises, including the standard literary convention of character/ author substitution.

Therefore, by adopting the role of teller-of-tall-tales, Hurston takes on the role set aside in her community for black males. By exercising privileges traditionally identified as male, Hurston in a sense is able to impersonate or masquerade as male, at least from within the confines of certain social conventions. Personification is a concept, then, that appeals to Hurston because it lends itself so well to the structure and mechanism of impersonation; it allows a person to gain a certain power by taking on the characteristics of another. By writing texts characterized by personified images, Hurston achieves two purposes: she bucks the tradition that prohibited her from writing and from telling tall tales, and in the writing of these tales, she is able to impersonate the role of the male writer and so overturn the restrictions she labored under as a child. Nevertheless, the storytelling is not re-gendered, for Hurston is a woman telling tales about women. And neither does she monopolize the tradition for women; instead, storytelling is rendered gender neutral, while the power of the imagination to remake the world is again reconfigured.

NOTES

I presented a version of this essay to The City College of New York's Faculty Colloquium in 1991. Many thanks to Kimberley Benston, Joseph Brown, Joshua Wilner, Marcellus Blount, and James deJong for their very helpful suggestions and emendations.

1. Robert Stepto, *From Behind the Veil* (Urbana: University of Illinois Press, 1979), 166. All subsequent references will be indicated parenthetically as Stepto.

2. Henry Louis Gates Jr., *The Signifying Monkey* (Oxford: Oxford University Press, 1988), pp. 207–211. Gates's essay on Hurston represents a virtual compendium of the commentary on Hurston and her use of free indirect discourse.

3. Mae Gwendolyn Henderson, for example, says "Janie, the protagonist in . . . *Their Eyes Were Watching God,* demonstrates how the dialectics/dialogics of black and female subjectivity structure black women's discourse." "Speaking in Tongues: Dialogics, Dialectics, and the Black Woman's Writer's Literary Tradition," in *Changing Our Own Words: Essays on Criticism, Theory, and Writing by Black Women,* ed. Cheryl A. Wall (New Brunswick: Rutgers University Press, 1989), p. 21.

4. In fact, Hurston deliberately problematizes the issue of male/female roles. Gates says that she uses "two chiasmuses in her opening paragraphs" of *Their Eyes Were Watching God.* "The subject," he says, "of the second paragraph of [the novel] (women) reverses the subject of the first (men) and figures the nature of their respective desire in opposite terms" (Gates, *The Signifying Monkey,* 171). On chiasmus in Hurston's novel, Gates refers his readers to Ephi Paul, "Mah Tongue is in Mah Friends's Mouf," unpublished essay. But also see Maria Tai Wolff, "Listening and

Living: Reading and Experience in *Their Eyes Were Watching God,*" in *Black American Literature Forum* 16 (spring 1982): p. 30.

5. Claire Crabtree indirectly responds to an article by Lloyd W. Brown on the ambiguous nature of the ending of *Their Eyes Were Watching God* in which the death of Janie's lover, Tea Cake, has been difficult to rationalize. "The apparent weakness of the ending of the novel," says Crabtree, "is perhaps explained by the possibility that Hurston, as a feminist, did not want Janie to find fulfillment in a man, but rather in her new-found self." See Claire Crabtree, "The Confluence of Folklore, Feminism and Black Self-Determination in Zora Neale Hurston's *Their Eyes Were Watching God,*" *Southern Literary Journal* 17 (1985): p. 65; see also Lloyd W. Brown, "Zora Neale Hurston and the Nature of Perception," *Obsidian* 4 (winter 1978): pp. 39–45; and S. Jay Walker, "Zora Neale Hurston's *Their Eyes Were Watching God:* Black Novel of Sexism," *Modern Fiction Studies* 20 (1974–1975): pp. 519–527.

6. See particularly, Mary Helen Washington, "The Black Woman's Search for Identity: Zora Neale Hurston's Work," *Black World* 21 (August 1972): pp. 68–74.

7. Zora Neale Hurston, *Dust Tracks on a Road* (1942; reprint, Urbana: University of Illinois Press, 1970), xxxv. All subsequent references will be given parenthetically as *DTOAR.*

8. Nellie McKay, "Race, Gender, and Cultural Context in Zora Neale Hurston's *Dust Tracks on A Road,*" in *Life/Lines: Theorizing Women's Autobiography,* edited by Bella Brodzki and C. Schenck (Ithaca: Cornell University Press, 1988), pp. 175–188. All subsequent references will be given parenthetically as McKay.

9. Elizabeth Fox-Genovese, "My Statue, My Self: Autobiographical Writings of Afro-American Women," in *Reading Black, Reading Feminist,* edited by Henry Louis Gates Jr. (New York: Meridian, 1990), pp. 176–177. References will be noted parenthetically as Fox-Genovese.

10. But my discussion is not as concerned with the personality of Hurston, the historical personage, as it is with her creative impulses, and only then to the extent such impulses are described in her own work. Nevertheless, it seems worth pointing out, as Lorraine Bethel does, that one can see "Hurston's Black woman-identification not only in her words, but in her visual appearance as well. . . . The pictures we have show her as a naturally handsome woman who confronted sexual/gender conventions even in the way she dressed—frequently in rakish hats and in pants—and acted on the street, smoking publicly at a time when it was not considered ladylike. I see her as refusing to mutilate or alter either her mind or her body to achieve someone else's standard of what she should be as a Black woman." See "'This Infinity of Conscious Pain': Zora Neale Hurston and the Black Female Literary Tradition," in *All the Women Are White, and All the Blacks Are Men, But Some of Us Are Brave: Black Women's Studies,* ed. Gloria T. Hull, Patricia Bell Scott, and Barbara Smith (Old Westbury, N.Y.: The Feminist Press, 1982), p. 184.

11. Here, in a heavily glossed passage from the last page of *Their Eyes Were Watching God,* is Hurston's metaphor of ego concealment/camouflage and expansion/magnification, expressed more provocatively and beautifully than anywhere else in her work: "Here was peace. She pulled in her horizon like a great fish-net. Pulled it from around the waist of the world and draped it over her shoulder. So much of life in its meshes! She called in her soul to come and see," *Their Eyes were Watching God* (1937; reprint, Urbana: University of Illinois Press, 1978), p. 286. References will be given parenthetically as *TEWWG.*

12. I intend to keep my use of the term prosopopoeia to a minimum because it can be defined much too broadly. Oliver Goldsmith, for example, once said, "the enchanting use of the prosopopoeia, [above all] is a kind of magic, by which the poet gives life and motion to every inanimate part of nature." I borrowed this quotation from Bertrand H. Bronson, "Personification Reconsidered," *ELH* 14 (September 1947): p. 170.

13. Paul de Man, "Autobiography as De-facement," *Modern Language Notes,* 94 (1979): p. 921. See also James Krasner, "The Life of Women: Zora Neale Hurston and Female Autobiography," *Black American Literature Forum* 23 (spring 1989): p. 113.

14. Zora Neale Hurston, *Jonah's Gourd Vine* (Philadelphia: Lippincott, 1934). All references are to this edition and will be given parenthetically as *JGV.*

15. This is an intimacy often noted in discussions of Hurston's second novel, *Their Eyes Were Watching God,* as well. "Throughout *Their Eyes Were Watching God,*" says Callahan, "Hurston works out the relationship between her voice and Janie's on grounds of cooperation and support—that condition of intimacy sought by women." See John F. Callahan, *In the African-American Grain: Call-and-Response in Twentieth-Century Black Fiction* (Middletown, Conn.: Wesleyan University Press, 1988), p. 119. See also Gates, *The Signifying Monkey,* p. 211.

16. In other words, from a psychological view point, Amy's image of God represents an act of projection which can be depicted in fiction either by using the language of prosopopoeia or by creating a personified image. But even before Amy creates her own anthropomorphic image, "God himself," as Bronson reminds us, "is himself a personification" (167).

17. Paul Ricoeur, "The Metaphorical Process as Cognition, Imagination, and Feeling," in *On Metaphor,* edited by. Sheldon Sacks (Chicago: University of Chicago Press, 1978), p. 153.

18. Amy's activity, according to a Renaissance rhetoric, would be described as pathopoeia, "an expression of vehemente affections and perturbations," in Earl R. Wasserman's paraphrase, "whereby the passions of the mind, such as anger and hope, are personified." See Wasserman's "The Inherent Values of Eighteenth-Century Personification," *PLMA* 65 (1950): p. 441.

19. Calvin Hall and Gardner Lindzey, *Theories of Personality* (New York: Wiley, 1957), p. 139. All other references will be given parenthetically as Hall and Lindzey. Personification, however, is rarely spoken of in the same breath as projection, possibly to avoid a confusion of linguistic modes. Yet as a psychological defense projection may be understood as the psychic equivalent of personification, setting personification's projective, psychic, and defensive qualities in relief.

20. Of course, we must take care: personification is a difficult convention upon which to theorize, for, like allegory, from which it is oftentimes almost indistinguishable, personification contains an "attractive but disturbing violence in the relation between ideal agency and empirical consciousness." At least this is what Steven Knapp believes was Coleridge's complaint against it. See Knapp's *Personification and the Sublime: Milton to Coleridge* (Cambridge: Harvard University Press, 1985), p. 5.

21. Later, for example, in Hurston's third novel, *Moses, Man of the Mountain* (1939; reprint, Urbana: University of Illinois Press, 1984), "the Moses of the Old testament," as Blyden Jackson puts it in his introduction, "and the Moses of Negro myth, legend, and song are *superimposed* to create a new 'reading' of the Exodus

Story," (back cover, emphasis mine). In this "superimposition," Hurston *projects* both black language and black American socio-political concerns onto a Biblical tale. But inasmuch as this novel is written as an extension of black aspirations, at least as Hurston sees them, *Moses* offers a cast of characters in the act of personifying such black aspirations as well. Moses, for instance, is a historical/mythical symbol, but superimposed upon this symbol are the aspirations of black men made known not so much in Moses's actions as in his speech. Hurston demonstrates the flexibility of such a language and the breadth of its applicability; this demonstration is the primary significance of such a superimposition or personification of projected images.

22. Michael Awkward, *Inspiriting Influences: Tradition, Revision, and Afro-American Women's Novels* (New York: Columbia University Press, 1989), p. 19.

23. Wasserman notes that "since personification is a vehicle for artistic communication, it is, like all other vehicles, multivalent, the values depending upon the cargo the vehicle carries" (Wasserman, 436). Symbolism and allegory represent one strain of personification, while impersonation of (an)other's personality or outward characteristics and anthropomorphis describe a more theatrical manifestation of prosopopoeia.

24. Gordon E. Thompson, "The Uses of the Fantastic in the Works of Charles W. Chesnutt, Zora Neale Hurston, and Melvin B. Tolson" (Ph.D. dissertation, Yale University, 1987), pp. 93–192.

25. Kimberly Benston points out: "In creating the features of his face . . . by catching its reflection in some version of the other (be it racial, familial, or even psychical) the [African American] writer composes himself as a modal persona of a putative [black] culture." Benston introduces prosopopoeia here as a characteristic trope of the African American literary tradition. See Kimberly E. Benston, "Racing Tradition: Revisionary Scenes in African American Literature," *PMLA* 105 (January 1990): p. 99.

26. One must note, however, that this rhetorical flourish is, in fact, articulated by the narrator but presented as Janie's thoughts in free indirect discourse. Gates describes this phenomenon as it operates in Hurston's romance thus: "Free indirect discourse in *Their Eyes* reflects both the text's theme of the doubling of Janie's self and that of the problematic relationship between Janie as a speaking subject and spoken language . . . [that] serves to disrupt the reader's expectation of the necessity of the shift in point of view from third person to first" (Gates, 207, pp. 209–10). *Their Eyes* is a historical memoir Janie relates to Phoebe, her best friend. Arguably, the "buzzard" tale could be conceived as an embellishment Janie creates while relating her tale to Phoebe; or contrarily, the tale could be thought of as having been created by the narrator to depict Janie's musings when she is forced to remain at home.

27. Zora Neale Hurston, *Seraph on the Sewanee*, (New York: Scribner's, 1948).

28. Zora Neale Hurston, *Spunk, The Selected Short Stories of Zora Neale Hurston* (Berkeley: Turtle Island Foundation, 1985), p. 38.

29. bell hooks, *Talking Back: Thinking Feminist, Thinking Black* (Boston: South End Press, 1989), p. 9.

30. These thematic associations and preoccupations are also reflected in Hurston's earliest fictions. For instance, in *Their Eyes Were Watching God*, the buzzard fable that Janie preoccupies herself with in response to being forced to stay at home comes quickest to mind. While the rest of the town participates in the mule's mock funeral, Janie's tale not only allows her to imagine herself transported to the

site of the funeral, but it also allows her to make up a tale about personified, or at the very least, talking vultures.

31. Throughout *Dust Tracks*, Hurston, according to Fox-Genovese, "provides numerous clues that her primary identification, her primary sense of herself, transcends gender" (Fox-Genovese, 176). Hurston's attachment to folk tales and the recitation of folk tales goes beyond anthropological curiosity and aesthetic appreciation; investigating her commitment to the tall tale also reveals sexual undertones that appear crucial to Hurston's continual trafficking in folk material.

32. Elsewhere, McKay says: "the events of both the private and public life are never fully explored in the autobiography . . . she constructs . . . an intellectual rather than an emotional self—a fully-formed philosophical self." See "Autobiographies of Hurston and Brooks" in *Wild Women in the Whirlwind*, edited by Joanne M. Braxton and Andree Nicola McLaughlin (New Brunswick: Rutgers University Press, 1990), p. 275.

33. Zora Neale Hurston, "John Redding Goes to Sea," *Opportunity*, January 1926, p. 16; hereafter cited in the text as "John Redding."

34. "[P]ersonification," says Geoffrey H. Hartman, "is at least distantly related to the ritual assumption of god or ancestor via his mask." See Hartman's *Beyond Formalism: Literary Essays: 1958–1970* (New Haven: Yale University Press, 1970), p. 331. Hartman's statement is made in the context of Romantic poetry and the role of the pastoral. In fact, though I have had little to say about the pastoral in Hurston, any casual reader will notice her strong attachment to pastoral images. The very fact that she has characters named "Tea Cake" and "Vergible Woods," who works in the fields, is telling. But it also offers us a clue as to why Tea Cake is presented as Janie's near perfect lover and is then shot by her: Tea Cake represents for Janie the very image of love; he is a "glance from God." With Tea Cake's death, Janie "assumes" a certain godhead by taking on male attributes, permission given her by Tea Cake alone of all the people in her life. Thus, in the imaginary universe of the romance, a woman is able to effect the transfer of "gendered" attributes from a male figure to a female figure. See also Henry Louis Gates Jr. "Dis' and 'Dat': Dialect and the Descent," in *Afro-American Literature: The Reconstruction of Instruction*, edited by Robert B. Stepto and Dexter Fisher (New York: Modern Language Association, 1978), pp. 89–119.

35. See de Man, 921.

36. And this expanding drive is also expressed well in the language of personification. As Wasserman points out, "It was assumed by almost all eighteenth-century rhetoricians . . . that the artistic use of this figure [personification] effectively conveyed to the reader the passionate transport of the author." These men were not talking about physical travel. But, nevertheless, note as well the "sublime" character of personification that offers an "extension of the imagination to its farthest reaches as it strives to realize that which distends the mind or exceeds its capacity" (Wasserman, 441).

37. These ideas were clarified by my reading of a very interesting paper presented at The City College of New York's American Studies Seminar in March 1992 by Fran Bartkowski (Rutgers University) entitled "Travelers v. Ethnics: Discourses of Displacement." See also Mary G. Mason, "Travel as Metaphor and Reality in Afro-American Women's Autobiography, 1850–1972," *Black American Literature Forum* 24 (summer 1990): pp. 337–356.

38. This is fortuitous in light of Kimberly Benston's reading of African American literature as a prosopopoeic "translation into the visible of an endless procession of virtual selves" (99).

39. Krasner, 117.

40. Zora Neale Hurston, *Mules and Men* (1935; reprint, Bloomington: Indiana University Press, 1978), p. 134.

41. See also Cheryl A. Wall, "Mules and Men and Women: Zora Neale Hurston's Strategies of Narration and Visions of Female Empowerment," *Black American Literature Forum* 23 (winter 1989): pp. 661–680.

JOHN LOWE

From Mule Bones to Funny Bones:
The Plays of Zora Neale Hurston

Zora Neale Hurston has recently been rescued from literary oblivion and installed as a major figure in the American literary canon. Her stature thus far, however, has stemmed from her success as a novelist, especially in her masterwork, *Their Eyes Were Watching God* (1937). Some Hurston aficionados were therefore surprised when the play she coauthored with Langston Hughes, *Mule Bone*, had its Broadway debut in 1991. Did Hurston write plays as well? Indeed she did. In fact, one of her first publications was a play, and she never gave up trying to mount a successful production.

As a preacher's daughter, Hurston came by her dramatic gifts naturally. John Hurston, born a slave, overcame his humble origins by marrying Lucy Potts, the daughter of a well-to-do farmer and by heeding a call from God. A strapping man, he was a commanding figure in the pulpit and made the most of his booming voice and musical gifts. Zora Neale was born on either 7 January or 15 January 1891 in Notasulga, Alabama, not far from Booker T. Washington's Tuskegee Institute. She was the sixth of John and Lucy's children. One son, Isaac, died in childhood, and three more sons were born after the family relocated in Eatonville, an all-black town in central Florida, in the early 1890s. In her autobiography, Hurston vividly recalls learning the dynamics of African American performance style from the men swapping lies on the porch of Joe Clarke's general store.

Southern Quarterly: A Journal of the Arts in the South, Volume 33, Number 2–3 (Winter–Spring 1995): pp. 65–78. © 1995 Southern Quarterly/Southern Mississippi.

Hurston's apparently happy life fell apart in 1904 when her mother died. She did not get along with her stepmother and eventually left Florida as a lady's maid for a traveling Gilbert and Sullivan company, thus inaugurating her theatrical experiences. After a series of jobs and a sequence of college courses at Morgan State and Howard University, Hurston won a scholarship to Barnard College, where she studied with Ruth Benedict and Franz Boas, the founders of American anthropology. While in New York she also met the leading figures of the New Negro literary movement and soon became one of the leading "niggerati," as she called them, herself. One of her several contributions to the Harlem Renaissance, as it has become known, was a play, *Color Struck*, which she published in a short-lived magazine, *Fire!!* She also submitted a play, "Spears" (since lost), to *Opportunity*'s writing contest in 1925; the piece was awarded an honorable mention.

Aside from the material surrounding *Mule Bone*'s publication and premiere, some brief commentary by her biographer, Robert E. Hemenway, and articles by Adele Newsome on "The Fiery Chariot" and Lynda Hill on plays that dramatize Hurston's life and work, virtually nothing has been written on Hurston as dramatist. One finds some insight into her dramatic program, however, by examining the nature of her few published and several unpublished plays, a sequence initiated with *Color Struck*.

This four-scene play initially depicts a group of laughing, animated friends boarding the Jim Crow railway car in Jacksonville enroute to a cakewalk contest in St. Augustine in 1900. The crowd predicts that John and Emma will win: "They's the bestest cakewalkers in dis state" (7). When these two appear, however, they argue because the dark Emma thinks brown-skinned John has been flirting with the mulatto Effie. Throughout the play, Emma's jealousy and morbid self-hatred keep her from accepting John's love. Her tragedy, however, is played out in the early scenes against the boisterous comedy enacted by her friends, and the lovingly detailed cakewalk contest in scenes 2 and 3. Joe Clarke, mayor of Eatonville, who plays a prominent role in much of Hurston's fiction, appears for the first time here. Emma, jealous again, refuses to perform with John, who goes on anyway, partnering Effie. As Emma watches, they win the contest.

The fourth and final scene takes place twenty years later. Emma is revealed nursing her light-skinned, invalid daughter when John enters. Although he has not seen her since the cakewalk and has since been married and widowed, he still loves Emma. She supposes he married a light-skinned woman, but John says he chose a dark wife because he longed for Emma. He teases her when he discovers her invalid teenage daughter is nearly white. He tells her he will stay with the girl while Emma goes for the white doctor she insists on. Instead of going for the doctor, however, Emma doubles back and accuses John of lust for her daughter. Disgusted, John leaves. The doctor arrives, but he is too late to save Emma's daughter and tells her that she might have lived had she sent for him sooner. The play's melodrama makes it top heavy, but it succeeds in suggesting the creativity and exuberance of African American culture and in sketching in the parameters of color prejudice within the African American community.

Hurston was asked to contribute a piece to Charles S. Johnson's *Ebony and Topaz: A Collectanea*, an anthology of black writing that appeared in 1927, and she chose a play. *The First One: A Play in One Act* is set in the Valley of Ararat three years after the flood and features Noah, his wife, their three sons (Shem, Japeth and Ham), Eve, Ham's wife and the sons' wives and children. This was the first of several pieces that Hurston would set in biblical times, frequently in black dialect. Here, however, Hurston uses standard speech. As the play opens, Noah and everyone else stand fuming because Ham, the way-ward son, is once again late for the annual commemoration of the delivery from the flood. Ham comes in playing a harp, dressed in a goat-skin and a green wreath, obviously linking him with both Orpheus and Bacchus. Shem's wife criticizes Ham because he doesn't bring an offering and because, unlike his brothers who toil in the fields, he merely tends flocks and sings. After a brief ceremony, the characters recall the flood and the deliverance in dramatic language. Noah calls upon Ham to play and sing to help them forget. Noah gets drunk to forget the images of the dead faces that floated by the ark. When Ham, also inebriated, laughingly reports on his father's nakedness in the tent—"The old Ram . . . he has had no spring for years." Shem's jealous wife seizes the opportunity and wakes Noah, reporting the deed but not the identity of the perpetrator. Noah, enraged, roars that "His skin shall be black . . . He and his seed forever. He shall serve his brothers and they shall rule over him" (55). Later, all involved are appalled and try to reverse the curse, but Ham comes in laughing, unaware that he has been turned black. His son has changed color as well. Noah banishes them, fearing that blackness is contagious. Ham, rather than show dismay, laughs cynically, saying "Oh, remain with your flocks and fields and vineyards, to covet, to sweat, to die and to know no peace, I go to the sun" (57).

Two things are worth noting about this play. First is that the origin of a race is in its founding father's joke. Second, the ending suggests that "The First [Black] One," a being who knows the true value of life, is superior to whites. Thus Hurston's playlet both embraces and inverts the traditional in-terpretation of the biblical passage upon which it is based.

In the meantime, Hurston continued her education at Columbia. En-couraged by Boas, she began a series of trips to Florida to gather folklore materials. This work was facilitated for years by the sponsorship of a wealthy white woman, Mrs. Osgood Mason, who also supported the careers of Hur-ston's gifted friends, the writers Langston Hughes and Alain Locke, as well as the musician Hall Johnson, who was active in the Broadway theater. All of them called Mrs. Mason "Godmother."

Even during the years of this patron's largesse, Hurston had to scramble to make ends meet. In 1931 she was hired to write some sketches for *Fast and Furious,* a black musical review produced by Forbes Randolph. She also appeared as a pom-pom girl in a football sketch and helped direct the show, which folded after a week. Her next theatrical adventure was writing sketches for the revue *Jungle Scandals,* which also closed quickly. Hurston had nothing but scorn for both of these shows and saw an opportunity to correct their errors with a musical of her own. Accordingly, she sought out Hall Johnson, who had directed the chorus of the wildly successful *Green Pastures* in 1931. Hurston thought that the play, written by a white man, Marc Connelly, was a dreadful hash of black culture, but she knew Johnson was master of his craft. She decided to set a single day in a railroad work camp to music. At first she thought of calling it *Spunk* but settled on *The Great Day.* Johnson worked on the project desultorily, but finally withdrew, only to filch some of Hurston's material for his production *Run Little Chillun,* which opened to favorable reviews in 1931.

In spite of these early disappointments, Hurston persevered. By pawning some of her possessions to raise funds and wheedling the final backing from Godmother, *The Great Day* was presented at New York's John Golden Theater on 10 January 1932. It used a concert format, and Alain Locke wrote the program notes. In the first part of the program, the audience saw workers arising and going to the job, singing songs as they laid track, returning to their homes where their children played folk games, and listening to a preacher's sermons accompanied by spirituals. Part 2 presented an evening's entertainment at the local "jook" (nightclub), consisting mainly of blues songs, ending with half the cast doing a blues song, half singing *Deep River.* No theatrical producer came forward to offer an extended run and the show lost money, even though it attracted a good crowd and favorable reviews. Godmother refused to let Hurston ever again put on the play as written and also forbade the theatrical use of other portions of *Mules and Men.* Hurston did succeed in mounting an edited version of *The Great Day* at Manhattan's New School on 29 March 1932. A program of this production survives, and *Theatre Arts* published a photo of the cast.

The next year, back home in Florida, Hurston and her friend Robert Wunsch of the Rollins College English department produced a January performance of the revised *The Great Day* to great acclaim, using a new title, *From Sun to Sun.* A second performance was given in February. In this form, the musical was mounted in a number of other cities in Florida, including Eatonville. Two years later, Hurston repeated the show in abbreviated concert form at Fisk University in Nashville and followed with a performance in Chicago, using still another title, *Singing Steel,* casting it with aspiring singers from the YWCA. Once again the show received good reviews, but, more importantly, officials from the Rosenwald Foundation, impressed by Hurston's research, offered to sponsor her return to Columbia to work on a PhD in anthropology.

We have no script for these musicals, but the Library of Congress owns tapes of many of the musical numbers. A version was pieced together for a performance at the 1993 Zora Neale Hurston Festival of the Arts in Eatonville.

Hurston did write down a one-act play that was part of the Rollins *From Sun to Sun* performance in 1933. The unpublished version, now in the Hurston Collection of the University of Florida, "The Fiery Chariot," creates a seven-page drama out of an old folktale. The play takes place in Dinah and Ike's slave cabin. Initially Ike comically wars with his little son over a baked sweet potato but soon switches to a comic duel with Dinah, who criticizes Ike in lively vernacular for praying every night to God to come get him in his fiery chariot. "Ah betcher God gits so tired uh yo' noise dat when He sees you gittin' down, he gwan in his privy house and slam de door." Ole Massa hears Ike praying and appears before the door wearing a sheet, claiming to be the Lord come in his chariot. Ike hides under the bed and tells Dinah to tell him he isn't there. Ole Massa says Dinah will do, and Ike urges her to go. When Dinah reveals Ike, he comes out and quivers at the sight of the Lord in his white sheet and stalls by saying he needs to put his Sunday shirt on. Then it's his Sunday pants. Finally, he persuades Ole Massa to step back some and bolts out the door and away. When Ike's son asks if God will catch him, Dinah answers, "You know God aint got no time wid yo' pappy and him barefooted too." Although the play builds on an old comic tradition, it has serious undertones. Ike prays for death because Ole Massa works him so hard; Ole Massa's decision to take Dinah instead verges toward the habit actual owners had of appropriating the bodies of their female slaves. Finally, Ike's clever method of escaping Ole Massa/God links him with the heroics of the legendary trickster slave, High John de Conquer.

The most important Hurston play is a collaboration with Langston Hughes, *Mule Bone,* which they wrote in 1930 but never produced, as the authors had a "falling out" right after it was written and never reconciled. In 1985 Henry Louis Gates, Jr. read the play at Yale and began a campaign to have it produced, but the revival almost did not come about. A staged reading before one hundred prominent black writers and theater people in 1988 led over half of them to urge the project be shelved, partly because its humor seemed stereotypical—it made extensive use of vernacular and racial humor, including the word "nigger." Changes were duly made, and *Mule Bone* was finally brought to the New York stage in March 1991, edited and revised by George Houston Bass, Ann Cattaneo, Henry Louis Gates, Jr., Arnold Rampersad and the director, Michael Schultz. Taj Mahal provided the musical numbers, which included lyrics drawn from some poems by Hughes. Bass wrote a "frame" story involving Hurston herself, who pronounced to the audience that the evening's event was a result of her scientific folklore expeditions.

In both the original and revised versions, the plot is based on Hurston's short story "The Bone of Contention," which detailed the falling out of two friends who quarrel over a turkey one of them has shot. In the three-act version, the two men, Jim Weston, a musician, and Dave Carter, a dancer, form a musical team. They quarrel over a flirtatious local domestic worker, Daisy Taylor, who skillfully plays them off against each other. The real voice in the play, however, belongs to the community. The men on Joe Clarke's porch and the women who stroll by offer a continual stream of commentary on the triangle, tell jokes and stories, and play local card games and checkers. A political parallel emerges in the Reverend Simms's public campaign to unseat Joe Clarke as mayor. Even children contribute, playing out classic African American folk games for the audience. The community takes sides according to religious denominations after Jim (a Methodist) knocks Dave (a Baptist) out with a mule bone. Act 2 largely consists of the "trial," held at the Macedonia Baptist Church, presided over by Mayor Clarke. But his leadership is challenged by Reverend Simms, who later spars with Reverend Childers. Their rivalry is matched by the wickedly comic duel between the Methodist Sister Lewis and the Baptist Sister Taylor, who signify to each other to beat the band, seemingly setting off various other quarrels. A continuing joke is the general ineffectiveness of the town marshall, Lum Boger, to coerce anyone, of any denomination. The latter proves that the mule bone is indeed a dangerous weapon by quoting Samson's story from the Bible. Clarke rules that Dave be banished for two years.

The brief third act focuses on the romantic triangle. After toying with the rivals, Daisy chooses Jim and demands that he take a good job as the white folks' yardman. When Jim refuses, she sidles up to Dave, but he too rejects her. The play ends with the two men back together, determined to make the town accept them both.

Mule Bone enjoyed limited success at the box office. It closed on 14 April 1991 after twenty-seven previews and sixty-seven performances. Although a few critics found it funny and historic (Kissel), an "exuberant" theatrical event (Beaufort) and a "wonderful piece of black theater" (Barnes), it was deemed "an amiable curiosity" (Winer), "one of the American theater's more tantalizing might-have-beens" (Rich), "pleasant but uneventful" (Wilson) and a "theatrical curio" (Watt) by other critics, who found it charming but dramatically deficient.

During the thirties, Hurston spent most of her time in Florida writing her novels, two books of folklore and working for the Federal Writers' Project. In October 1934 she wrote from Chicago to her friend James Weldon Johnson about a visit she had just made to Fisk University. There, President Jones asked Hurston to consider attending Yale Drama School for a year to study directing and the allied dramatic arts as preparation for establishing an experimental theater at Fisk. The idea, Hurston wrote, was "to create the Negro drama out of the Negro himself" (Yale, James Weldon Johnson Collection). Despite this and other ambitious but ultimately unrealized plans to create a new and authentic "negro drama," Hurston wrote mostly nonfiction afterward, but did publish an autobiography in 1942 and a final novel in 1948.

Hurston's only other full-length play, *Polk Country: A Comedy of Negro Life on a Sawmill Camp with Authentic Negro Music in Three Acts* was written in collaboration with Dorothy Waring and copyrighted in 1944, but it has never been published or produced. Although like *Mule Bone* it lacks a compelling story line, it demonstrates that Hurston never gave up trying to achieve her dream of the "real Negro theater" she had outlined to Hughes in 1928: "We shall act out the folk tales, however short, with the abrupt angularity and naivete of the primitive 'bama Nigger" (Yale, James Weldon Johnson Collection). *Polk County* attempts to meet this goal with a combination of humor, folklore and music. It clearly comes mainly from Hurston's own work as folklore collector in the real Polk County, and whatever the mysterious Dorothy Waring contributed must have been marginal.

Mule Bone has recently been published, and the debate still rages about Hughes's role in composing it. Conversely, *Polk County* is little known and, in some ways, represents a more intriguing turn in Hurston's dramatic career. Accordingly, I will treat it here more exhaustively than *Mule Bone*, which, in any case, demands a more complicated analysis than I can provide here.

The subtitle of *Polk County*, "A Comedy of Negro Life on a Sawmill Camp with Authentic Negro Music," speaks to Hurston's longstanding disdain for adulterated forms of African American music. The "scene and setting" section that introduces the piece describes the lush Florida landscape, replete with Spanish moss, cypress, scrubby palmettos and bull alligators. The workers' quarters are described in some detail, too. The impermanence of the scene dominates:

> No fenced in yards, few flowers, and those poorly tended. Few attempts at any kind of decoration or relief of ugliness. Everyone lives temporary. They go from job to job, or from job to jail and from jail to job. Working, loving temporarily and often without thought of permanence in anything, wearing their switch-blade knives and guns as a habit like the men of the Old West, fighting,

cutting and being cut, such a camp where there is little law, and the
peace officers of state and county barred by the management, these
refugees from life see nothing unlovely in the sordid camp. They
love it and when they leave there, will seek another place like it.

Hurston underlines the importance of this seemingly casual tableau:

Such a place is the cradle of the Blues and work songs.

Accordingly, the scenarios she foregrounds often center on love, anguish,
jealousy and betrayal—and skew the traditional notions of gender roles to
do so. The women, for instance, are said to be

misfits . . . seldom good looking, intelligent, or adjustable . . . They
too pack knives. No stigma attaches to them for prison terms. In
fact, their prestige is increased if they have made time for a serious
cutting. It passes for bravery—something to give themselves a
rating in their small world, where no intellectual activities exist.
Hence the boastful song: I'm going to make me a graveyard of my
own, etc.

The story line is simple. A mulatto, Leafy Lee, has wandered down from
New York hoping to learn the blues. This device runs throughout the play and
provides the rationale for the insertion of most of the musical numbers. Leafy
is befriended by the dominant personality in the camp, Big Sweet, who uses
her fists and knife to protect Leafy and to maintain order when the white
Bossman isn't around. Clearly, Leafy represents a fictional equivalent of Hurston herself, whose attempt to collect folklore under the protection of the real
Big Sweet is detailed in *Mules and Men*. *Polk County*, however, makes more
out of Big Sweet's role as *teacher*. As she tells Leafy, "I aim to put *my* wisdom
tooth in your head. I mean to be your fore-runner like John the Baptist." And
in many ways, Big Sweet seems like Hurston, too, especially in her declaration "It matters a difference where I go, just so I go laughing."

Big Sweet's man Lonnie is friends with My Honey, a guitar player, who
is sought after by Dicey, a sour, scheming, dark-complexioned woman. Significantly, Dicey's plans to break up Big Sweet and Lonnie find temporary
success only when she can involve the white Quarters Boss. In the course of
the play, Dicey's strategy of setting the other characters against each other
fails, and Leafy and My Honey marry, setting a new "civilizing" standard the
other characters intend to follow.

Despite its many grimly realistic and naturalistic aspects, the play is by
no means intent on slice-of-life theatrics. *Polk County* might more properly

be termed a musical comedy with surreal touches, in that the opening page lists twenty-seven "Vocal and Instrumental Numbers." The play opens with Lonnie waking the quarters up with a ritual comic chant, as he raps on the porches with a stick. The work song obviously has elements of the spirituals in it, for it begins with "Wake up, Jacob! Get on the rock /Taint quite day, but it's five o'clock!" After this religious opening, however, he shifts to a reference to quotidian toil: "Wake up bullies! Day's a'breaking / Get your hoecake a'baking, and your shirt-tail shaking!" Then the social order weighs in: "It know you feel blue / I don't want you, but the Bossman do!" This is followed by a comic reference to the natural world: "What did the rooster say to the hen? / Aint had no loving in the lord knows when." In fact, the stage directions indicate that at this point a rooster and his hens should cross the stage, and they have *lines* to say. Clearly we are in the world of magic realism, 1940s style. The animals parody the humans: When the rooster dances around a hen, coaxing "How about a lil' kiss?" she replies, evasively "I want some shoes," a motif Hurston frequently uses with "round-heeled" women, most notably with Ora, the vixen who appears at the end of *Jonah's Gourd Vine* and in the story of Aunt Ca' line in "The Eatonville Anthology." The comic interplay between the chickens is quite intricate and leads up to the rooster complaining "You Polk County hens always hollering for shoes! Why I have to buy you shoes to love you? You get just as much out of it as I do. Aw, cutta-cut cut!" The rooster's suggestion that one hen represents all those in Polk County mirrors a hen's earlier, parallel suggestion: "These Polk County roosters! They want plenty loving, but they don't buy you no shoes." Moreover, the "chicken theme" reappears in more human form later, when Big Sweet says of her rival "Ella Wall aint no big hen's biddy, if she do lay gobbler's eggs."

The anthropomorphic play here creates an interesting affinity with the animal cast of Janacek's opera *The Cunning Little Vixen* (1924), while the several descriptions of lights slowly going on, breakfast sounds and so on from the morning sequence might stem from a similar scene in Gershwin's *Porgy and Bess* (1935). The surreal quality of these moments in *Polk County* relate to those (quite a few) devoted to Lonnie's readings of his extravagant dreams and visions. In one, he tells us, he rode to heaven on a crow, "diamond-shining black. One wing rests on the morning and the other brushes off the sundown." Throughout the play, Lonnie compares himself to High John the Conquer, the mythic folk hero who similarly looms larger than life and enjoys magical powers in the natural world. All these "magic realism" touches appear only to be submerged by the play's basically realistic veneer, but the play ends, as we shall see, with an expressionistically surreal display.

Whatever the mode at work at any given moment, however, the play ultimately stands or falls on the strength of its many striking characters. Like *Mule Bone*, *Polk County*'s cast is large: sixteen named characters and many others play parts. Hurston, obviously profiting from her experiences with *From Sun to Sun,* included twenty-seven vocal and instrumental numbers. Virtually all of the human characters reprise roles they played in Hurston's book of folklore, *Mules and Men* and thus are presumably based in fact.

The Hurston we see here is franker than she was in earlier works, especially about both racial attitudes and sexuality. Dicey, for instance, is described in the cast list as a

> homely narrow-contracted little black woman, who has been slighted by Nature and feels "evil" about it. Suffers from the "black ass." Her strongest emotion is envy. . . Yearns to gain a reputation as "bad" (the fame of a sawmill camp) to compensate for her lack of success with men . . . Being short, scrawny and black, a pretty yellow girl arouses violent envy in her.

Throughout the play, Leafy and My Honey's courtship has a communal dimension, affording much commentary from the cast on the nature of love. Leafy up to this point plays out a parallel to the role Hurston herself played in Polk County in *Mules and Men.*

Interestingly, Lonnie's "visions" involve African retentions and dreams of liberation and glory. The community attends to these visions eagerly, and they look forward to Lonnie's cheering music. As one character claims, everyone would leave the place if Lonnie wasn't there, suggesting that he parallels the role Tea Cake plays on the Muck in Hurston's novel *Their Eyes Were Watching God,* but also pointing to the key role African American cultural traditions have played in making harsh work bearable.

On the other hand, Hurston signals that dreams can be dangerous. One manifestation of Big Sweet's violent power emerges when we learn she regularly "lams" Lonnie to bring him back to reality:

> I just sort of taps him once in a while. You see, Lonnie got his mind way up in the air, and I taps him to make him know that the ground is here right on, and that there's minks on it trying to take advantage of him all the time. They cant fool *me.* Lonnie dreams pretty things. Thats what make I love him so.

Furthermore, her "lamming" Lonnie finds exponential expansion in her general role as disciplinarian for the community. As Sop-the-Bottom asserts, "More men makes time [work] now than they used to cause Big Sweet keeps a lot of 'em from cutting the fool and going to jail." This thematic device, especially as it focuses on Lonnie's dreams/madness, recalls that used in Hemingway's powerful story "The Battler" (1925), and the similar situation in Steinbeck's *Of Mice and Men* (1937). In both of these tales, violence on the part of a loving "caretaker" becomes necessary to still a dreaming and disturbed personality.

Another echo of an earlier Hurston work is heard in the name of Leafy Lee. Janie's mother in *Their Eyes*, also a mulatto, is named Leafy. Here this gentle ingenue yearns to be a blues singer and much of the second act is devoted to using her "lessons" as occasions for song.

Another character who has a counterpart in *Their Eyes* is Sop-the-Bottom. Here he appears as one with a "big appetite, a rather good gambler at Georgia Skin but not above being sharp with less efficient players. Not really wicked, but considers himself smart." Sop plays a more sinister role in *Their Eyes;* conversely, Ella Wall, a figure recycled from *Mules and Men,* becomes far more menacing in *Polk County.* The cast list presents her as "primitive and pagan," yet one who "has the air of a conqueror. She is strutting and self-assured and accustomed to the favors of men which she in return grants freely. She practices Voodoo and feels she leads a charmed life."

As in *Mules,* the real dynamo of the comedy is Ella's nemesis, Big Sweet, who is "two whole women and a gang of men." Although she can physically dispatch any enemy, it is her arsenal of verbal taunts that makes her truly formidable and entertaining. Kicking Nunkie, she emphasizes her actions with words:

> You multiplied cockroach! I'll teach you to die next time I hit you.
> . . . Beating my Lonnie out of his money. Gimmie! If you don't, and
> that quick, they going to tote you through three yards—this yard,
> the churchyard, and the graveyard.

Here, as in many other scenes, Big Sweet appropriates traditionally male modes of action, talk and stance. When she finally gets caught in the meshes of Dicey's scheme, she fights her way out after finding inspiration in the example of the legendary hero, High John de Conquer. Like him, she possesses an arsenal of comic one-liners: "If God send me a pistol, I'll send him a man!" or "Pulling after a man that dont want you, is just like peeping in a jug with one eye; you can't see a thing but darkness." But then, even minor characters are blessed with pithy expressions: Laura tells Lonnie, "You got a grin on you like a dead dog in the sunshine."

The richly metaphoric humor of the backwoods community is not unique to the black workers. The white Quarters Boss, who in some ways is sympathetically drawn, can signify with the best of them. Mocking the community's defense of Big Sweet, he declares,

> Thats all I can hear from most of you. Big Sweet aint never done
> a thing but praise the Lord. Her mouth is a prayer-book and her

lips flap just like a Bible. But where do all these head-lumps come
from that the Company Doctor is always greasing? . . . How can I
keep order like that?

This comic passage underlines, however, the way in which Big Sweet has
operated within the community *precisely* to keep order, which obviates
the need for white interference and dominance. Hurston thus uses comic
exchanges to illustrate quite serious points.

Despite her role as villain, Dicey is portrayed somewhat sympathetically,
in that she resembles the despairing Emma of *Color-Struck* in her bitterness
over color: "I know I aint yellow, and aint got no long straight hair, but I got
feelings just like anybody else." She tries to gain revenge with her knife and
through association with the rough and ready Ella Wall, who is brought in
toward the end of the play for a dramatic showdown with Big Sweet. Ella
also presides over a compelling hoodoo scene in the woods, providing more
exotica.

Big Sweet plays a more complex role here than in *Mules and Men*. For
instance, she wistfully explains to maidenly Leafy just how she lost her virgin-
ity and how she became accustomed to "careless love." She also claims that
God directed her to kick the "behinds" of people who try to take advantage
of folks. Nor is this introspective moment atypical, despite the overwhelming comedy of the play. A minor character, Laura B., comments at one point
"Everybody is by themselves a heap of times, even when they's in company."
Later, Lonnie sings movingly of the dangers and hardships of sawmill work:
"keep on like that until you die . . . Just moving around in the cage."

The dangers of *Polk County* are not confined to the machinery. Still
another name repeated from *Their Eyes* is Nunkie. In the earlier book she
is a woman; here Nunkie is a man, a "no-good gambler—shifty and irre-
sponsible. His soul is as black as his face and his face is as black as the sins
he commits," a description that partakes of the stereotypical concepts of
blackness. As many of these descriptions suggest, throughout these opening pages, Hurston emphasizes the danger and violence of the scene and
even claims that "at least one person is killed every pay night." Polk County
clearly represents a "backwoods" counterpart to the more refined community of Eatonville and seems equivalent to many other fictional backwoods
communities created by other southern writers, such as those in the books of
Hurston's sometime friend and fellow chronicler of Florida, Marjorie Kin-
nan Rawlings (especially in *South Moon Under*, 1933), or the Frenchmen's
Bend tales of William Faulkner. In these types of narratives, the frontier
ethos provides a sharper edge to the dramatic action, an exotic and legendary setting and more possibilities for violence, conflict and, ultimately,
"civilizing" redemption.

One should not, however, assume that these "backwoods" people come off as barbarians; far from it. Hurston wants us to perceive that they have a vivid culture and works out various stratagems to *make* us see it. As in *Mule Bone,* children play typical African American games as part of the display of everyday life in the Quarters. Also as in *Mule Bone,* the central scenes are communal. In the latter play, the key conflict is the quarrel between the Methodists and Baptists that accompanies Jim's "trial." Here the chief battles take place in the Quarters jook, which is elaborately described, and in the woods, where Ella and her partisans' hoodoo fails to conjure Leafy and My Honey's marriage. A feast follows, along with Lonnie's pronouncement "You can git what you want if you go about things the right way."

The pattern of the play—order, chaos, order, concluding with a marriage—is that of the traditional stage comedy, but Hurston reinvents it with her transposition of the genre into the register of a dialect-driven, black backwoods culture, one rich in linguistic, cultural and dramatic nuance. As in virtually all of her works, the folk humor generates the dynamism, which buoys and amplifies every page and scene. A few examples will suffice. Hurston mines the "I'm so . . . that . . ." of African American jokes here, after Sop-the-Bottom sings his "I'm going to make me a graveyard of my own." Do-Dirty starts it by saying "I'm so mean till I'll kill a baby just born this morning," followed by Few Clothes's escalation "Man, I'm mean! I have to tote a pistol with me when I go to the well, to keep from gitting in a fight with my ownself. I got Indian blood in me. Reckon that's how come I'm so mean," and all the other men say that they have some in them too. This sequence relates to others in the African American comic repertory that Hurston used tirelessly, such as the "so ugly that . . ." or "so black that . . ." comic sequences. Interestingly, she radically transforms one version of the tradition. She always deplored the "Black Black woman" jokes that focused on the supposed evil of darker women. Here she subtracts the color component, but leaves the rest. When Sop-the-Bottom brags, "I shacked up with a woman once that was so contrary she used to sleep humped up in bed so you couldnt find no way to stretch out comfortable to sleep," Lonnie ups the ante by claiming "I done seen 'em dreaming. They dont never dream about roses and scenery and sunshine like a sweet woman do. Naw, they dreams about hatchets and knives and pistols, and ice-picks and splitting open people's heads."

A second example, also centered in communal comic exchange, appears when the men talk about how Lonnie was ripped off by the dirty dealing of Nunkie the night before, using comic proverbs and folk sayings to connote a serious sequence of events. They saw it happening, but didn't tell Lonnie. As Few Clothes says, "I aint no bet-straightener. Its more folks in the graveyard right now from straightening bets than anything else. Blind me aint got no business at the show." They prophesy that Big Sweet will take care of Nunkie.

FEW CLOTHES: [S]he bound to find it out. My woman done found it out and she wouldnt let her shirt-tail touch her till she run tell Big Sweet all she know.

SOP: He [Nunkie] claim that his knife going to back Big Sweet off him. Claim he aint scared, but I know better. He's talking at the big gate.

DO-DIRTY: "Before she turn him loose she'll make him tell her that she is Lord Jesus, and besides her there is no other.

Amazingly, despite the relatively naturalistic presentation of most of the play, it ends expressionistically. After the feast and the commitment of the previously lawless community to marriage and stability, a huge rainbow descends and all get on board, plates in hand, with Lonnie singing "I ride the rainbow, when I see Jesus," the song he sang as he made his entrance at the beginning of the play. With the presence of his fellow "riders" on the rainbow, his individual song becomes communal. The curtain falls as the rainbow ascends.

Hurston never found the rainbow herself. In the fifties she drifted from job to job, while working on various manuscripts. When she died in 1960, she was living in a county charity facility. She never achieved the dream of founding a new "Negro" dramatic movement. Her life, however, had been highly dramatic and despite its end, fulfilling.

As these brief descriptions of her plays suggest, Hurston devised some inventive dramatizations of African American folk life and customs. White theatrical producers of her time, however, wanted the tried and true formulas when they dared present plays with predominantly black casts. They had no interest in experimenting with Hurston's authentic modes.

To be fair, however, it should be borne in mind that Hurston's emphasis on group culture and interaction led her to sacrifice a focus on strongly individual central plots, the basic staple of mainstage American theater. Moreover, although she sought to provide an alternative to contemporary, often racist, stereotypes of blacks, today's audiences are likely to find even *her* versions embarrassing throwbacks to an earlier time, when African Americans themselves used forms of address and metaphor that have now been discarded. The fact that *Mule Bone* had to be edited prior to production and then failed to attract an audience offers illustration of this point.

Hurston's fiction has taken a central place in the American literary canon, but it seems unlikely that her plays will be produced in the near future, largely because, for many readers, they seem to move uncomfortably close to stereotypes, even though Hurston felt she was doing just the opposite in her own day and time. In the more expansive mode of her fiction she was able to burst through into fully-fleshed characterizations, something that eluded her as dramatist. Finally, for many, the plays' small-town settings, situations and language simply seem dated when placed next to those of contemporary African American dramas and comedies. Thus despite their many charms and innovations, Hurston's work for the theater appears headed for the "historical curiosity shelf." It seems likely, however, that her fiction and her own lively autobiography will continue to furnish subjects for the American stage.

This condition could change, however, if there were published editions of all of Hurston's plays, and directors and producers who were capable of meeting the challenges that Hurston's scripts present. Literary critics could hasten this project by moving beyond *Their Eyes* and *Dust Tracks* into a wide-ranging discussion of the totality of Hurston's work, including the dramas. Ultimately, however, we will never know now effective her "genuine Negro drama" is unless producers come forward. Only then, with her words quickened into theatrical life, will we really be able to judge the success of dramatist Zora Neale Hurston's attempt to "let the people sing."

Archival Sources

The manuscripts of most of Hurston's plays, published and unpublished, are in the James Weldon Johnson Memorial Collection, Yale Collection of American Literature, Beineke Rare Book and Manuscript Library, Yale University. "The Fiery Chariot" manuscript is in the Hurston Collection of the University of Florida. One version of *Mule Bone* is at the Moorland-Spingarn Research Center, Howard University. Letters by Hurston, Langston Hughes and Carl Van Vechten related to *Mule Bone* are also at Yale.

Published Plays

Color-Struck: A Play. Fire!! Nov. 1926: 40–45.
The First One: A Play in One Act. Ebony and Topaz: A Collectanea. Edited by Charles S. Johnson. New York: National Urban League, 1927, 53–57.
Mule Bone: A Comedy of Negro Life. Coauthored with Langston Hughes; Edited by George Houston Bass and Henry Louis Gates, Jr. New York: HarperCollins, 1991.

Unpublished Plays

The Fiery Chariot. Play in one act. Hurston Collection, University of Florida.
Polk County: A Comedy of Negro Life on a Sawmill Camp, with Authentic Negro Music. Play in three acts written with Dorothy Waring, 1944. James Weldon Johnson Collection, Beineke Library, Yale University. Cited by permission.

Musical Productions

The Great Day. Originally performed at the John Golden Theater, New York, 10 Jan. 1932. Also titled, in later productions, *From Sun to Sun* and *Shining Steel.*

Relevant Essays and Articles by Hurston (Selected)

"Characteristics of Negro Expression." *Negro: An Anthology.* Edited by Nancy Cunard. London: Wishart, 1934, 39–46.
"Folklore and Music." (unpublished essay, 22 pages). Florida Historical Society Papers, University of South Florida.

Works Cited

(All reviews of "Mule Bone" cited below are in *New York Theatre Critics' Reviews* L11, 1 (191): 390–391. Original source page numbers are not provided.)
Barnes, Clive. "'Mule Bone' Connected to Funny Bone." *New York Post* 15 Feb. 1991.
Beaufort, John. "'Mule Bone' Debuts after 60 Years." *Christian Science Monitor* 26 Feb. 1991.
Gates, Henry Louis, Jr. "Why the Debate Over *Mule Bone* Persists." *New York Times Book Review* 10 Feb. 1991: 5, 8.
Hemenway, Robert E. *Zora Neale Hurston: A Literary Biography.* Urbana: University of Illinois Press, 1977.
Hill, Lynda. "Staging Hurston's Life and Work." *Acting Out: Feminist Performances.* Edited by Lynda Hart and Peggy Phelan. Ann Arbor: University of Michigan Press, 1993, 295–313.
Kissel, Howard. "Folk Comedy Tickles Funny 'Bone.'"*Daily News* (New York) 15 Feb. 1991.
Newson, Adele S. "The Fiery Chariot." *Zora Neale Hurston Forum* 1.1 (1986): 32–37.
Rich, Frank. "A Difficult Birth for 'Mule Bone.'" *New York Times* 15 Feb. 1991.
Watt, Doug. "Second Thoughts on First Nights." *Daily News* [New York] 22 Feb. 1991.
Winer, Linda. "A Precious Peek at a Lively Legend." *New York Newsday* 15 Feb. 1991.

Plays Based on Hurston's Life and Works

Holder, Geoffrey. *Zora Neale Hurston.* Unpublished.
Spiesman, Barbara. *A Tea with Marjorie and Zora.* Rawlings Journal I (1988): 67–100.
Wolfe, George C. Spunk: *Three Tales by Zora Neale Hurston, Adapted by George C. Wolfe. Two by George Wolfe* by George Wolfe. Garden City, NY: Fireside Theatre, 1991, 65–132.

SUSAN E. MEISENHELDER

Conflict and Resistance in
Zora Neale Hurston's Mules and Men

While *Mules and Men* seems (and was, in fact, read by most of her contemporary reviewers as) a straightforward depiction of the humor and "exoticism" of African American folk culture, Zora Neale Hurston carefully arranged her folktales and meticulously delineated the contexts in which they were narrated to reveal complex relationships between race and gender in Black life. Underscoring the traditional subversive role of African American folklore, she highlights the continuing role folktales play in Black people's struggles with economic and racial oppression. Hurston also details the function of folklore in conflicts between Black men and Black women, showing both how men use folktales to reinforce and legitimate oppression of women and how women use them to fight against a subservient role and to assert their power.

In her introduction to *Mules and Men*, Zora Neale Hurston stresses the difference between the unreflective immersion in Black folklife of her childhood and her later understanding of it:

> When I pitched headforemost into the world I landed in the crib of negroism. From the earliest rocking of my cradle, I had known about the capers Brer Rabbit is apt to cut and what the Squinch Owl says from the house top. But it was fitting me like a tight

Journal of American Folklore, Volume 109, Number 433 (1996): pp. 267–288. Copyright © 1996 American Folklore Society.

chemise. I couldn't see it for wearing it. It was only when I was off in college, away from my native surroundings, that I could see myself like somebody else and stand off and look at my garment. Then I had to have the spy-glass of Anthropology to look through at that. (Hurston 1935: 3)

As Hurston suggests here, she is more than a passive transcriber of folktales in *Mules and Men*. Distanced from the culture she depicts and trained as an anthropologist to analyze it, she shapes her material in order to reveal the warp and woof of the fabric she saw. While *Mules and Men* seems (and was, in fact, seen by most reviewers as) a straightforward, nonthreatening depiction of the humorous and exotic side of Black culture in the rural South, Hurston offers in veiled form a complex analysis of race and gender in Black life.[1]

Part of the reason Hurston takes an indirect approach to race stems from her dependence on white figures who exerted considerable control over her work. Hurston's patron, Charlotte Osgood Mason, for instance, literally owned Hurston's material and consistently pushed Hurston to express only the "primitivism" she saw in Black culture. Hurston's struggle with Franz Boas in her research and writing of *Mules and Men* is less well-known, but as the correspondence between him and Hurston (housed in the archives of the American Philosophical Society) indicates, his control over her fieldwork at this time in her career was just as intrusive as that exerted by Mason. In addition to letting her know what she was to focus on in her research (May 3, 1927) and treating her as an aid or informant rather than a researcher in her own right (May 17, 1929), Boas also clearly had his own analysis of the material Hurston was collecting even before she finished.[2] In a letter of May 3, 1927, he expressed an opinion about African influences at odds with Hurston's own: "We ought to remember that in transmission from Africa to America most of the contents of the culture have been adapted from the surrounding peoples while the mannerisms have, to a greater extent, been retained." Aware of Boas's power to validate or dismiss the significance of her research, Hurston responds by posturing as deferential, requesting permission to express her own conclusions. As she looks over her material, she writes to him on April 21, 1929:

Is it safe for me to say that baptism is an extension of water worship as a part of pantheism just as the sacrament is an extension of cannibalism? Isn't the use of candles in the Catholic church a relic of fire worship? Are not all the uses of fire upon the altars the same thing? Is not the Christian ritual rather one attenuated nature-worship, in the fire, water, and blood? Might not the frequently mentioned fire of the Holy Ghost not be an unconscious fire worship. May it not be a deification of fire?

> May I say that the decoration in clothing is an extension of the primitive application of paint (coloring) to the body?
>
> May I say that all primitive music originated about the drum and that singing was an attenuation of the drum-beat?

In his reply of April 24, 1929, Boas refuses Hurston's "request," suggesting that she may not say these things because her questions "contain a great deal of very contentious matter." Hurston's tentative tone reflects her awareness of Boas's power but not her acquiescence to it. That it represents the mask she donned to deal with a powerful mentor rather than her own uncertainty is clear from a letter she wrote Langston Hughes nine days after her letter to Boas:

> I am convinced that Christianity as practiced is an attenuated form of nature worship. Let me explain. The essentials are a belief in the Trinity, baptism, sacrament. Baptism is nothing more than water worship as has been done in one form or the other down thru the ages... I find fire worship in Christianity too. What was the original purpose of the altar in all churches? For sacred fire and sacrifices BY FIRE. . . . Symbols my opponents are going to say. But they cannot deny that water and fire are purely material things and that they symbolize man's tendency to worship those things which benefit him to a great extent. . . . You know of course that the sacrament is a relic of cannibalism when men ate men not so much for food as to gain certain qualities the eaten man had. Sympathetic magic pure and simple. *They have a nerve to laugh at conjure.* (April 30, 1929, Yale, quoted in Hemenway 1978: xix–xx)

Hurston had her own anthropological views to express in *Mules and Men* as well.[3] What she discovered when she looked at her culture through the spyglass of anthropology was that the folktales she had always heard were not merely amusing stories or even relics of slavery, but living forces, strategies used in her own day for dealing with power inequities. As she emphasized in "Characteristics of Negro Expression," "Negro folklore is not a thing of the past" (Hurston 1983: 56) but testimony to the power of her own contemporaries to do battle in a world of inequality. Aware of the social significance of Black folktales, Hurston uses her "spyglass" in *Mules and Men*, relating tales to analyze the culture in which they operate.

Faced with the dilemma of how to present her analysis in a way that could bypass the censoring eye of her mentors and unsympathetic white readers, Hurston adopted a strategy of masking social conflict and critical commentary with humor. The persona she creates is crucial to this project. By presenting herself as a lovable "darky," one who thanks white folks for "allow-ing" her to collect folklore and who praises the magnanimity of her patron Mrs. Mason, she appears a narrator with no racial complaints or even awareness. Pouring on the "charm of a lovable personality" commented on by Boas in his preface (Hurston 1935: x) and by reviewers, Hurston paints herself as an Uncle Remus figure pleased to entertain the white world with her tales.[4] Making no controversial statements and, in fact, offering little explicit analysis, she plays an extremely nonthreatening role: lovable, entertaining, and intellectually mute.

Hurston reminds us in *Mules and Men,* however, that Black humor is richly multifaceted, reflecting a wide range of emotions: "The brother in black puts a laugh in every vacant place in his mind. His laugh has a hundred mean-ings. It may mean amusement, anger, grief, bewilderment, chagrin, curiosity, simple pleasure or any other of the known or undefined emotions" (1935: 67–68). Much of the humor in *Mules and Men* reflects this complexity rather than the primitive simplicity and carefree gaiety seen by reviewers. Hurston also hints at the complex ambiguity of folktales themselves in discussing the Black person's strategy for deflecting the probe of white cultural analysis:

> The Negro, in spite of his open-faced laughter, his seeming acquiescence, is particularly evasive. You see we are a polite people and we do not say to our questioner, "Get out of here!" We smile and tell him or her something that satisfies the white person because, knowing so little about us, he doesn't know what he is missing. The Indian resists curiosity by a stony silence. The Negro offers a feather-bed resistance. That is, we let the probe enter, but it never comes out. It gets smothered under a lot of laughter and pleasantries.
>
> The theory behind our tactics: "The white man is always trying to know into somebody else's business. All right, I'll set something outside the door of my mind for him to play with and handle. He can read my writing but he sho' can't read my mind. I'll put this play toy in his hand, and he will seize it and go away. Then I'll say my say and sing my song." (Hurston 1935: 4–5)

While Hurston makes these comments to convince readers that they are read-ing the unvarnished truth in *Mules and Men,* that she is initiating them into the Black world, her remarks provide an interesting comment on her strategy in the work.[5] She uses "feather-bed tactics" in her rendition of Black folktales, placing her "lovable personality" and the seemingly simple, humorous stories of her informants as a "play toy" in the hands of her white readers.

As Hemenway suggests in his introduction (Hemenway 1978: xxiii), Hurston's "cultural messages" in *Mules and Men* are "coded" ones, similar to

Black proverbial expressions or "by-words," which as one man explains, "all got a hidden meanin'" (Hurston 1935: 134). She conveys her controversial cultural messages not by explicitly analyzing folktales but by embedding them in social contexts that underscore issues of race and gender.[6] Undoubtedly aware that the context of Joel Chandler Harris's tales had defused the racial conflict and Black resistance in them, Hurston embeds her tales in situations that highlight this function of Black folklore. Her mode of presentation in *Mules and Men* is thus crucial. As Boas notes in his preface, it was a novel one; "by giving the Negro's reaction to every day events," by placing tales in "the intimate setting in the social life of the Negro" (Hurston 1935: x), Hurston is able to convey her commentary without asking permission or offending her mentors.

While Boas rather dimly praises this aspect of *Mules and Men* in his preface, his correspondence with Hurston reveals her trials in getting him to write it. Fully aware what his stamp of approval would mean for her work's acceptance, she pleads with him to write an introduction: "I am full of terrors, lest you decide that you do not want to write the introduction to my 'Mules and Men.' I want you to do it so very much" (August 20, 1934). From her extensive experience with Boas's scientific "rigor," Hurston was clearly aware that the novelistic frame for her tales might present a potential problem for Boas. She is, therefore, extremely careful in her arguments to give an explanation for its necessity in the book:

> Mr. Lippincott likes the book very much and he will push it. His firm, as you know probably publishes more text-books than any other in America and he is conservative. He wants a very readable book that the average reader can understand, at the same time one that will have value as a reference book. I have inserted the between-story conversations and business because when I offered it without it, every publisher said it was too monotonous. Now three houses want to publish it. So I hope that the unscientific matter that must be there for the sake of the average reader will not keep you from writing the introduction. It so happens that the conversations and incidents are true. But of course I never would have set them down for scientists to read. I know that the learned societies are interested in the story in many ways that would never interest the average mind. He needs no stimulation. But the man in the street is different.

Foisting responsibility for "unnecessary" elements in her work onto her publishers and further implying they are anthropologically insignificant, Hurston ends this letter with her familiar strategy of ingratiation:

> So *please* consider all this and do not refuse Mr. Lippincott's request
> to write the introduction to *Mules and Men*. And then in addition,
> I feel that the persons who have the most information on a subject
> should teach the public. Who knows more about folk-lore than you
> and Dr. Benedict? Therefore the stuff published in America should
> pass under your eye. You see some of the preposterous stuff put out
> by various persons on various folk-subjects. This is not said merely
> to get you to write the introduction to my book. No. (August 20,
> 1934)

Hurston's strategy of deferential humility, of course, worked. She was able
to publish her work with this crucial contextual material and to get Boas's
(albeit brief and rather condescending) approval in the preface.[7]

The "between-story conversations and business," the contexts in which
tales are narrated, are central in *Mules and Men*, for they show how vital and
socially meaningful folklore is in the lives of her rural Black contemporaries.
While Hurston's collection reproduces a wide variety of folktales, the types
told by her informants arise out of their immediate social situations. One set
of tales, those told at the sawmill in Polk County (chapters four and five),
provides an important commentary on the situation of Black workers in the
South. Hurston sets up this work scene to emphasize white domination and
control of these men's lives. Arriving at work to find no straw boss, the men
think they will be given a day off but are disappointed when the foreman
orders them on to the mill to see if they are needed there (1935: 74). Telling
tales all the way, they walk the long distance to the mill, only to be summarily
dismissed by the mill boss (1935: 100). Like mules, the men are moved from
one work location to the next, never informed of the white boss's plans.

Frustrated by this dehumanizing situation, the men often use traditional
tales in this section to critique white power figures and to reassert their own
humanity. After general speculation that the boss is absent due to illness, one
man sneers, "Man, he's too ugly. If a spell of sickness ever tried to slip up on
him, he'd skeer it into a three weeks' spasm" (1935: 73). This last comment
leads into a series of exaggeration stories, in which the workers try to top one
another's stories about men who are "so ugly." As a later series of exaggeration
stories told while fishing shows (1935: 106), this traditional genre is often a
form of fun-filled verbal play engaged in for its own sake. In a work context,
however, it is used specifically to lampoon a white power figure. Similarly,
the men deal with their frustration and anger when the foreman announces
that they must report to the mill through another series of exaggeration tales
about mean men, initiated by one man's comment, "Ain't dat a mean man? No
work in the swamp and still he won't let us knock off." The tales that follow
detail one straw boss "so mean dat when the boiler burst and blowed some

of the men up in the air, he docked 'em for de time they was off de job" and a road boss so mean "till he laid off de hands of his watch" (1935: 75).

Significantly, stories about "slavery days" are most common in this section of *Mules and Men*. Often focusing on the trickster figure John, these tales depict the slave's strategies for dealing with apparent powerlessness.[8] Many of them graphically demonstrate the impossibility of open defiance and the need for indirection in battling oppressive whites. While the Black man may pray in private for God "to kill all de white folks" (1935: 96), a different approach is required in their presence. Hurston most explicitly shows the strategic necessity of indirect defiance in the tale "Big Talk," told in the Polk County section. In the first half of this tale, one slave brags to another that he "cussed" Massa with no punishment. When another slave complains that Ole Massa "come nigh uh killin'" him (1935: 83) for similar behavior, the first slave exclaims, "Ah didn't say Ah cussed 'im tuh his face. You sho is crazy. Ah thought you had mo' sense than dat. When Ah cussed Ole Massa he wuz settin' on de front porch an' Ah wuz down at de big gate" (1935: 83–84). As this tale suggests, open defiance, with death as the price, is the strategy of fools; indirection, on the other hand, is a crucial strategy for survival and for victory. As one listener remarks, such foolhardiness is not the hallmark of the Black folk hero John: "'Dat wasn't John de white folks was foolin' wid. John was too smart for Ole Massa. He never got no beating!" (1935: 85).

The slavery stories in these two chapters, the bulk of the ones told in *Mules and Men,* function as a model for these men in surviving their own oppression. Unable to openly defy their bosses, they too "talk by the big gate" in the tales they narrate, reliving the slave's psychic victory. Tales related in this section also solidify the group, uniting the men, who at least twice respond to stories by moving "closer together" (1935: 73–74) in spiritual opposition to their bosses. By placing most John stories in this section, by having them told against a backdrop of economic slavery, Hurston reinforces the contemporary subversive import of these tales. As she suggests in her essay "High John de Conquer," in which she analyzes the dynamics of these stories, a John story "was an inside thing to live by. It was sure to be heard when and where the work was the hardest, and the lot most cruel. It helped the slaves endure" (1983: 69). In the Polk County section of *Mules and Men,* Hurston demonstrates that John did not die with Emancipation, but "retire[d] with his secret smile into the soil of the South and wait[ed]" (Hurston 1983: 78), reemerging—even in the 1920s—when needed to help Black people deal with oppression. By not analyzing in *Mules and Men* how these tales work, by inserting her extremely brief description of John only in her glossary, and by giving tales innocuous titles that mask their thematic import, Hurston hoped to recreate the plantation dynamics of the John tales. Like Massa and Ole Miss, her contemporary white readers could hear the tales without understanding their subversive import.[9]

The complex ambiguity of these tales is evident in one John story narrated in this section, "Ole Massa and John Who Wanted to Go to Heaven," a favorite of Hurston's told elsewhere as "The Fiery Chariot." While the tale seems to poke fun at the Black man through a series of racist stereotypes, a different kind of humor derives from the depiction of John as a trickster who not only outruns the Lord but also verbally outwits him. While an escape is obviously uppermost in his mind, he engineers it by feigning concern for the Lord's interests. He begins with a short appeal to decorum: "O, Lawd, Ah can't go to Heben wid you in yo' fiery chariot in dese old dirty britches; gimme time to put on my Sunday pants" (1935: 77). When this strategy is exhausted because "John didn't had nothin' else to change" (1935: 77), he lays the groundwork for his escape by appealing to "facts" God cannot possibly deny, God's superiority (1935: 77) and the Black man's inferiority (1935: 77–78). John's last plea is a rhetorical flourish, demonstrating that what Hurston has called in "Characteristics of Negro Expression" (1983) the Black person's "will to adorn" often derived not just from love of the poetic possibilities of words but from an awareness of their strategic rhetorical value. Here John calls on metaphor, double descriptive, and parallelism for perhaps the most serious persuasive motive—to save his own life:

> O, Lawd, Heben is so high and wese so low; youse so great and Ah'm so weak and yo' strength is too much for us poor suffering sinners. So once mo' and agin yo' humber servant is knee-bent and body-bowed askm' you one mo' favor befo' Ah step into yo' fiery chariot to go to Heben wid you and wash in yo' glory—be so pleased in yo' tender mercy as to stand back jus' a li'l bit further. (Hurston 1935: 78)

Just who in this scene is "brighter" becomes quite complicated when "Ole Massa stepped back a step or two mo' and out dat door John come like a streak of lightnin'" (1935: 78).[10] While Hurston deliberately leaves unstated the meaning of everybody's "Kah, Kah, Kah," their "laughing with their mouths wide open" (1935: 78), the context of their own feelings of impotence in this section strongly suggests their delight in the Black man's wiliness and the white's gullible vanity.[11] Many of the tales that follow repeat this theme and function psychologically to remind men of their humanity, no matter how mulish their existence.

In the social context that Hurston so carefully details before the stories are narrated, tales often acquire more subversive social commentary than their amusing (and sometimes even racist) surface might at first suggest. One such tale is "Deer Hunting Story," told at the end of chapter four. On the surface, the story might appear a racist story of the Black man's stupidity. Massa instructs the Black man to shoot the deer when he "skeer[s]" him up, but when the deer runs by, the Black man does nothing (1935: 82). When questioned by Massa, the slave claims to have seen no deer: "All Ah seen was a white man come along here wid a pack of chairs on his head and Ah tipped my hat to him and waited for de deer" (1935: 82). While one listener finds this tale proof that "some colored folks ain't got no sense" (1935: 82), the context in which this tale arises, one that highlights the men's awareness of the economic oppression Blacks experience, points to another reason for the slave's inactions.[12] First of all, the tale follows Jim Presley's suggestion that they should not worry about work since "de white folks made work" (1935: 80) and two tales, "Why the Sister in Black Always Works the Hardest" (1935: 80–81) and "De Reason Niggers Is Working So Hard" (1935: 81), that pinpoint the role of whites in Black oppression. As Jim Presley's comment immediately before the story suggests, in a world of harsh racial and economic inequalities, one in which "ought's a ought, figger's a figger; all for de white man, none for de nigger" (1935:81), the Black man who works diligently only serves the white man's interests rather than his own. With the literal context of the men's own slow walking to avoid work borne in mind, the story emerges as one extolling the subversive virtues of laziness, an indication of the slave's clever strategies for avoiding work through the appearance of stupidity.[13]

Although the large number of stories lampooning whites and showing the superior wit of Blacks depict the sawmill workers emotionally resisting their own masters, Hurston is careful not simply to romanticize Black response to white oppression. As she demonstrates, the conflict between the desire to see oneself as human and the pressure to accept white definitions of oneself as a mule is an intense one. She highlights this struggle several times in the men's conversations between tales, casting Jim Allen as the mouthpiece for white psychological control. In contrast to men like Jim Presley, who argues for the virtues of "laziness"—"Don't never worry about work. . . . There's more work in de world than there is anything else. God made de world and de white folks made work" (1935: 80)—Jim Allen repeatedly urges the men to hurry to work (1935: 80, 91, 95). The other men's defiance of this attitude finds voice in Lonnie Barnes's heated and insulting response: "Aw naw—you sho is worrysome. You bad as white folks" (1935: 95).

The conflicting reactions of Black people to white power—clever defiance or defeated acceptance—which these conversations embody is also reflected in the tales told in this section. Significantly, in addition to John stories, the section of *Mules and Men* set in the work context of Polk Country also has the harshest examples of self-denigrating tales narrated in the entire book.[14] Through her careful attention to context, Hurston suggests that these tales constitute another Black response to oppression. For instance, an abrupt change of mood occurs as the men arrive at the mill:

> Well, we were at the mill at last, as slow as we had walked. Old Hannah was climbing the road of the sky, heating up sand beds and sweating peoples. No wonder nobody wanted to work. Three fried men are not equal to one good cool one. The men stood around the door for a minute or two, then dropped down on the shady side of the building. Work was too discouraging to think about. Phew! Sun and sawdust, sweat and sand. (1935: 90–91)

Even John tales cannot totally erase this stark reminder of oppression. Facing the reality of the mill, some men tell self-degrading tales, the bitterest, "From Pine to Pine Mr. Pinkney," showing the destructive psychological effects of white oppression. The story of an escaped slave, Jack, caught because another slave helps the master, the tale ends with a depressing reminder of the men's own slavery symbolized by the mill: "So they caught Jack and put uh hundred lashes on his back and put him back to work" (1935: 93). As the men sit outside the mill in the heat, conscious that they too are "caught" by the boss, awaiting at least a figurative "hundred lashes" on their backs, they tell another tale about a Black man who avoided work through laziness, one that places the man's subversive "laziness" in a broader and harsher economic context. When the white man's back was turned, this Black man "would flop down and go to sleep. When he hear somebody comin' he'd hit de log a few licks with de flat of de ax and say, 'Klunk, klunk, you think Ah'm workin' but Ah ain't' " (1935: 99–100). The white man, however, gets the last laugh when the Black man comes to collect his pay: "De white man stacked up his great big ole silver dollars and shook 'em in his hand and says, 'Clink, clink you think I'm gointer pay you, but I ain't' " (1935: 100).

While these stories reveal harsh economic realities, the power of white definitions of Blackness, and the divisiveness of oppression, Hurston refuses to let these stories stand as the last word. By embedding them in the context of John stories and by ending this section with tales such as "The Fortune Teller" and "How the Negroes Got Their Freedom" which focus on Black men winning from whites, she emphasizes the power of Black people to resist psychological oppression even in the face of racist definitions and economic exploitation. Significantly, she ends this section with "Member Youse A Nigger," the story of a slave who, instead of outwardly defying white definitions (and risking death), simply dons the mask of subservience as he steps toward freedom. Such stories graphically demonstrate to the Black men hearing them the psychic freedom that can be enjoyed even when they are defined by whites as mules. As Hurston suggests in "High John de Conquer," the spiritual freedom depicted and experienced in hearing these stories is extremely important: these tales of John "fighting a mighty battle without outside-showing force, and winning his war from within" are meaningful victories showing a Black hero "really winning in a permanent way, for he was winning with the soul of the Black man whole and free. So he could use it afterwards" (Hurston 1983: 70–71). While the mill and its definitions of Black men still await them, such stories allow the workers to enter inured from the most devastating effects of spiritual enslavement.

When the workers in Polk County finally do get their day off to go fishing, they narrate tales quite different from those told at work. In the midst of this relative freedom (emphasized in Hurston 1935: 102, 123), the men tell not John tales, but light-hearted fish tales (1935: 103–104) and exaggeration stories (1935: 123–125) that demonstrate their delight in verbal play for its own sake. They also engage in traditional verbal contests, vying with one another for the best tales about the hottest weather (1935: 106), the biggest mosquito (1935: 108–109), the richest and poorest land (1935: 109–110). The delight in these tales ("everyone liked to hear about the mosquito" [1935: 109]) and the laughter they elicit ("they laughed all over themselves" [1935: 109]) are psychologically quite different from the enthusiastic response to the earlier John tales. Hurston also places in this fishing context etiological tales that reveal a freed imagination tackling profound philosophical issues. These stories (1935: 104–106, 111–116) of "how everything started" (1935: 127) also demonstrate a different kind of Black cultural creativity that flourishes outside the range of white control.

When the figure John (or Jack) does appear in this fishing section, he is a quite different hero than the "doubleteened" trickster focused on at work. In the last tale narrated before the men return home, "How the Lion Met the King of the World," John, who brags that he is "King of de World," must fight both the bear and the lion to prove his boast. Tackling them in cosmic warfare unseen "since de mornin' stars sung together" (1935: 142), he easily emerges the victor, not through cunning but through brute strength. Even the mighty lion affirms the godlike power of this Black figure: he knows he has met the King "'cause he made lightnin' in my face and thunder in my hips" (1935: 143). A similar kind of tale, "Strength Test between Jack and the Devil," the only one told at the jook that night and the last one narrated in the Polk County section, paints a similar picture of the Black hero created outside the psychic perimeter of white oppression. In a decidedly Black milieu (which Hurston carefully details), this formidable figure, who matches the devil's strength picking up trees and a mule under each arm, is depicted finally as even stronger than the devil.

The effects of freedom from white control on the storytelling imagination of Black people are also evident in chapter ten when Hurston goes
to Mulberry, Pierce, and Lakeland. In her "between-story business" Hurston
contrasts this environment with the oppressive one at the sawmill camps:

> The company operating the mines at Pierce maintains very
> excellent living conditions in their quarters. The cottages are on
> clean, tree-lined streets. There is a good hospital and a nine-months
> school. They will not employ a boy under seventeen so that the
> parents are not tempted to put minors to work. There is a cheerful
> community center with a large green-covered table for crap games
> under a shady oak. (1935: 166)

In this comparatively benign context, the stories told are not ones in
which Blacks must use indirect ways to maintain power against whites.
When whites are again on the periphery, the storytellers focus instead on
etiological tales that evoke "blow-out laughs" (1935: 167) and on "skeery
lies" (1935: 183) about supernatural experiences. Black figures focused on
in this section include ones of mythic proportions and strength like Big
Sixteen (1935: 172) as well as hoodoo doctors like High Walker "who had
[supernatural] power" (1935: 184) and Raw Head, "a man dat was more'n
a man" (1935: 174) with the cosmic power of Moses. Out of range of white
control, in a world as characterized by Nanny, "where de black man is in
power" (1935: 29), Black people feel their power not just to understand the
cosmos but to control it.

The battle between Blacks and whites is not the only one waged in
Mules and Men. Paying equal attention to power struggles between Black
men and women, Hurston repeatedly underscores not only how men oppress women (and use folktales to legitimate it) but also how women fight
against their subservient role, in ways both direct and more subversive.[15]
While the sexism in many men's comments and behavior is often undeni-
able, Hurston never explicitly comments on it, choosing instead (as she did
in treating race issues) to contextually embed her treatment of gender im-
balances and conflicts. One such instance is the argument that takes place
between Good Bread and Mack Ford over Good Bread's size. Rather than
straightforwardly exposing the sexism in Mack Ford's attitudes, Hurston
simply narrates the conversation without evaluation or comment. The episode begins with Mack Ford addressing Hurston: "Zora, why do you think
de li'l slim women was put on earth?" (1935: 170). When Hurston responds
to his answer that "dese slim ones was put here to beautify de world," with
the comment, "De big ones musta been put here for de same reason" (1935:
170), Ford responds that they were put here "to show dese slim girls how far

they kin stretch without bustin'" (1935: 170). While Good Bread takes this joke as the personal insult about her size that it is (serious enough for her to pull out her knife), Hurston inserts no explicit evaluation but rather shows the men cracking more jokes at Good Bread's expense. When Mack chides her that "you done set round and growed ruffles round yo' hips" (1935: 170) and Mah Honey gets in the last word with "Hey, lady, you got all you' bust in de back!" (1935: 171), these comments appear to be simple, good-natured fun: "Everybody laughed" (1935: 171). Like much laughter of "the brother in black," however, this humor carries a complex message. That this scene reflects sexual inequality rather than harmless fun or Good Bread's insecurity is revealed in the next folktale narrated. The story of Big Sixteen (1935: 172–173), who is so "big and strong" (1935: 172) that he can carry a mule under each arm and is feared even by the devil, it shows a mythic admiration for male strength and power. As the preceding "between-story conversation and business" reveals, however, a "big and strong" woman is often a source of scorn. The men hate not only her size but the equality with men that she also asserts in her overalls (1935: 171), "bull woofin'" (1935: 171), and "loud talk[ing]" (1935: 171).

Hurston uses her folk material in other ways to dramatize the gender battles waged in the community. Given the different social positions of women and men, it is not surprising that they often know and tell different stories. For instance, one man responds to a story told by Gold with the comment, "'Tain't no such story nowhere. She jus' made dat one up herself" (1935: 33). In Gold's defense, Armetta breaks in, "Naw, she didn't. . . . Ah *been* knowin' dat ole tale" (1935: 33), supported by another woman's "Me too" (1935: 33). Generally, men tell stories that reflect and reinforce their power over women while women tell stories that "strain against" it. Even when men and women hear the same tales, they often draw different meanings from them that reflect their contrasting interests in much the same way that Blacks and whites may see different significances in many of the John tales.[16]

Hurston uses both of these techniques to deal with two major areas of conflict between women and men: work and love. The tale that most starkly delineates the male perspective on work is "Why the Sister in Black Works Hardest," told by Jim Allen in Polk County. According to Allen's rendition of the tale, God originally put work in a box. Unaware of its contents, Ole Massa orders the Black man to carry it, who then orders his wife to do so. When the Black woman gets the box, she opens it eagerly. The tale ends with its moral: "So she run and grabbed a-hold of de box and opened it up and it was full of hard work. Dat's de reason de sister in black works harder than anybody else in de world. De white man tells de nigger to work and he takes and tells his wife" (1935: 81). While this tale (accurately, for Hurston) places Black sexual inequality in a larger context of racial oppression, a comparison between this rendition of the tale and the one Nanny gives in *Their Eyes Were Watching God* reveals two quite different versions of the same basic tale. Explaining to Janie why she must marry Logan Killicks, Nanny concludes:

> Honey, de white man is de ruler of everything as fur as Ah been able tuh find out. Maybe it's some place way off in de ocean where de black man is in power, but we don't know nothin' but what we see. So de white man throw down de load and tell de nigger man tuh pick it up. He pick it up because he have to, but he don't tote it. He hand it to his women-folks. De nigger woman is de mule uh de world so fur as Ah can see. (Hurston 1978: 29)

Whereas Nanny's version paints the Black woman as a victimized mule, Allen's tale, with its parallels to the story of Pandora's box, legitimates the Black woman's oppression by making her, through her own curiosity, responsible for it. Told in the context of the workers' racial oppression in Polk County, the tale ironically reveals another way in which Black men assert their own humanity: they can see themselves as men by making Black women mules. Told by Jim Allen, the most psychologically oppressed Black man in the group, the tale in context finally exposes racial inequality and insecurity as the foundation of Black male oppression of Black women.

In her depiction of the men's return to the quarters after having been sent home by the straw boss, Hurston reveals how this male point of view is played out in the social life of the community:

> When Mrs. Bertha Allen saw us coming from the mill she began to hunt up the hoe and the rake. She looked under the porch and behind the house until she got them both and placed them handy. As soon as Jim Allen hit the step she said:
>
> "Ah'm mighty proud y'all got a day off. Maybe Ah kin git dis yard all clean today. Jus' look at de trash and dirt! And it's so many weeds in dis yard, Ah'm liable to git snake bit at my own door."
>
> "Tain't no use in you gittin' yo' mouf all primped up for no hoein' and rakin' out of me, Bertha. Call yo' grandson and let him do it. Ah'm too ole for dat," said Jim testily.
>
> "Ah'm standin' in my tracks and steppin' back on my abstract— Ah ain't gointer rake up no yard. Ah'm goin' fishin'," Cliffert Ulmer snapped back. "Grandma, you worries mo' 'bout dis place than de man dat owns it. You ain't de Everglades Cypress Lumber Comp'ny sho nuff. Youse shacking on one of their shanties. Leave de weeds go. Somebody'll come chop 'em some day."

"Naw, Ah ain't gointer leave 'em go! You and Jim would wallow in dirt right up to yo' necks if it wasn't for me."

Jim threw down his jumper and his dinner bucket. "Now, *Ah'm* goin' fishin' too. When Bertha starts her jawin' Ah can't stay on de place. Her tongue is hung in de middle and works both ways. Come on Cliff, less git de poles!" (Hurston 1935: 100–101)

Unlike Tea Cake in *Their Eyes Were Watching God,* secure enough in his racial and sexual identity to labor beside Janie both in the field and in the home, Jim Allen refuses any association with "women's work." Clifford's sneering reminder that the Everglades Cypress Company owns the place further demonstrates that the men see this work, like their own at the mill, as toil for white men. They fail, however, to acknowledge the female needs this labor serves, emphasized in Bertha's comment, "Ah'm liable to git snake bit at my own door." Thus, the "laziness" that functioned as a subversive strategy against white power at the mill actually furthers female oppression at home. The dynamics of male oppression are also highlighted here in Jim's changed behavior. Unable to feel "like a man" at work, he becomes one at home by imperiously tossing his load to a Black woman. While he takes off fishing, his wife, left behind as a mule alone in her work, pays the price for his psychological freedom.

As Big Sweet's fighting over Joe Willard's infidelity demonstrates, love is also a major struggle between men and women in *Mules and Men.* In the several courting conversations she narrates, Hurston demonstrates how male and female perspectives differ: in men's comments and tales, love is often a game with women as the sexual prize. One story told by a man, in fact, bespeaks an attitude toward love frequently expressed by men. In this courtship story, a man woos a woman by pointing to a farm, cattle, sheep, and hogs and telling her, "All of these are mine" (1935: 179). When she goes home with him, only to find it a "dirty li'l shack" (1935: 179) and berates him for his lies, he responds, "I didn't tell you a story. Everytime I showed you those things I said 'all of these were mine' and Ah wuz talkin' bout my whiskers" (1935: 179). While such insincerity is a source of humor for men, several episodes in *Mules and Men* reveal it as frequently the norm in courting. As Hurston's own experience demonstrates (1935: 68–70), a woman's ability to protect her own interests often depends on recognizing such "woofing" for the "aimless talking" (1935: 253) that it is.

Men's view of love as a game and fidelity as a trap is clear in Willie Sewell's boast: "Ya'll lady people ain't smarter *than* all men folks. You got plow lines on some of us, but some of us is too smart for you. We go past you jus' like lightnin' thru de trees. . . And what mek it so cool, we close enough to you to have a scronchous time, but never no halter on our necks. Ah know they won't git none on dis last neck of mine" (1935: 38). The conflict between men's and women's interests is highlighted in Gold's retort, "Oh, you kin be had . . . Ah mean dat abstifically" (1935: 38), and Willie's rejoinder, "Yeah? But not wid de trace chains. Never no shack up. Ah want dis tip-in love and tip yo' hat and walk out. Ah don't want nobody to have dis dyin' love for me" (1935: 38). The disagreement does not end with the conversation between this man and woman; instead, it plays itself out through the tales that follow. Jack Oscar Jones reinforces the male perspective with his "speech about love" (1935: 38), actually a poem about a man having concurrent love affairs with three women. Refusing to allow this version of the male-female relationships to go unchallenged, Shug responds to Jack's paean to philandering with the comment, "Well, de way Ah know de story, there was three mens after de same girl" (1935: 40). She then proceeds with the story of the heroic feats three men perform to win the hand of a girl in marriage. Told in another context, this tale might seem simply another mythic story of heroic Black deeds, similar to those told in chapter ten. In the male-female battle out of which it grows, it more accurately demonstrates the women's use of folktales to elevate their status. Reversing the numbers and the roles here, showing men eager for marriage, Shug paints the men in her tale delivering on their promises, performing heroic labors and even "female" tasks to prove their love.

Men, on the other hand, use folktales to counter women's assertions of equality and to reinforce the status quo. Three tales told at the end of chapter seven, "The Son Who Went to College," "Sis Snail," and "Why the Waves Have whitecaps," narrated in the context of heated arguments between men and women, become charged with gender-specific meanings.[17] The scene begins with one of the battles between Big Sweet and Joe Willard over his infidelity. Introducing his contribution to a series of stories about dogs, Gene Oliver comments, "Talkin' 'bout dogs, . . . they got plenty sense. Nobody can't fool dogs much" (1935: 133).[18] Recognizing Gene's "by-word" reference to men, Big Sweet changes the direction of the conversation with her own "signify[ing]" (1935: 133) comment: "And speakin' 'bout hams, . . . if Joe Willard don't stay out of dat bunk he was in last night, Ah'm gointer sprinkle some salt down his back and sugar-cure his hams" (1935: 133). The interchange between her and Joe Willard that follows highlights Big Sweet's verbal dexterity in asserting her own interests:

> Joe snatched his pole out of the water with a jerk and glared at Big Sweet, who stood sidewise looking at him most pointedly.
> "Aw, woman, quit tryin' to signify."
> "Ah kin signify all Ah please, Mr. Nappy-chin, so long as Ah know what Ah'm talkin' about."
> "See dat?" Joe appealed to the other men. "We git a day off and

figger we kin ketch some fish and enjoy ourselves, but naw, some wimmins got to drag behind us, even to the lake."

"You didn't figger Ah was draggin' behind you when you was bringin' dat Sears and Roebuck catalogue over to my house and beggin' me to choose my ruthers. Lemme tell *you* something, *any* time Ah shack up wid any man Ah gives myself de privilege to go wherever he might be, night or day. Ah got de law in my mouth."

"Lawd, ain't she specifyin'," sniggered Wiley. (1935: 133–134)

Joe's "appeal" to the men does not go unheeded, for they immediately launch into a series of stories told specifically to denigrate women. Jim Allen introduces the first with the telling comment, "Well, you know what they say—a man can cakerlate his life till he git mixed up wid a woman or git straddle of a cow" (1935: 134). As astute in interpreting words as she is in speaking them, Big Sweet decodes the gender equation thinly veiled in Allen's signifying comment: "Who you callin' a cow, fool? Ah know you ain't namin' my mama's daughter no cow" (1935: 134). The context of this tale highlights it as a parable about male oppression of women. Echoing the same kind of sexual innuendo seen in the song about Ella Wall who "rocks her rider/From uh wall to wall" (1935: 159), the "inside meaning" of this story of a man riding a cow to tame her is a thinly veiled male commentary on the sexual and emotional dynamics of relationships between women and men. The son has the original insight on how to cure this cow from kicking: "Mama, cow-kickin' is all a matter of scientific principle. You see before a cow can kick she has to hump herself up in the back. So all we need to do is to take the hump out the cow's back" (1935: 135). His cure for this unruly behavior is also highly symbolic: "All we need to keep this animal from humping is a weight on her back" (1935: 136). While not entirely successful, the plan to burden the cow with the weight of a male rider reveals a male perspective on relationships with women that involves female dehumanization and domination.[19] The men immediately launch into another tale commenting on relationships between men and women. The story of Sis Snail in another context might appear a rather innocuous animal tale. Here, however, the gender dynamics of the preceding arguments highlight the male attitudes toward women evident in the tale:

> You know de snail's wife took sick and sent him for de doctor. She was real low ill-sick and rolled from one side of de bed to de other. She was groaning "Lawd knows Ah got so much misery Ah hope de Doctor'll soon git here to me."
>
> After seben years she heard a scufflin' at de door. She was real happy so she ast, "Is dat you baby, done come back wid de doctor?

Ah'm so glad!"

He says, "Don't try to rush me—Ah ain't gone yet." He had
been seben years gettin' to de door. (Hurston 1935: 137)

While men's failure to support women is humorously rationalized and
legitimized in this tale, it is an ironically accurate reflection on the level of
support Jim Allen and other men offer their wives.

The last tale, innocently cast as an etiological tale with the title "Why
the Waves Have Whitecaps," is firmly grounded in thinly veiled stereotypes
of women. The wind and the water are both cast as women who, "jus' like all
lady people," spend much time "talk[ing] about their chillun and brag[ging]
on 'em" (1935: 138). The tale, significantly narrated by Jim Allen's grandson
and protégé, is much more than a parable of women's vanity, however; for
their maternal devotion takes a most sinister turn. When Mrs. Wind's children ask Mrs. Water for a drink, she drowns them. The tale ends with an
explanation of the origin of white caps:

> Mrs. Wind knew her chillun had come down to Mrs. Water's
> house, so she passed over de ocean callin' her chillun, and every time
> she call de white feathers would come up on top of de water. And
> dat's how come we got white caps on waves. It's de feathers comin'
> up when de wind woman calls her lost babies.
>
> When you see a storm on de water, it's de wind and de water
> fightin' over dem chillun. (Hurston 1935:139)

Here, as in much European folklore, women's actions are described as the
root of human and cosmic discord.

Although Hurston relentlessly exposes the sexism in the Black world
described in *Mules and Men,* she holds firmly to an ideal of equality between
men and women. As Cheryl Wall (1989: 377–378) has pointed out, Hurston
smuggles in a religious and metaphysical affirmation of men and women as
equal partners by inserting the sermon "Behold the Rib" (1935: 148–150).
Although spoken to an unenthusiastic audience who does not even comment
on the preacher's message or respond to his good "strainin' voice," this speech
represents the ideal against which relationships between men and women
are measured in *Mules and Men.* The female character who comes closest
to achieving this ideal even in the face of male efforts at domination is, of
course, Big Sweet, a woman who "didn't mind fightin'; didn't mind killing and
didn't too much mind dyin'" (1935: 159) to protect herself and those she loves.
Hurston is careful not to paint Big Sweet as simply racially defiant and dan-
gerously violent. Rather, she stresses in the character of Big Sweet a fusion,
suggested even in her name, of traditional male toughness and female tender-

ness. The value Big Sweet places on generous support for another is indicated in her selfless support of Hurston—"You come here tuh see and lissen and Ah means fuh yuh tuh do it" (1935: 186), she promises her—and in the tale she narrates about the mockingbird. Telling about the death and damnation of an evil man who was only good to birds, Big Sweet stresses the selfless devotion evident in the birds' herculean labor:

> De birds all hated it mighty bad when they seen him in hell, so they tried to git him out. But the fire was too hot so they give up—all but de mockin' birds. They come together and decided to tote sand until they squenched de fire in hell. So they set a day and they all agreed on it. Every Friday they totes sand to hell. And that's how come nobody don't never see no mockin' bird on Friday. (Hurston 1935: 103)

Hurston emphasizes the value women place on selfless devotion and supportive friendship by suggesting (as she often does to highlight gender issues) that the men do not know this story. When Big Sweet comments before telling her tale, "Oh you know how come we don't hear no birds. It's Friday and de mocking bird ain't here" (1935: 102), Eugene reveals his ignorance of the tale with the comment, "What's Friday got to do with the mockin' bird?"—an attitude reiterated by Joe Wiley: "Dat's exactly what Ah want to know" (1935: 102). Hurston also suggests that the men do not understand the tale's significance after they hear it. Joe Wiley's "chuckl[ing]" comment, "If them mockin' birds ever speck to do dat man any good they better git some box-cars to haul dat sand. Dat one li'l grain they totin' in their bill ain't helpin' none" (1935: 103), reveals how totally he has missed the tale's emotional point. Only sensitive to the tale's personification, he can only make the weakest of interpretive stabs at the tale's meaning: "But anyhow it goes to show you dat animals got sense as well as peoples" (1935: 103). He then launches into a tale, jarring with the empathy and pathos of Big Sweet's, about a catfish that drags a fisherman into deep water and drowns him (1935: 103).

Although Big Sweet represents the ideal Black woman for Hurston—tender and supportive with those she loves, ruthless when necessary for her own survival or that of her loved ones—she is, nevertheless, an ideal.[20] She herself suggests that not every Black woman can be so direct in asserting her rights when she warns Hurston not to "let [her] head start more than [her] rump kin stand" (1935: 187). For women of less titanic proportions the strategies necessary to battle sexual inequality are often more indirect ones. Oppressed by men within their own communities, they must often act in ways that echo those used by Blacks in battling racial oppression. These parallels are emphasized in the story Mathilda Moseley tells early in the book, in "Why Women Always Take Advantage of Men" (1935: 33–38). Again, Hurston highlights the role women's stories play in attacking sexism by detailing the discussion that prompts Mathilda to tell this tale, a conversation peppered with derogatory comments about women and male bragging about their superiority. To counter these comments, Mathilda launches into a story that, first of all, reinforces the message of the "Behold de Rib!" sermon. Women are not "naturally" inferior to men, she points out, because originally "de woman was just as strong as de man and both of 'em did de same things. They useter get to fussin' 'bout who gointer do this and that and sometime they'd fight, but they was even balanced and neither one could whip de other one" (1935: 33–34). In her female version of the creation myth, Eden is destroyed by male perfidy when the man asks God for more strength so he can "whip" the woman and "make her mind" (1935: 34).

When the man swaggers home to announce, "Ah'm yo' boss" (1935: 35), the woman, as feisty as Big Sweet, heroically fights back. Now physically "double-teened," however, she finds herself a mule in relation to her husband. "Long as you obey me," he warns, "Ah'll be good to yuh, but every time yuh rear up Ah'm gointer put plenty wood on yo' back and plenty water in yo' eyes" (1935: 35). Determined to regain her strength, the woman (after God refuses her request) finally goes to the devil. Significantly, it is the devil, "a powerful trickster" (1935: 254), who helps women in their battles with Black men just as he often helps Black men in their struggles with whites. Teaching her to be a cunning trickster herself, counseling her to ask God for his keys, he promises that in an indirect fashion, she can "come out mo' than conqueror" (1935: 35). After securing the keys to the kitchen, the bedroom, and the cradle, she returns to the devil, who instructs her not to "unlock nothin' until [her husband] use his strength for yo' benefit and yo' desires" (1935: 36). Unable to "rear up" (1935: 35) in open defiance of her rider, the woman, like High John, nevertheless wins without "outside show of force," as Mathilda's self-satisfied conclusion suggests:

> de man had to mortgage his strength to her to live. And dat's why
> de man makes and de woman takes. You men is still braggin' 'bout
> yo' strength and de women is sittin' on de keys and lettin' you blow
> off till she git ready to put de bridle on you. (Hurston 1935: 38)

With the woman holding the bridle now rather than wearing it, the mule and rider motif shifts starkly at this point in the tale. As the last sentence suggests, this female trickster, despite apparent inequality, exercises considerable control in her relationship with men. So do the women in *Mules and Men*. That they use similar strategies for survival and victory over their oppressors can be seen in Mrs. Allen's response to her husband's refusal to clean the yard: instead of foolishly confronting her husband physically, she uses one of her keys. When the men return from fishing, "The fishermen began scraping fish and hot grease began to pop in happy houses. All but the Allen's. Mrs. Allen wouldn't have a thing to do with our fish because Mr. Allen and Cliffert had made her mad about the yard" (1935: 147).

As this tale suggests, Hurston treats race and gender as complexly inter-related issues in the Black world she describes. Gender inequality is not only grounded in racial inequality (the Black woman's burden can, after all, be traced back to the white man who originally orders the Black man to pick it up); it also operates in strikingly parallel ways in *Mules and Men.* Hurston's ambiguous title captures the richness of her analysis. A world controlled by whites, one (like that of the sawmill) in which Black men are economically oppressed and socially defined by them, is a world of mules and men. Tragi-cally, for Hurston, when Black men draw their self-concepts from white people and make themselves feel like men by slipping their halters onto Black women, the Black community becomes another world of mules and men. Hurston's analysis of power relations between Black and white or be-tween Black men and women is, however, even more complex, for it involves not just grimly detailing oppression but also enthusiastically depicting resis-tance to it. As many folktales suggest, any world of mules and men is poten-tially unstable. As Black men in their relationships with whites and Black women in their relationships with Black men repeatedly show, mules are not simply brutalized beasts of burden who silently endure their slavish existence; they can often be fractious beasts who throw off their burdens and their riders or subtle tricksters who more slyly slip their halters.[21]

NOTES

1. Her contemporary reviewers in mainstream periodicals (for instance, Brick-ell 1935, Chubb 1936, Daniels 1935, MacGowan n.d.), universally responding to the work enthusiastically, appreciated its light-hearted exterior. For Sterling Brown, however, these apparent qualities indicate Hurston's lack of critical awareness. In his view the humor Hurston conveys in describing "a land shadowed by squalor, poverty, disease, violence, enforced ignorance, and exploitation" is only one side of the story. *Mules and Men,* he concludes, "should be more bitter; it would be nearer the total truth" (Brown 1936, in Hemenway 1978: xxv–vi).

2. Boas, like Mason, also inserted himself into Hurston's financial arrange-ments. After receiving notice from a finance company that Hurston had applied for a loan, he writes to her:

> You certainly ought to have written to me about this matter so that I may know why you want the money and whether there is any hitch with your arrangements. It worries me particularly as you want to repay it in eight

monthly installments, because that obscures the whole situation. I wish you
would write to me definitely why you want this money and I shall delay
replying to the Corporation until I hear from you. Perhaps you can explain the
matter in a night letter. (March 24, 1927)

In her reply, Hurston dutifully explains her need for a car to carry out her
research and adds a subtle, characteristically double-edged "apology": "I had no idea
that [this matter] would cause you any worry at all. In fact, I thought I was doing
business with the Martin-Nash Motor Company" (March 29, 1927).

Hurston was not the only one of Boas's female protégés to note his powerful
control. Margaret Mead, for instance, comments on his "authoritative and uncompromising sense of what was right" (1966: 4) and the "austerity of his fundamentally
paternal relationship to his students" (1966: 9).

3. Despite Boas's admonitions, Hurston managed to smuggle her views on
fire and water symbolism into *Mules and Men*. At the beginning of part two, she
states that Hoodoo "adapts itself like Christianity to its locale, reclaiming some of its
borrowed characteristics to itself. Such as fire-worship as signified in the Christian
church by the altar and candles and the belief in the power of water to sanctify as
in baptism" (1935: 193). The correspondence between Hurston and Boas (F.B. to
Z.N.H. [September 12, 1934] and Z.N.H. to F.B. [October 23, 1934]), indicat-
ing that Boas was originally sent only the folklore section to read before deciding
whether to write a preface, raises the possibility that Hurston did not want him to
see parts she knew he would find problematic.

4. Most reviewers—including Brock (1935), Chubb (1936), Fallaize (1936),
Gannett (1935), MacGowan (n.d.), Moon (1935), and Stoney (1935)—made this
explicit comparison in discussing Hurston's work.

5. Many reviewers, including Chubb, Moon, MacGowan, Brickell, and
Stoney, expressed their delight in being brought "inside" Black folklife. Some
reviewers even felt free to evaluate Hurston's own firsthand knowledge; for instance,
MacGowan commented that "those who know their Negro will scarcely doubt a line
of [*Mules and Men*]" (n.d.:n.p).

6. The anthropological significance of the social context in which Hurston
embedded her tales has only really begun to be appreciated recently. John Roberts,
reviewing *Mules and Men* for the *Journal of American Folklore*, argues that Hurston's
"narrative structure" "provided her with a unique opportunity to present storytelling
context. In the process, she demonstrated a folkloristic sophistication and sensitivity
to folklore processes shared by few of her contemporaries" (1980: 464). Specifically,
he suggests that the dialogue is central, for from it "one also gains insights into how
the participants viewed the role of the tales within their own experience" (1980:
464). Dana McKinnon Preu has also stressed the importance of social context for
interpreting tales in *Mules and Men* (1991).

7. Hurston worked hard to convince Boas of her scientific rigor. In one letter,
for instance, she stresses her painstaking approach to transcribing folktales:

I have tried to be as exact as possible. Keeping to the exact dialect as closely as
I could, having the story teller to tell it to me word for word as I wrote it. This
after it has been told to me off hand until I know it myself. But the writing
down from the lips is to insure the correct dialect and wording so that I shall
not let myself creep in unconsciously. (October 20, 1929)

Despite these claims, Hurston most likely took some literary license in recasting the tales she heard. A comparison with her version of traditional tales in other anthologies often shows how much more unified and artistically developed Hurston's versions are. In his review, Roberts questions the absolute "authenticity of the transcription," finding it quite unlikely that Hurston could have transcribed tales in some of the "tense situations" described (1980: 464). Evidence of how widespread and traditional most of the tales narrated in *Mules and Men* are and how Hurston's versions differed from others can be seen by examining such Black folktale anthologies as those by Botkin (1945), Courlander (1976), Puckett (1926), Dorson (1956a, 1956b), Jones (1925), Brewer (1958, 1968), Fauset (1927), Dance (1978), Hughes and Bontemps (1971), and Lester (1969). It is also interesting that a number of the stories in *Mules and Men* also appear in unpublished material of the Florida Writers Project on which Hurston worked. Hemenway (1976) has reprinted a number of these tales.

8. For discussion of this traditional figure in Black folklore, see Brewer 1959, Weldon 1959, Anderson 1961, and Dorson 1956: 124–170.

9. Hurston's narrative strategy in *Mules and Men* is deeply indebted to the trickster tradition in Black folklore. Barbara Johnson (1985), bell hooks (1990: 138), and Susan Willis (1987: 29–31) have pointed to trickster elements in specific tales and their relation to Hurston's subversive strategy in *Mules and Men*.

10. Another tale, "The First Colored Man in Massa's Houses" (1935: 85–86), one that also demonstrates how central mimicry of the master's language is for effective masking, has been discussed by Hemenway (1978: xxii–xxiii). As he argues, the tale not only lampoons white pretensions but also shows the slave, despite his subservient behavior, as not at all duped by them.

11. Hurston reinforces this lampooning of whites by including two tales—"How the Negro Got His Freedom" (1935: 88–90) and "God an' de Devil in de Cemetery" (1935: 93–95)—that depict the white master as more superstitious than the slave.

12. Susan Willis has given a detailed reading of the tale "How Jack Beat the Devil" (Hurston 1935: 518) to show how Hurston's tales often reflect economic realities (Willis 1987: 40–44). This one, she argues, highlights Jack's oppression, revealing that "everything Jack does is contained by the system of capital that is in no way influenced or affected by the forms of exchange employed by Jack" (1987: 40).

13. The ludicrous portrait of the white master, indistinguishable from a deer when adorned "'wid a pack of chairs on his head" (1935: 82), is also an important element in the subversive humor of this tale.

14. In *Shuckin' and Jivin'* Daryl Dance provides numerous examples of self-degrading tales built on white stereotypes of Blacks (1978: 77–100).

15. Both Mikell (1983) and Willis (1987) have pointed to Hurston's treatment of gender issues in *Mules and Men*. Mikell argues, for instance, that Hurston portrays women in her anthropology as both subject and object (1983: 31), while Willis points out that many women in Hurston's tales are not "stereotypically subservient" (1987: 43) but intelligent and clever. Mary Katherine Wainwright (1991) and Cheryl Wall (1989) have also discussed the battles between the sexes in *Mules and Men*.

16. Hurston's contribution to anthropological understanding of Black women's folklore was significant and original. Ferris (1972) has pointed out the lack of women's stories in the literature and attributes it to the fact that most collectors have been male.

17. Dance provides examples of many Black folktales about women (1978: 110–142) and discusses the sexist stereotypes on which they are built.

18. Drawing from Black folklore and blues lyrics, Hurston often uses the dog in her fiction and in *Mules and Men* to symbolize oppressive masculinity. See "Risqué Tales," chapter fifteen of Dance 1987, for numerous examples of the male represented as a dog in Black folk culture.

19. This tale is richly complex. Told by Jim Allen, it mirrors his relationship with his burdened wife and again dramatizes the racial component in Black women's oppression. As the man who feels most heavily the weight of white oppression, Allen must "ride" a woman to feel himself less like a mule. The most racially oppressed man in the community is, not coincidentally for Hurston, the most sexist.

As Hurston often does, she also here hints at the complexity of cow/mule image. The man in the tale "rides" (1935: 136) the woman, but she is a "fractious" beast and takes off with her rider who is hardly in control of the situation. Oppression of any form is rarely without some subversive element in Hurston's work.

20. The strength and compassion evident in Big Sweet's character are important features of Hurston's ideal Black woman. Marie Leveau, for instance, the famed two-headed doctor described in the hoodoo section of *Mules and Men* is powerful, godlike, yet loving (1935: 201–204).

21. As Dundes points out, the mule metaphor in Black folklore is a richly complex one, symbolizing the Black person's slavish existence but also his or her "mother wit," strength, and stubbornness (1973: 37 n.). Despite the obvious allusion, Hurston's title has prompted some interesting comments. Missing the metaphorical significance entirely, MacGowan suggests that "the few mules that appear in the pages supply the comic relief and the alliteration for a snappy title" and uses the mule metaphor as the basis for a condescending conclusion about Black life: "If voodoo, or hoodoo, does persist with the force that Miss Hurston claims, it is evidence that a race will cling for generations, even in a changed environment and under benign influences, to the beaten tracks of the past. Therein men are mules" (n.d.: n.p). In a scathing critique of the book, Harold Preece points to the title as evidence of Hurston's racial self-hatred. He understands the "resentment of some Negro circles toward the work of Miss Hurston," for "when a Negro author describes her race with such a servile term as 'Mules and Men,' critical members of the race must necessarily evaluate the author as a literary climber" (Preece 1936: 37).

WORKS CITED

Anderson, John Q. 1961. Old John and the Master. *Southern Folklore Quarterly* 25: 195–197.

Botkin, B. A., ed. 1945. *Lay My Burden Down, A Folk History of Slavery.* Chicago: University of Chicago Press.

Brewer, J. Mason. 1958. *Dog Ghosts and Other Texas Negro Folk Tales.* Austin: University of Texas Press.

———. 1968. *American Negro Folklore.* Chicago: Quadrangle Books.

———. 1959. John Tales. *Publications of the Texas Folklore* Society 24: 170–189.

Brickell, Herschel. 1935. A Woman Writer and Her People. *New York Post,* October 26: 7.

Brock, H. I. "The Full, True Flavor of Life in a Negro Community." *New York Times Book Review,* November 10 (1935): p. 4.

Brown, Sterling. Review of *Mules and Men.* James Weldon Johnson Collection, Beinecke Library, Yale University, 1936.

Chubb, Thomas Cadecot. 1936. Review of *Mules and Men*. *North American Review* 241: 181–183.

Courlander, Harold. 1976. *A Treasury of Afro-American Folklore*. New York: Crown Publishers.

Dance, Daryl Cumber. 1978. *Shuckin' and Jivin': Folklore from Contemporary Black Americans*. Bloomington: Indiana University Press.

Daniels, Jonathan. 1935. Black Magic and Dark Laughter. *Saturday Review of Literature* 12 (October 19): 12.

Dorson, Richard. 1956a . *American Negro Folktales*. Greenwich, Conn.: Fawcett Publications.

———. 1956b. *Negro Folktales in Michigan*. Cambridge, Mass.: Harvard University Press.

Dundes, Alan. *Mother Wit from the Laughing Barrel: Readings in the Interpretation of American Folklore*. Englewood Cliffs, NJ.: Prentice-Hall, 1973.

Fallaize, E. N. Negro Folklore. Review of *Mules and Men*." Manchester Guardian, April 7, 1936: 7.

Fauset, Arthur Huff. 1937. Negro Tales from the South. *Journal of American Folklore* 40: 213–303.

Ferris, William R., Jr. 1972. Black Prose Narratives in the Mississippi Delta. *Journal of American Folklore* 85: 140–151.

Gannett, Lewis. 1935. Books and Things. Review of *Mules and Men*. *New York Herald Tribune,* October 11: 27.

Glassman, Steve, and Kathryn Lee Seidel, eds. 1991. *Zora in Florida*. Orlando: University of Central Florida Press.

Hemenway, Robert. 1976. Folklore Field Notes from Zora Neale Hurston *Black Scholar* 7: 39–47.

———. 1978. Introduction. In *Mules and Men*. Zora Neale Hurston. Bloomington: Indiana University Press.

hooks, bell. 1990. *Yearning: Race, Gender, and Cultural Politics*. Boston: South End Press.

Hughes, Langston, and Bontemps, Arna, eds. 1971. *The Book of Negro Folklore*. New York: Dodd, Mead and Company.

Hurston, Zora Neale. 1935. *Mules and Men*. Philadelphia: J. B. Lippincott.

———. 1978. *Their Eyes Were Watching God: A Novel*. Urbana: University of Illinois Press.

———. 1983[1943] High John de Conquer. In *The Sanctified Church*, pp. 69–78. Berkeley: Turtle Island Press.

———. 1983. Characteristics of Negro Expression. In *The Sanctified Church*, pp. 41–78. Berkeley: Turtle Island Press, 1983.

Johnson, Barbara. 1985. Thresholds of Difference: Structures of Address in Zora Neale Hurston. *Critical Inquiry* 12: 278–289.

Jones, Charles C. 1925. *Negro Myths from the Georgia Coast, Told in the Vernacular*. Columbia, S.C.: The State Company.

Lester, Julius. 1969. *Black Folktales*. New York: Richard W. Baron.

MacGowan, Gault. n.d. Negro Folklore. Review of *Mules and Men*. Schomburg Collection, New York City Library.

Mead, Margaret. 1966. *An Anthropologist at Work: Writings of Ruth Benedict*. New York: Houghton Mifflin.

Mikell, Gwendolyn. 1983. The Anthropological Imagination of Zora Neale Hurston. *Western Journal of Black Studies* 7: 27–34.

Moon, Henry. 1935. Big Old Lies. Review of *Mules and Men*. *New Republic* 85 (December 11): 142.

Preece, Harold. 1936. The Negro Folk Cult. *Crisis* 43: 364, 374.
Preu, Dana McKinnon. 1991. A Literary Reading of *Mules and Men*, Part I. In *Zora in Florida*, ed. Steve Glassman and Kathryn Lee Seidel, pp. 46–61. Orlando: University of Central Florida Press.
Puckett, Newbell Niles. 1926. *Folk Beliefs of the Southern Negro*. Chapel Hill: University of North Carolina Press.
Roberts, John. 1980. Review of *Mules and Men*. *Journal of American Folklore* 93: 463–467.
Stoney, Samuel Gaillard. 1935. Wit, Wisdom, and Folklore. Review of *Mules and Men*. *Books*, October 13: 7.
Wainwright, Mary Katherine. 1991. Subversive Female Folk Tellers in *Mules and Men*. In *Zora in Florida*, ed. Steve Glassman and Kathryn Lee Seidel, pp. 62–75. Orlando: University of Central Florida Press.
Wall, Cheryl. 1989. *Mules and Men* and Women: Zora Neale Hurston's Strategies of Narration and Visions of Female Empowerment. *Black American Literature Forum* 23: 661–680.
Weldon, Fred O. 1959. Negro Folktale Heroes. *Publications of the Texas Folklore Society* 21: 170–189.
Willis, Susan. 1987. *Specifying: Black Women Writing the American Experience*. Madison: University of Wisconsin Press.

MICHAEL AWKWARD AND

MICHELLE JOHNSON

Zora Neale Hurston

Side-splittingly funny and moving moments in *In Search of Our Mothers' Gardens* offer a record of Alice Walker's search for Zora Neale Hurston's final resting place during the early 1970s, a search that took her, ultimately, to a Fort Pierce, Florida, burial ground filled with unchecked vegetation and inhospitable spirits. In large part because of Walker's efforts to recover her authorial forebear's discarded literal and literary body and Robert Hemenway's seminal contribution, *Zora Neale Hurston: A Literary Biography*, scholars over the last two decades have had access, if not to Hurston's literal body, to the lively, complex spirit manifested in her literary corpus.

Unsure about the precise location of Hurston's body, Walker nonetheless sumptuously marks her closest approximation of Hurston's resting place with a tombstone made of Ebony Mist that inscribes the younger writer's sense of her forebear's place in the American literary firmament:

ZORA NEALE HURSTON
"A GENIUS OF THE SOUTH"
NOVELIST FOLKLORIST
ANTHROPOLOGIST
1901   1960

Prospectus for the Study of American Literature: A Guide for Scholars and Students, edited by Richard Kopley. New York: New York University Press, 1997. © 1997 New York University Press.

As remarkable as Walker's gesture still appears to us more than two decades after Hurston's rediscovery—particularly in light of Harold Bloom's popular speculations on the anxiety of literary influence—we are struck nonetheless as much by what Walker's inscription fails to record as by its rich recognitions. We now know, for example, that Hurston was born at least a decade before 1901, and that she contributed significantly to other discursive forms, particularly the essay (some of whose best examples Walker made widely available through a Feminist Press collection of Hurston's writings, *I Love Myself When I Am Laughing*) and autobiography (which Walker does not mention apparently because, as she acknowledges in her writings, she dislikes the liberties that Hurston takes with the narrative of her self-making).

If we see Walker's list as not only partial, but also motivated by the contingencies of value that, according to Barbara Herrnstein Smith, condition all evaluative acts, then we can respond to the strategic partiality of scholarly renderings of Hurston's thematics, racial and gendered politics, aesthetics, and formal and disciplinary negotiations. Like Whitman's famous persona, Hurston was a vast figure containing multitudes, including sometimes perplexing contradictions. Explorations of her work must attend to its formulation on race and gender. To do Hurston justice, however, scholarship must operate with as expansive a concept of African Americanist and feminist—or, as we will argue below, gender—studies as possible.

Scholars taking up the subject of Zora Neale Hurston's work and life must be concerned with investigating more fully all of her texts and the expansive contexts in which she and her texts were produced. These scholars should aim for richer assessments of the individual texts themselves, of their relations to one another and to the work of black diasporic and other American writers, and of the fullness of Hurston's achievement.

Assessments of the nature of Hurston's current status vary widely. For example, as late as 1990, Robert Hemenway, using academic rank as a measure of canonicity, argued that Hurston "has a precarious hold at the untenured assistant professor level—the jury being still out on the nature of her achievement," while Ernest Hemingway is "good, but not of the first rank (an associate professor, who seems to repeat himself)" (30). Using the same two figures' "contrasting fortunes," however, Wendy Steiner asserted just five years later that Hurston's work has become central to literary and cultural studies in the academy, whose abiding methodologies privilege the return of the repressed, the suppressed, and marginalized, while an already well-known Hemingway's "virile chest-thumping and despair have become clichéd" (148). We believe that Hurston's place is much more secure than her distinguished biographer suggests (perhaps in an attempt to make no more than modest claims for the impact of his own contributions to American literary history). But while she is now widely recognized as an important, canonical writer, the celebration of Hurston may be short-lived if, as in Steiner's rendering, our attention is confined primarily to one text—*Their Eyes Were Watching God*—and to revisiting already much-traveled interpretive ground pertaining to that novel's narrative strategies, its representation of black gender relations, and the issue of a black woman's search for voice.

Nevertheless, we recognize that the canonicity of that text and the cult of personality that has developed around Hurston—as represented in the Broadway plays, festivals, T-shirts, postcards, and other paraphernalia that celebrate her colorful personality—have had significant benefits for Hurston scholarship, not the least of which is the fact that others of her texts are now widely available for the first time. Indeed, the shift in Hurston's fortunes has been accompanied by a shift in her publishers from the University of Illinois Press to HarperCollins (which has, under Henry Louis Gates, Jr.'s editorship, reprinted virtually all of her writings) and, in 1995, the Library of America, for whom Cheryl Wall has contributed a beautiful two-volume set of Hurston's writings, *Novels and Stories* and *Folklore, Memoirs, and Other Writings* (in which all of Hurston's work referred to in this essay is collected). If it is true that, as Hurston's best-known protagonist, Janie of *Their Eyes Were Watching God*, says of her dead husband, Tea Cake, "he could never be dead until she herself had finished feeling and thinking" (183), then clearly Hurston has achieved a level of literary immortality virtually unprecedented for American writers of African descent.

But we encounter competing versions of Hurston circulating in the popular and critical imaginations—the black feminist par excellence, the race woman, the diasporic visionary whose anthropological work anticipated and helped clear the way for current fascination with notions of a Black Atlantic inspired in part by Paul Gilroy, the controversial iconoclast, the cultural nationalist, the politically naive conservative, the literary foremother. These competing versions make it seem at times that her readers and scholars have been even less reliable in their location of the body of Hurston's work than Walker was in discovering her literal body's remains, and that the perhaps unresolvable identities hamper our ability to discover the meaning of her work.

If, as Steiner claims, Hemingway's value to Americanist scholarship has diminished because his meanings are overdetermined, part of Hurston's importance may well lie in the fact that, with each new significant scholarly discovery, her corpus resists such stock—and, of course, even in Hemingway's case, patently simplistic—representations. Hence, we make no effort here to resolve the contradictions between the available versions of Hurston. We are, nevertheless, convinced that the future research likely to be influential in the resolution of these contradictory narratives must engage the entirety of her discursive project. We recognize, however, that in its concentration on selected works, Hurston scholarship is not significantly different from that of the other writers included in this volume. (Critical work on Hurston texts other than *Their Eyes Were Watching God* is clustered primarily around the folklore collection *Mules and Men,* which is viewed by many as a model of participatory ethnographic narrative, and the autobiography *Dust Tracks on a Road,* whose most insightful critics see it as a provocative rendering of subjective indeterminacy.)

Whereas it may not be possible effectively to enliven the clichéd understandings of the works of a figure such as Hemingway—as Michael Reynolds argues in this volume, scholars seem generally unprepared to engage Hemingway either from a postmodernist or a "serious gender studies" perspective— perceptions of Hurston are still being actively formed and re-formed, established, debated, and defended. We believe that because of these still-active debates, future scholarship has the capacity to impact the shape and direction not only of Hurston's career and the analyses of black and women's texts, but, among other things, of American modernism, gender and cultural studies, and autobiographical and narrative theory.

Consider, for example, the potential fruits of exploring Hurston's work in the context of the widely accepted view that one of the great modernist subjects is "the exploration and questioning of the relations between the sexes" (Steiner 147). Scholarship on *Their Eyes Were Watching God* has for some time now been focused on what Carla Kaplan terms "the erotics of talk," a phrase that pertains in this context to Janie's desires to achieve verbal self-actualization—voice—and felicitous heterosexual coupling. Tracing what we might call a metaphorics of violence in Hurston's texts—and it appears in nearly all of the fictive texts and in the anthropological and autobiographical works as well—encourages not merely a recognition of a pattern evident throughout her corpus, nor simply more persuasive readings of Janie's murder of her third husband, Tea Cake, but a first step toward a comprehension of violence's transracial and transgendered significance to a modernist project framed by two brutal world wars, the bloody dismantling of Jim Crow, and the volcanic discord that accompanied the boisterous struggles for women's, gay and lesbian, and other minority civil rights.

Further, given the centrality of the image of pollination to the novel, both in the much-discussed backyard scene, in which Janie experiences nature orgasmically, and in her "love thoughts" about Tea Cake, whom she believed could be the bee to her blossom, Janie's childlessness is a subject that scholars might profitably explore. Indeed, one issue that has barely been discussed in examinations of Hurston's fictive rendering of Eatonville is its strange absence of children. Given the concern of modernist texts such as Hemingway's *A Farewell to Arms* and black texts such as Nella Larsen's *Quicksand* and James Weldon Johnson's *The Autobiography of an Ex-Colored*

Man with the procreative consequences of sexual expression, scholars must begin to explain what it means for our understanding of Hurston that what Ann duCille and others demonstrate to be this novel's powerful critique of the institution of marriage fails, in its rendering of Janie's travails, to consider the pleasures and dangers of reproduction.

Hurston scholarship would profit not only by exploring underexposed topics in much-discussed texts, but also by an active decentering of facets of her personality and work that scholars have already located and examined. At the same time, we need to expand our vision so as better to contextualize her corpus vis-à-vis the historical and cultural patterns that both inform it and against which it struggles. While we have become entranced by her striking personality, the compelling themes she engages, and the maverick quality of her methodology and behavior, we must remind ourselves that much of Hurston's genius is firmly rooted in the clarity of vision that compelled her to document and refigure multiple components of American cultures. Because Hurston explored important aspects of black culture in the 1920s, 1930s, and 1940s, we run the risk of obscuring much of the nature of the dynamic shifts within black culture if we limit the body of Hurston scholarship to analyses of gender and culture.

We are calling, in other words, for a more energetically historicized, contextualized, and comparativist Hurston scholarship. And while the type of project we envision will undoubtedly present challenges to some literary scholars because of her work in other forms, the shift in focus of many literary critics to Cultural Studies suggests that investigators are quickly becoming more intellectually adroit at exploring new contexts. Exploration needs to include examining her work in relation both to African American and/or women's literature and culture and to white and/or male American authors and anthropologists. Such examination will undoubtedly yield marked refigurations of our understanding of a number of discourses.

Because Hurston engaged and recorded the dynamic nature of African American cultures as both an author of fiction and an anthropologist, literary scholars must more fully engage her nonfiction. The lack of fuller attention to Hurston's anthropological work and the ways in which it informs her fiction results in part from the fact that her work's most influential scholarly investigator, Robert Hemenway, concludes in "Eatonville Anthology" that Hurston was primarily a "creative artist." That assertion suggests that her ultimate movement away from anthropology can be seen as a function of both her fundamental ambivalence about the tenets of anthropology and her commitment to the creative venture. The discourse on the partial truths possible in anthropological investigation and on the blurred lines between creative and scientific ethnography has grown since the publication of Hemenway's essay, allowing us to recognize the fluidity of Hurston's negotiations of these narrative forms more acutely than her biographer was able to in 1972.

By examining Hurston's role as anthropologist, we can more clearly discern the similarities to and deviations from, the practices of other anthropologists such as Franz Boas, Ruth Benedict, Hortense Powdermaker, Katherine Dunham, and Jane Belo. We can begin to understand more fully the ways in which Hurston uses her ethnographies and fiction to engage issues posited by her contemporaries who were also concerned with a systematic investigation of culture. But at the same time that we compare these methodological and theoretical approaches, it is imperative that we discern Hurston's relationships with key anthropologists, such as Boas, and lesser-known anthropologists, such as Jane Belo. Assumptions that Boas greatly influenced Hurston because she studied under him need to be tested systematically by means of close comparisons of the two figures' anthropological output and theorizing. If, in fact, Boas was such a great influence on her anthropological work, we need to understand why in her letters to Langston Hughes she credits Hughes, rather than Boas, with ideas for the structure and content of her Southern folklore collecting.

And while we must explore Boas's influence on Hurston's work, we must also discern the extent to which Hurston's findings may have influenced Boas's and his colleagues' approaches to cultural analysis. We know, for instance, that Boas introduced Otto Klineberg to Hurston, whom she put in touch with informants in the South. In order to gain a clearer understanding of the contours of her contributions to the development of American cultural analysis, we need to examine Klineberg's research to determine Hurston's influence on its direction and outcome.

Even as we seek to understand Hurston's texts in the context of her anthropological setting, we must also situate her work within African American cultural experiences and the ideological perspectives that seek to explain them. At least since the pioneering work of Melville Herskovits, a foundational ideological concern in the study of African American cultures has been the extent to which cultural beliefs, forms, and norms originating in Africa are manifest throughout the African diaspora in general and in the United States in particular. Advocates of the "tabula rasa" perspective, such as E. Franklin Frazier, and scholars who argue for the retention of West African beliefs and practices, such as Herskovits, debated energetically such issues as African American acculturation and the manifestations of African cultural and spiritual tenacity during the first half of the twentieth century.

In the coming years, we must establish more convincingly Hurston's early and influential membership in the African retention school. Hurston not only argued for the influence of West African ritual throughout the diaspora, but also carefully documented African-inflected rituals that appear in the Americas. Because of the careful work of Gwendolyn Midlo-Hall, we now are aware, for instance, that the specific practices that Hurston attributes to Dr. Grant and Dr. Duke in "Hoodoo in America" and *Mules and Men*, respectively, are linked to a Senegambian tradition of acknowledging the living spirit of roots and plants prior to harvesting them for human use. Hurston's work may hold further examples of the ways in which West African traditions are retained in African American cultures, and while her corpus provides the anthropologist or historian with documentation of Africanist presence in African American cultures, it also illuminates aspects of the world view that Hurston brings to her fiction.

Hoodoo appears as a theme in Hurston's work from her first published short story, "John Redding Goes to Sea" in 1921, and continues to be featured in her series "Hoodoo and Black Magic" until the year before her death. We must therefore explore the ways in which she understood and crafted the results of her lengthy and extensive field work, and engage in a sustained discussion of Hurston and her work on Hoodoo and Voodoo. Her representations of Hoodoo shift from rendering it as a limiting superstition in "John Redding Goes to Sea," to figuring it as a destructive social and spiritual force in *Jonah's Gourd Vine*, to positing it as a liberatory practice in *Moses Man of the Mountain*. Our consideration of her shifting perspectives raises critical questions of ideology, methodology, and epistemology.

When considering Hurston's cultural and intellectual context concerning Hoodoo and Voodoo, we must also carefully clarify how her relationships with Langston Hughes and Carter G. Woodson may have informed her research on such foundational issues as methodology and access to practitioners. Likewise, we will benefit from a clearer understanding of how Hurston compares with other contemporaries, such as Rudolph Fisher, Richard Wright, and Claude McKay, who, in varying degrees, discuss Hoodoo, "superstition," and Obeah. It will also be crucial to explore how negritude writers treat African spirituality particularly, since thinkers such as Senghor insist that McKay and Hughes are influential figures in their intellectual development. Moreover, we will benefit from extending the conversation that Hurston started in her critical review of Robert Tallant to determine how her conclusions about Hoodoo and Voodoo compare with those of other Hoodoo, Root Medicine, and Voodoo scholars like Lyle Saxon and Katherine Dunham.

We must not only establish a diasporic cultural connection and assert the influence of West African traditions in these cultures, but also consider how Hurston engages another primary theme in African diasporic studies: slavery. Hurston commented on the results of slavery in her short stories, novels, essays, and ethnographies, yet her perspectives range from recognizing the horror and the resultant rage in "Magnolia Flower" to claiming that slavery was a necessary price to pay in exchange for some benefits of western culture in "How It Feels to Be Colored Me." We must carefully examine the original material that Hurston collected and published in the admittedly heavily plagiarized "Cudjo's Own Story of the Last African Slaver." Through this project we can discern how her research connects with other folklore collections that reconstruct the lives of African Americans who were formerly enslaved.

Earlier we argued that it is crucial for scholars to focus their critical attention beyond *Their Eyes Were Watching God* to a wider range of fictive texts. We want to suggest below how an expansive vision might further enliven Hurston scholarship by situating her work in the context of a number of central literary, critical, and cultural concerns. Take, for instance, the example of *Moses Man of the Mountain,* which, despite Hemenway's insistence that it is one of Hurston's masterpieces, has received scant critical attention, in part because this eclectic novel is difficult to place comfortably in the same context as the most widely discussed Hurston works, which can be more easily situated in terms of extant discussions of African American culture, feminist discourse, or other popular contemporary theoretical concerns.

While a closer reading of even the more widely discussed Hurston texts might cause us to question the insistence of scholars during the previous three decades that Hurston is a feminist thinker in a late twentieth-century sense, certainly a sophisticated gender analysis—one that benefits from, among other things, an emerging, increasingly complex men's studies—could be brought usefully to bear in explications of *Moses Man of the Mountain.* Perhaps because Hurston draws so heavily from an established patriarchal biblical tradition, she offers an undoubtedly masculinist treatment of Moses, whom she renders as a paternalistic nationalist, but critiques only minimally for such perspectives. Yet, given the context of her larger body of work, a detailed analysis of gender in Hurston requires more sustained treatments of *Moses* and its female characters Miriam, Zipporah, and Jochebed.

The method and outcome of cross-cultural analysis in the diaspora are subjects to which we can usefully return to expand upon (among other recent revisitings) Ann duCille's provocative investigation of Hurston's last novel, *Seraph on the Suwanee.* Before duCille, before—for that matter—Hemenway, Hurston's engagement of white characters was read as an appeal to a white audience and an abandonment of African American cultural tradition. Given contemporary interest in the politics of race and gender, a compelling point of entry might be to discuss why and how she felt qualified to write a novel about capitalism, class, sexuality, violence, gender, and culture among Florida whites. Indeed, a careful examination of this text in the context of her later essays that criticize racism in the United States may reveal a more complicated notion of how she viewed relationships between southern African Americans and whites and provide an illuminating reading of *Seraph on the Suwanee*.

Revisiting Hurston's neglected work suggests another area for fruitful research: Hurston's relationship to other insightful investigators of twentieth-century American Southern culture, including William Faulkner, Carson McCullers, and Flannery O'Connor. Analysis of this relationship should also extend the transracial gaze to white efforts to "write" black culture and other African American efforts to "write" white culture, such as those found in works by Richard Wright, Eugene O'Neill, Julia Peterkin, Sherwood Anderson, Ann Petry, and Lorraine Hansberry.

Close attention to the figuration of violence in *Seraph* is crucial to our understanding of that novel, though quite a number of critics go to great lengths to minimize its significance or ignore it altogether. For example, Lillie Howard ignores the most blatant act of what she calls "chauvinism," and, as recently as 1994, John Lowe suggests that Hurston did not, in fact, intend to suggest that Jim rapes Arvay. The question of sexual and emotional violence emerges when we consider Jim and Arvay's relationship, and might be seen profitably in the context of other depictions in Hurston's corpus. Hurston examines the ways in which fear, insecurity, habit, love, illusion, and sexual fulfillment both inform and disrupt notions and/or experiences of "true love." While we may find the romantic/sexual relationships in Hurston's texts upsetting, even unsettling, we must examine their tensions and question Hurston's recurring rendering of these tensions.

Reading *Seraph on the Suwanee* against other texts by African American authors who explore white culture is just one possibility as we consider the many writers with whom Hurston bears comparison. Highlighting the artistic and ideological differences between Hurston and Richard Wright, scholars have put forward important comparisons of their work as well as of their various criticisms of one another. As well, critics have provided numerous comparisons between Walker's *Color Purple* and Hurston's *Their Eyes Were Watching God*. While these are important comparisons, and each of these authors' works, particularly Wright's, encourage even deeper critical investigation, Hurston's corpus calls for a broader cast of authors against which to examine a wide range of themes and approaches.

For example, though scholars have emphasized Hurston's and Langston Hughes's friendship and the ensuing schism over the authorship of their co-authored *Mule Bone*, virtually no comparative analysis of their creative output exists. Likewise, Hurston's oeuvre should be related to that of other writers of the twenties and thirties, including Claude McKay, Rudolph Fisher, Nella Larsen, and Jean Toomer, in order to investigate more fully, among other topics, the ways in which these authors represent their central characters' relationships to African American folk culture.

Additionally, because of the significance of Hurston's environmental awareness and use of nature imagery, her work also carries with it important correlations with and divergences from that of nineteenth-century authors such as Charles Chesnutt, Ralph Waldo Emerson, Henry David Thoreau, and Sarah Orne Jewett. By exploring connections between her work and that of her contemporaries of the first half of the twentieth century such as Toomer, Willa Cather, Meridel Le Sueur, William Faulkner, Ann Petry, and John Steinbeck, we can begin to examine how these writers' notions of nature, industry, modernity, and culture intersect with or differ from Hurston's. Finally, just as critics have explored connections between Walker and Hurston, we must investigate the extent to which her work compares with that of contemporary writers such as Toni Cade Bambara, Gloria Naylor, Paule Marshall, Ishmael Reed, and Randall Kenan, in part to understand precisely how important themes that Hurston addressed such as spirituality, enslavement, gender, and relations to the natural world are taken up by subsequent African American authors.

Hurston is a writer whose stock rose in the academy to some extent as a consequence of the spaces created for previously marginalized texts by poststructuralist theorists and by feminist and Afro-Americanist scholars. Scholarship on her work should strive to render the meanings of her career as faithfully as possible. But it should also recognize that we are doomed to offer biased, incomplete, and limited readings that, like Hurston's own perspectives on crucial matters such as slavery, are neither definitive nor immutable. While it is our duty as Hurston scholars and "witnesses for the future" to collect and make Hurston's work available to subsequent generations, our activities do not ensure—Walker's memorable formulation notwithstanding—that by "collect[ing them] again . . . , bone by bone" (92) we will achieve a unified vision of their significance and power.

Walker's osseous image foreshadowed developments at the 1991 Eatonville Festival of the Arts, where some of its organizers discussed moving what Walker marked as Hurston's remains from their Fort Pierce location to Eatonville in an effort to prevent developers from destroying the center of her imaginative and anthropological universe. This plan seems the ultimate in—and certainly, from a variety of vantage points, the most self-serving of—Hurston recovery projects. While it appears that this effort has been abandoned, it speaks to the intensity of the urges of Hurston's biological and spiritual successors to make use of and reclaim her, bone by bone, in a quite literal sense. And if this use of Hurston's remains appears unseemly, we should keep in mind that Hurston herself never recoiled from the subject of death. From her first short story, "John Redding Goes to Sea," to *Seraph on the Suwanee,* Hurston examined the ways in which the lifeless body is read and interpreted by those whom its spirit leaves behind.

As we embark upon future projects in Hurston scholarship, we must be careful about the uses to which we are willing to put her bodily remains to serve our own interests. Yet we must also remember the crucial components of Hurston's work that symbolically embrace an Africanist notion of the simultaneous existence of life and death. Hurston leaves us what is no longer a living body, yet through our efforts to invigorate the body of Hurston scholarship, we can uncover new life and new meanings for the living.

Works Cited

Anderson, Sherwood. *Dark Laughter.* New York: Boni & Liveright,1925.

Bambara, Toni Cade. *The Salt Eaters.* New York: Vintage, 1980.

Benedict, Ruth. *Race and Racism.* 1945. London: Routledge & Kegan Paul, 1983.

Bloom, Harold. *The Anxiety of Influence.* New York: Oxford University Press, 1973.

Boas, Franz. *Anthropology and Modern Life.* New York: Norton, 1962.

Cather, Willa. *Sapphira and the Slave Girl.* 1940. New York: Vintage, 1975.

Chestnutt, Charles. *The Conjure Woman.* 1899. Ann Arbor: University of Michigan Press, 1969.

duCille, Ann. *The Coupling Convention.* New York: Oxford University Press, 1994.

Dunham, Katherine. *Island Possessed.* Garden City, NJ: Doubleday, 1969.

Frazier, E. Franklin. *Black Bourgeoisie.* New York: Free Press, 1957.

Gates, Henry Louis, Jr. *The Signifying Monkey: A Theory of Afro-American Literary Criticism.* New York: Oxford University Press, 1989.

Gilroy, Paul. *The Black Atlantic.* Cambridge: Harvard University Press, 1994.

Hansberry, Lorraine. *Les Blancs.* New York: Random House, 1972.

Hemenway, Robert. "The Personal Dimension in *Their Eyes Were Watching God*," in *New Essays on "Their Eyes Were Watching God,"* edited by Michael Awkward. Cambridge, MA, and New York: Cambridge University Press, 1990, pp. 29–50.

———. *Zora Neale Hurston: A Literary Biography.* Urbana: University of Illinois Press, 1977.

———. "Zora Neale Hurston and the Eatonville Anthology," *The Harlem Renaissance Remembered,* edited by Arna Bontemps. New York: Dodd, Mead, 1972, pp. 190–214.

Hemingway, Ernest. *A Farewell to Arms.* New York: Scribners, 1929.

Herskovits, Melville. *The Anthropology of the American Negro.* New York: Columbia University Press, 1930.

Holloway, Joseph. ed. *Africanisms in American Culture.* Indianapolis: Indiana University Press, 1990.

Howard, Lillie. *Zora Neale Hurston.* Boston: Twayne, 1980.

Hurston, Zora Neale. *Dust Tracks on a Road.* 1942. Urbana: University of Illinois Press, 1984.

———. *Folklore, Memoirs, and Other Writings,* edited by Cheryl A. Wall. New York: Library of America, 1995.

———. "Hoodoo in America." *Journal of American Folk-lore* 44 (1931): pp. 317–417.

———. *I Love Myself When I Am Laughing-and Then Again When I Am Looking Mean and Impressive,* edited by Alice Walker. Old Westbury, NY: Feminist Press, 1979.

———. *Jonah's Gourd Vine.* 1934. New York: HarperCollins, 1990.

———. "Magnolia Flower," in *The Complete Short Stories,* edited by Henry Louis Gates, Jr., and Sieglinde Lemke. New York: HarperCollins, 1995, pp. 33–40.

———. *Moses Man of the Mountain.* 1939. New York: HarperCollins, 1990.

————. *Mules and Men*. New York: HarperCollins, 1990.

————. *Novels and Stories*, edited by Cheryl A. Wall. New York: Library of America, 1995.

————. Review of *Voodoo in America*, by Robert Tallant. *Journal of American Folk-lore* 60 (1947): pp. 436–438.

————. *Seraph on the Suwanee*. 1948. New York: HarperCollins, 1990.

————. *Their Eyes Were Watching God*. 1937. New York: Perennial, 1990.

Hurston, Zora Neale, and Langston Hughes. *Mule Bone*. New York: HarperCollins, 1993.

Jewett, Sarah Orne. *The Country of Pointed Firs and Other Stories*. 1896. Garden City, NY: Doubleday Anchor Books, 1954.

Johnson, James Weldon. *The Autobiography of an Ex-Colored Man*. 1912. New York: Hill & Wang, 1960.

Kaplan, Carla. *The Erotics of Talk*. New York: Oxford University Press, 1995.

Kenan, Randall. *Visitation of Spirits*. New York: Anchor, 1989.

Klineberg, Otto. *Race and Psychology*. Paris: Modern Sciences, 1951.

Larsen, Nella. *Quicksand and Passing*. 1929. New Brunswick, NJ: Rutgers University Press, 1986.

Le Sueur, Meridel. *I Hear Men Talking and Other Stories*. Minneapolis: West End Press, 1984.

Lowe, John. *Jump at the Sun: Zora Neale Hurston's Cosmic Comedy*. Urbana: University of Illinois Press, 1994.

Marshall, Paule. *Praisesong for the Widow*. New York: Dutton, 1983.

McKay, Claude. *Banana Bottom*. New York: Harper, 1933.

Midlo-Hall, Gwendolyn. *Africanisms in Colonial Louisiana: The Development of Afro-Creole Culture in the 18th Century*. Baton Rouge: Louisiana State University Press, 1992.

Naylor, Gloria. *Mama Day*. New York: Vintage, 1988.

O'Neill, Eugene. *The Emperor Jones*. Cincinnati, OH: Stewart & Kidd, 1921.

Peterkin, Julia. *Scarlet Sister Mary*. Indianapolis: Bobbs-Merrill, 1928.

Petry, Ann. *The Street*. Boston: Houghton Mifflin, 1946.

Powdermaker, Hortense. *After Freedom: A Cultural Study in the Deep South*. 1939. New York: Russell & Russell, 1986.

Saxon, Lyle, Edward Dreyer, and Robert Tallant, eds. *Gumbo Ya-Ya: Folk Tales of Louisiana*. 1945. New York: Pelican, 1991.

Senghor, Leopold. *Afrique Africaine*. Lausanne: Clairefontaine, 1963.

Smith, Barbara Herrnstein. *Contingencies of Value*. Cambridge, MA: Harvard University Press, 1988.

Steinbeck, James. *The Grapes of Wrath*. New York: Viking Press, 1939.

Steiner, Wendy. *The Scandal of Pleasure: Art in the Age of Fundamentalism*. Chicago: University of Chicago Press, 1995.

Thompson, Robert Farris. *Flash of the Spirit*. New York: Vintage, 1983.

Toomer, Jean. *Cane*. New York: Boni & Liveright, 1923.

Walker, Alice. *The Color Purple*. New York: Washington Square Press, 1982.

————. *In Search of Our Mothers' Gardens: Womanist Prose*. San Francisco: Harcourt Brace Jovanovich, 1983.

Wright, Richard. *Lawd Today*. New York: Walker, 1963.

CLAUDIA TATE

Hitting "A Straight Lick with a Crooked Stick": Seraph on the Suwanee, *Zora Neale Hurston's* Whiteface Novel

Arvay was pretty if you liked delicate-made girls. . . . She had plenty of long light yellow hair with a low wave to it with Gulf-blue eyes. Arvay had a fine-made kind of nose and mouth and a face shaped like an egg laid by a Leghorn pullet, with a faint spread of pink around her upper cheeks. . . . Arvay, young and white, and teasing to the fancy of many men. . . .
—Hurston, *Seraph* 4

I HAVE BEEN AMAZED by the Anglo-Saxon's lack of curiosity about the internal lives and emotions of the Negroes. . . .
—Hurston, "White," quoted in Walker 169; original emphasis

Despite the tremendous popularity of the works of Zora Neale Hurston over the last two decades, *Seraph on the Suwanee* (1948) is still a marginal work. In her fourth and last published novel, Hurston returned to the topic that claimed her lifelong interest—probing "what makes a man or a woman do such-and-so, regardless of his color" (*Dust* 151). But unlike Hurston's *Their Eyes Were Watching God*, published eleven years earlier, *Seraph* has

Journal for Theoretical Studies in Media and Culture, Volume 19, Number 2 (Winter 1997): pp. 72–87. Copyright © 1997 Wayne State University Press.

143

never enchanted its readers. In fact, the novel is generally understood by black literary scholars as a contrivance in Hurston's canon and in African-American literary scholarship.[1] This perspective undoubtedly results from Hurston's depiction of white protagonists instead of black ones. In the words of one prominent African-American literary scholar, Mary Helen Washington, *Seraph* is evidence of Hurston's "abandoning the source of her unique esthetic—the black cultural tradition" (21). Washington goes on to say that Hurston "submerged her power and creativity" in this work (21).

I hope to refute these contentions by demonstrating that *Seraph* is very much a part of Hurston's persistent and compelling investigations of female desire and racialized culture.[2] With this novel, I argue, Hurston tried to please a white popular audience and herself by conspicuously constructing *and* subtly deconstructing the novel's white patriarchal narrative of romantic love with a couple of canny jokes about that culture's idealization of passive female desire and its conflation of race and class. For the purposes of this essay, I want to concentrate on *Seraph's* investment in whiteness and only mention its critique of passive female desire, indeed female masochism, for the novel's white social milieu seems to be its most problematic feature. Before continuing my discussion, however, I must outline the plot of this under-read novel.

Seraph begins in 1905 in Sawley, a poor white town in Florida, and concludes around 1927 at sea, off the west coast of the state. The opening incident portrays the whole town's amusement in witnessing Jim Meserve court the peculiar Arvay Henson. On first seeing Arvay, Jim is sure that "[s]he just suited him . . . and was worth the trouble of breaking in" (8). However, Arvay believes that "this pretty, laughing fellow was far out of her reach," since she "was born to take other people's leavings" (24). To make matters worse, Arvay also suffers guilt from secretly "living in mental adultery with her sister's husband," Reverend Carl Middleton, on whom she has had a crush for five years (34). When he marries Larraine, however, whose robust manner and appearance everyone, including her parents, prefers to Arvay's slight form and timid manner, Arvay conceals her hurt feelings by "turning from the world" with "religious fervor" and then unconsciously repressing her sexual desire by developing hysterical convulsions (3).

In record time Jim proposes to Arvay, and she accepts even though she expects him to jilt her. Her insecurity then makes her behavior contradictory and causes Jim to think she has insufficient love for him. To remedy this dilemma, two weeks before their wedding day, Jim rapes Arvay and marries her immediately afterward without coercion. Arvay does not realize that this scenario is Jim's attempt to show his satisfaction with her and to bind her to him. She merely concludes that his extravagant charity causes him to marry her. The failure to recognize their mutual insecurities binds them in a sado-masochistic cycle of sexual aggression and submission, which the rape foreshadows. This defensive pattern of erotic attachment defines their marriage for more than twenty years.

Their first child, Earl, probably conceived during the rape, is retarded and slightly deformed. His abnormality suggests Hurston's censure of the rape. Weak and fearful of almost everything, he projects Arvay's insecurity. Even though she and Jim have two more children, Angeline and James Kenneth (called Angie and Kenny), who are not just normal but smart, very good-looking, and self-confident, Arvay devotes most of her energy to Earl, as her penance for "the way [she] used to be" (69). Since she cannot recognize her own virtues, she regards Earl as her child, while perceiving Angie and Kenny as Jim's children. When Earl is about eighteen, he sexually assaults a neighbor girl and is killed by a local man in an attempt to escape. Earl's death frees Arvay of her guilty burden but she continues to suffer acute insecurity.

During the marriage, Jim pushes his family up the social ladder. Although Arvay enjoys the financial security of Jim's ambition, she recognizes neither his motive nor his struggle to succeed. Entrenched in the passive-masochistic role of sexual submission, she cannot be confident of Jim's love. After Angie marries and Kenny goes to college, Arvay is relieved of most of her domestic duties. With time to reflect, she has more opportunity to justify her lack of esteem and to fantasize about Jim's abandoning her. According to her reasoning, she would then be free to return to her kind of folk in Sawley and live in confidence. Frustrated by Arvay's defensive behavior, Jim devotes more and more time to developing a shrimping business that takes him out of town. He also tries to invigorate the marriage by performing a stunt with a rattlesnake, but like his first effort to bind Arvay to him with rape, all he ends up doing is terrifying her. This final failure convinces him to leave her. Though he will support her indefinitely, he gives her one year to surrender passivity for "a knowing and a doing love" to save their marriage (262).

Before Arvay can plan a course of action, she receives a telegram from her sister stating that their mother is ill. Her mother's illness, which Arvay initially believes is not fatal, overshadows her "happy anticipation" of returning to Sawley. In her mind "[t]he corroding poverty of her childhood became a glowing virtue, and a state to be desired" (272). This idealization allows her to deny the pain of Jim's abandonment. Instead she imagines that she will leave him by returning to Sawley. When Arvay arrives at her former home, her idealization confronts reality. Larraine is a "ton of coarse-looking flesh," Carl is a "drab creature," and their daughters are "mule-faced and ugly enough" (pp. 274, 275, and 276). If the Middletons' appearances and the dilapidated childhood home, with its odor of rat urine, are insufficient to make Arvay consider her life with Jim as a tremendous improvement, the invectives of Arvay's dying mother, Maria Henson, sharpen this comparison. She tells Arvay, "You and Jim sure is raised your chaps to be nice and kind. 'Tain't that a'way with Larraine nor none of her whelps." She and Carl, Maria insists, are just "like turkey buzzards" (pp. 280, 278).

Maria confesses to Arvay a lifetime of unfulfilled aspirations, as if to justify her subsequent request of her daughter. She asks to be "put away nice" on Sunday "with a heap of flowers on my coffin and a church full of folks marching around to say me 'farewell.'" Arvay assures her that she can put her "dying dependence" in her (280). By keeping her "sacred promise" to her mother, Arvay nourishes her self-confidence.

This climactic event makes Arvay realize she has "sense enough to appreciate what [Jim's] done, and [is] still trying to do for [her]" (309). She resolves to win him back. Arvay soon joins Jim on board his shrimp boat, the *Arvay Henson*. She displays her courage and tells him how proud she is of him. Through indirect discourse, the text reveals that Arvay at last perceives the insecurity behind Jim's aggressive mask. She realizes she was just as unaware of his "inner" self as she had been of her own ability.

Seraph's focus on white protagonists and female masochistic desire are startling departures from the stories of black female self-definition that are so prominent in Hurston's other writings. In fact, so great are these departures that the novel's preoccupations appear as textual enigmas. By referring to psychoanalysis, a form of inquiry devoted specifically to interpreting concealed and puzzling meaning, I will attempt to unveil the novel's enigmatic whiteness to elucidate *Seraph's* meaning and clarify its relationship to Hurston's other works. Psychoanalysis allows me to establish a dialectic between *Seraph's* explicit surface content and its implicit deep significance, much as the human psyche constructs intelligible meaning by mediating between its conscious intentions and unconscious desire. By regarding the structure of *Seraph* "in some basic sense [like] the structure of the mind," I agree with Peter Brooks's claim that "there must be some correspondence between literary and psychic process"; that is, "aesthetic structure and form, including literary tropes, must somehow coincide with the psychic structures and operations they both evoke and appeal to" (pp. 24–25).[3] This viewpoint allows us to regard the discourses of *Seraph* as functioning like the conscious, preconscious, and unconscious domains of the psyche. By extending this argument, I will consider the novel's explicit and implicit discourses as analogous to those of Freudian joke-work, particularly those of the tendentious joke.

In Jokes and Their Relation to the Unconscious, Freud explains how the language of the joke initially incites bewilderment and subsequently produces illumination through the act of telling it. According to Freud, "jokes are formed in the first person" as *"a preconscious thought is given over for a moment to unconscious revision and the outcome of this is at once grasped by conscious perception"* (166; original emphasis). Like Freud's understanding of the tendentious joke, *Seraph* evokes pleasure by exploiting "something ridiculous in our enemy which we could not, on account of obstacles in the way, bring forward openly or consciously" (*Jokes* 103). Thus *Seraph "evade[s] restrictions and open[s] sources of pleasure that have become inaccessible"* (103; original emphasis).

When cast against Hurston's other writings, *Seraph's* discourse on whiteness is bewildering. By regarding it as a part of the text's preconscious, like that of the joke, undergoing silenced or unconscious revision, we can clarify its meaning. The unconscious here would include the novel's stylistic and structural elements—for example, its repetitive words, tropes, circuity, exaggeration, ellipses, suspension, anticipation, retraction, negation, digression, irony, and causality. Although joke-work and other forms of unconscious discourses make use of the same structural devices of condensation, indirect representation, and displacement, "the techniques [of jokes] are explicit and overt and their opposition to accepted modes of conscious thought [is] clearly recognizable" (Oring 7). Unlike banter, the pleasure of the fully formed joke derives from its circumventing the censor to consciousness to express a prohibited thought. Unlike the joke, which strives for intelligibility, unconscious discourses seek obscurity and expression. For this reason they are more heavily veiled.

Freudian psychoanalytic tenets about compulsive repetition also help me identify *Seraph's* recurring sentence—"I can read your writing"—as the inscription of the text's unstated demand that further directs my reading of its textual enigmas.[4] This sentence discloses Jim's ability to detect Arvay's desire despite her sexually repressed behavior; it also identifies the demand that Arvay fulfills at the novel's close when she accurately interprets Jim's concealed desire beneath his jesting, defensive behavior. Most important, though, this sentence demands that we examine *Seraph's* textual content, which, like Jim's joking behavior, is not transparent.

By realizing that *Seraph* is a tendentious joke that has much in common with the carnivalesque text, we can synthesize the incongruity of the novel's plot, surface elements, and rhetorical features to clarify its social critique. In psychoanalytic literary terms, we can interpret the novel's meaning not only by reading its conscious or explicit plot and dialogue, but also by deciphering its unconscious discourses of desire. Like Arvay, however, we readers will have to sweat because *Seraph* refuses to deliver its meaning in any simple way.

Seraph's white social milieu was probably the result not just of Hurston's effort to attract a Hollywood contract as a screenwriter, as several scholars have remarked, but also of a deliberate concession to publishers, who could not imagine a novel about a middle-class black family.[5] Shortly before Hurston began working on this novel, she tried to interest her publisher, Lippincott, in "a serious book [about a middle-class black woman] to be called *Mrs. Doctor*" (Hemenway 303).[6] No doubt Ann Petry and Dorothy West also encountered similar reluctance on the part of white publishers because they too were exploring the possibility of writing serious novels about the black middle-class. West's *The Living Is Easy* and Petry's *The Narrows* appeared in 1948 and 1953, respectively. However, both works went out of print soon after their first printings.[7] These circumstances suggest that the black and white reading public not only expected black characters in novels by black authors; they also expected black authors to represent a homogeneous black folk. While black stereotypes were undoubtedly a part of Hurston's problem with Lippincott, her biographer, Robert Hemenway refers to her editor's disappointment with "the sloppiness of the writing" and the "strained quality in the prose." Hemenway then explains that Hurston blamed the rejection on Lippincott's decision "that the American public was not ready" for a book on "the upper strata of Negro life" (393), Hurston gave up on the book, and on Lippincott, to write *Seraph* for Scribner's. While Hurston's hope to make money off an enlarged audience for the book no doubt was another reason for writing about white culture, this social milieu, I contend, is not a contrivance, as many scholars have argued, but the result of Hurston's complex reflections and unconscious longings.

When Hurston identifies Jim as Black Irish, she partly clarifies the novel's racial coding. According to David R. Roediger, the label "Black Irish" refers to a mixed black/white heritage, resulting from the preponderance of Irish "intermixing with shipwrecked slaves" (4). The label also invokes mid-nineteenth-century racial stereotypes associated with the Irish. According to popular racial wisdom, "an Irishman was a 'nigger,' inside out" (quoted in Roediger 133). Hurston's use of the term "Black Irish" suggests her familiarity with such stereotypes. *Seraph* draws on the derisive banter associated with the racialization of this ethnic stereotype to portray Jim and Arvay with white bodies and what her readers identify as black voices, because these characters speak recognizable Eatonville idioms (Eatonville was an all-black town). Thus Jim and Arvay seem to possess white exteriors and black interiors. In this respect, *Seraph* has two layers of meaning, which I attempt to read as a subversive and parodic joke by interpreting the literal and symbolic gap between these racial codes. The novel's unstated joke deconstructs absolute racial distinctions.

According to John Lowe, though, Jim and Arvay are decidedly white. Lowe insists that *Seraph* "is not simply a whitewashing of black characters," because "Crackers don't have a folk culture that memorializes actual events in history. Their stories and idioms bespeak a repository of folk wisdom, but one unconnected with history" (266). As evidence of this questionable insight, Lowe cites the following passage, which appears early in *Seraph:*

> Few were concerned with the past. They had heard that the
> stubbornly resisting Indians had been there where they now lived,

but they were dead and gone. Osceola, Miccanope, Billy Bow-Legs were nothing more than names that had even lost their bitter flavor. The conquering Spaniards had done their murdering, robbing, and raping and had long ago withdrawn from the Floridas. Few knew and nobody cared that Hidalgos under DeSoto had moved westward along this very route. (2)

Lowe argues that *Seraph's* lack of concern with the area's social history is indicative of its white social context: "Obviously, African Americans would have more cultural strength in this connection, as so much of their oral tradition is tied to history." He concludes that Arvay's "family in Sawley seems adrift in time, much like the Lesters of Caldwell's *Tobacco Road*" (266).

I find Lowe's conclusion curious and inaccurate. Hurston's other novels do not seem intricately tied to history. Each focuses on character development; historical events are not foregrounded. In *Their Eyes*, Nanny's "highway through de wilderness" speech situates the novel at the turn of the century (when *Seraph* takes place as well). After this temporal reference, *Their Eyes* is also "adrift in time," indeed so much that if we could not surmise Janie's age relative to Nanny's, the courthouse scene could be set in either 1910 or 1930. We can approximate dates only by referring to the novel's internal generational history relative to the Emancipation. The same is true of *Jonah's Gourd Vine:* Slavery is the only historical marker. In fact, the novel withholds the date of Lucy's death, telling us instead that Isis is nine when her mother dies. In *Seraph*, as in the other two novels, the narrator identifies a post-Reconstruction setting by referring to Jim's background: "fortunes of the War had wiped Jim's grandfather clean" (7). The narrator also informs us that Jim is twenty-five when he arrives in Sawley and near fifty when he leaves Arvay. Moreover, the inscription of Arvay and Jim's children's birth dates in a family Bible provides clear historical markers. This ritual informs us, for example, that Earl is born in 1906, nine months after the story begins.

Rather than being cast adrift in time, then, *Seraph* is more attentive to dates than are the other novels. In addition, Lowe does not present any examples of a historically informed black folklore from Hurston's works to support his argument. He simply assumes that the "black oral tradition is tied to history" (266). Hurston's use of this tradition in her writings reveals black and white folklife as tied respectively to the historical facts of slavery and the Emancipation on the one hand, and the consequences of the Civil War on the other. On the basis of these three of Hurston's four novels, there seems to be no reason to conclude that white culture is any more or less ahistorical than black culture.

We do know, however, that Hurston was emphatic in her denuncia-
tion of racial stereotypes. She contended that rural, poor people—black and
white—of the same southern region share the same dialect. In *Dust Tracks,*
she further explained that all Southerners have "the map of Dixie on [their]
tongue[s]." The "average Southern child, white or black, is raised on simile
and invective. . . . Since that stratum of the Southern population is not given
to book-reading, they take their comparisons right out of the barnyard and
the woods" (pp. 98–99). Given her reluctance to racialize southern dialect,
Hurston must have intended *Seraph's* white characters to sound like Eatonville blacks. This too was William Faulkner's intention in *The Sound and
the Fury* (1929) when he has two unnamed white northern characters tell
Quentin Compson that "He talks like they do in minstrel shows," by which
they mean that Quentin "talks like a colored man" (137). Similarly, as urban
blacks readily attest, when they speak the dialect associated with professional
whites, they are accused of speaking "white." Thus when Jim and Arvay speak
the phrases that the Eatonville blacks have already spoken in Hurston's earlier works, they must be speaking "black." Whether Sawley whites in fact
sounded like Eatonville blacks seems a moot issue because the racial valence
of the Eatonville dialect, designated as black in Hurston's prior publications,
remains black regardless of the racial identity of the speaker.

    Seraph invites us to see that conventional racial designations attributed
to dialects and speakers are based on erroneous assumptions. Just as Hurston
contended that poor blacks and whites living in the rural South spoke the
same dialect, she also maintained that race was cultural rather than biological: In the unexpurgated version of "My People, My People," for instance, she
insisted that "you can't tell who my people are by skin color" (*Dust* 216). If
appearance is an unreliable indication of race, what can be said of speech patterns, especially those of characters in a novel? Race for Hurston would seem
to be a questionable category. Indeed, her manipulation of allegedly fixed
racial designations of the body and the voice probably gave her a great deal of
pleasure. Nowhere would the pleasure be more intense than in *Seraph,* where
she subverts multiple racial expectations. Since the characters in *Seraph* sound
black, Hurston did not really abandon "the source of her unique esthetic—
black cultural tradition" insofar as language is the medium of culture.

    Despite Hurston's adoption of what we ultimately recognize as black
vernacular for her white characters, she nonetheless relied on the assumptions associated with the privilege of whiteness to stage her critique of
masochistic female desire. This setting facilitates her representation of the
patriarchal demands of romantic love by avoiding the black people's problematic relationship to interracial masculine authority. In this way Hurston
can connect Jim's love of Arvay and his financial success in Florida without
taxing the credibility of her white and black readers. Hurston uses money

similarly in "The Gilded Six Bits." But the few coins that Joe can bestow on Missie May make the act symbolic, whereas in *Seraph* Jim's economic gain is the physical proof that allows Arvay to set herself apart from her cracker background, a developmental process that Lowe has explained with the assistance of Freudian theory on melancholia and joking.

While in this instance I agree with Lowe's analysis[8]—that is, if one were going to psychoanalyze a character like a person—I am arguing that Hurston's use of Freudian psychology in representing a character like Arvay is part of her deliberate and subversive commentary on female masochism, of which Arvay's whiteness is a necessary part.[9] Unlike many contemporary feminists who still persist in discussing woman apart from her racial identity, Hurston realized that she could not depict a woman without racializing her body, even as she problematized the very effort.

By realizing that *Seraph* has textual subjectivity that is analyzable, we can construct the meaning of the text's whiteness and appreciate Arvay's flawed personality. She is, after all, a character whose newfound wisdom, at the novel's close, informs the reader how to decipher *Seraph's* meaning. Just as she learns to read Jim's jesting words, we must detect and read the novel's joking humor. For *Seraph* is a long satirical joke about notions of cultural and biological purity that probably serve Arvay's and possibly Hurston's aggressive ego defenses with pleasurable affect (Oring 97).

Psychoanalysis enables us to appreciate the double valences inscribed in this novel's metahumorous carnivalesque discourses. In addition to producing humor, these conciliatory and subversive discourses engender parody. In this way *Seraph* unsettles the unquestioned social relationships between blacks and whites, women and men. The novel foregrounds Jim and Arvay's unacknowledged dependency on black idiom, labor, companionship, and folk wisdom as well as their reliance on sadomasochism and sexual bondage. By also acknowledging Jim's successful business endeavors in language that seems like flattery, indeed cajolery, Arvay learns to manage Jim to her advantage. Compared to the spirited, aggressive, and censoring humor of Arvay's earlier invectives, however, her new language of sweet regard seems rather shallow.[10]

While the external whiteness of the novel's central protagonists controls the discourse of social mobility, Jim and Arvay's exploitation of black folk wisdom controls the novel's plot. For example, after listening to Joe Kelsey, his black friend, Jim finds what he believes to be a way of making Arvay love him—that is, by raping her just before marrying her, as discussed above. When Arvay returns from her mother's funeral, determined to win back her husband, for instance, she seeks the assistance of Joe's son, Jeff, and his wife, Janie, by taking "up an attitude that she would have died before adopting before she went away" (313). They respond to the changed Arvay by commenting:

"I declare, Miss Arvay, but you sure is folks."

"Sure is," Jeff added sincerely. "Just like Mister Jim, ain't she, Janie? And everybody knows that Mister Jim is quality first-class. Knows how to carry hisself, and then how to treat everybody. Miss Arvay's done come to be just like him."

The reflection upon her past condition escaped Arvay in the shine and the gleaming of the present. (314)

While the text preserves the class entitlements for racial demarcation, it signifies the mutual respect between the Meserves and the Kelseys, a perspective further emphasized on Jim's shrimp boats. When Arvay boards one of the boats, for instance, she notices "white and Negro captains were friendly together and compared notes. Some boats had mixed crews" (323). These factors, combined with the protagonists' speaking black but appearing white, suggest a masquerade. We see a connection here between the protagonists' psychic and social identities that becomes problematic when we try to place them in the novel's racially defined and polarized codes of the real South.

Racism not only segregated black people from white in the real South of Hurston's epoch; it also prescribed servility for all black subjects. For them to appear equal to white subjects in Western culture, they would have to assume white masks, as psychoanalyst Frantz Fanon has argued in *Black Skin, White Masks* (1952). Undoubtedly, Hurston could appreciate Fanon's contention because she seems to have masked Arvay and Jim in a related way.

Arvay's observations about her own changed racial perspective and the racial equality on the microcosm of the boats contribute to *Seraph's* racial fantasy. Hurston constructs this fantasy by violating the presumption of a black social context, thus periodically inverting the white social context so that in many ways it resembles the masquerade of Bakhtin's carnival. According to Bakhtin, the masquerade works out "a new mode of interrelationship between individuals, counterpoised to the all-powerful socio-hierarchical relationship of noncarnival life" (23). Like the participants of this carnival, the appearances, gestures, and speech of Arvay and Jim "are freed from the authority of all hierarchical positions" (Bakhtin 23).

Seraph's refusal to center a black social milieu—and its corresponding delight in repeatedly calling the white characters "Crackers" while self-consciously placing black folk idioms in their mouths—carnivalizes the presumption that discernible racial differences are the natural basis of segregation and discrimination. Such racist presumptions oppressed Hurston all of her life. Flaunting her circumvention of the racist social censor in *Seraph* must have given Hurston a great deal of pleasure.

Hurston seems to have been almost the only one to have appreciated *Seraph's* racial transgressions. Her black readers have been much too troubled by her switch to white characters to share this pleasure. And her white readers, who already enjoyed her apparent endorsement of dominant cultural myths about patriarchal virtue and female romantic submission in *Seraph,* probably would have liked it even better had she published the work under another name, thereby making the novel's connection to black culture less tangible.

Whether Hurston calculated correctly the demands of Hollywood we shall never know. She was falsely arrested for sexual misconduct shortly after the novel's publication. When the *Baltimore Afro-American,* in a sensational account of the indictment, used an excerpt from *Seraph* (Jim's statement "I'm just as hungry as a dog for a knowing and a doing love") to confirm Hurston's perverse sexual aggression, and subsequently defended its position by presuming Hurston's guilt, *Seraph* became entangled in the controversy. By the time the charge was dismissed, the damage was irreparable: Hurston and her readers neglected the novel .[11] Ironically, the novel that started out as Hurston's joke on her resistant readers ended up playing a cruel joke on her.

Seraph's whiteface masquerade can be seen as a mediation (indeed a deconstruction) of modern racial binary classifications. What initially appears as a regressive racial fantasy is actually a revolutionary text that condemns racial categories and restrictions. Like the "carnivalized" body that Bakhtin described, the white bodies of *Seraph's* protagonists, with their black speaking voices, are not closed, complete, defined, or totalized social entities. Since Arvay and Jim repeatedly transgress the boundaries of their presumed racial categories, they are neither entirely white nor black.

This radical commentary is lost on those who do not recall that all of Hurston's works refuse to consider race as a serious category. In "How It Feels to Be Colored Me," for example, Hurston insisted that "[a]t certain times I have no race, I am me" and "in the main, I feel like a brown bag of miscellany propped against a wall" (155). She further trivialized race by regarding it as a contest and by describing her colored body as painted: "[m]y face is painted red and yellow and my body is painted blue" (pp. 153, 154). *Seraph's* whiteface masquerade also engages in such racial bantering. Even as this masquerade performs the presumption of racial difference, it also symbolizes a revised social self and a reformed society in which race is not a fixed, quintessential characteristic.[12] The indeterminacy of race—the refusal of this novel to validate absolute racial distinctions between black and white dialect, culture, and people—is the basis of Seraph's subversion—its implicit joke on both black and white readers.

To be a joke, *Seraph* must have a punchline that defeats the censor, construed here as racist ideology. For "[a] joke without a punchline is no joke" (Oring 82). We can detect the punchline by looking for "what is seemingly incongruous" becoming "appropriate" (83). This novel appears to endorse two contradictory racial conventions: the segregation of black and presumably pure white bodies, on the one hand, and visibly white bodies talking black on the other hand. White readers have tended to read Jim's and Arvay's bodies as racially white and to disregard their black voices, even though both are the effects of language (Jim and Arvay are not real people but characters in a novel). Black readers have read these incongruities as contrivances to justify marginalizing the novel. Both groups of readers know how to interpret these apparent contradictions, however. For these characteristics identify racial hybridity that has been projected onto, and therefore inscribed in, textuality. According to real, time-honored racial conventions, white-black racial hybrids *must be* black. The punchline is then: These white folks are black! Much like *Puddn'head Wilson* (1894), by Samuel Clemens, in which the presumptions about the absolute meaning of racial difference turn out to be a cultural fiction, *Seraph* unsettles the validity of time-honored racial ideologies. This is *Seraph's* seditious joke on racialism, matched by its subtle but nonetheless radical critique of romantic love, which I discuss elsewhere.[13] In both instances, Hurston appears to uphold the racial and sexual conventions of her day. Yet she presents them in such a way that they insinuate their own internal contradictions and thereby collapse.

Notes

1. If African-American scholars mention *Seraph* at all, and many have not, they categorically regard it as the least of Hurston's works. For example, three black scholars writing in the wake of the Black Power and Black Aesthetic movements tie the novel's defects to its racial posture. Davis claims that the novel "lacks the racy Negro folk speech and seems more highly contrived. No matter how much Miss Hurston knew about Florida poor whites, she instinctively and naturally knew more about Florida Negroes, and the difference shows in this novel" (118). More recently, feminist literary scholars Wall and Washington endorse Davis's viewpoint. Wall contends that *Seraph* "represents an artistic decline" and that "Hurston was at her best when she drew her material directly from black folklore; it was the source of her creative power" (391). Washington speculates that Hurston wrote "this strange book to prove that she was capable of writing about white people." Washington goes on to judge the book as an "awkward and contrived novel, as vacuous as a soap opera" (21).

2. *Seraph* not only draws on Hurston's personal observations about what she calls the slavery of love in *Dust Tracks*, but also presents her critique of the orthodox Freudian viewpoint of masochism "as an expression of feminine nature," a perspective with which Hurston was undoubtedly familiar ("Economic Problem" 257). As John Lowe explains, "Freud was a favorite topic during the Harlem Renaissance and in New York intellectual society in general during the twenties and thirties" (271). "Hurston's mentor Boas," Lowe adds, "no doubt introduced her to Freud as early as the twenties, but other friends like Van Vechten were aficionados as well" (273).

3. Brooks contends "that the structure of literature is in some basic sense the structure of the mind—not a specific mind, but what the translators of the Standard

Edition of Freud's Works call 'the mental apparatus ([. . .]), a term which designates the economic and dynamic organization of the psyche, a process of structuration" ("The Idea" pp. 24–25).

4. For elaboration on the compulsion to repeat, see *Beyond* and "Remembering."

5. Wallace Thurman wrote several Hollywood screenplays featuring white characters to address class issues. As Klotman explains, Thurman, Langston Hughes, and Hurston learned "that the 'Negro' may have been in vogue in Hollywood in the thirties, but it was still the cardboard Negro, the Imitation Judge Priest-Green Pastures GWTW Negro" (quoted in Klotman 91).

6. According to her biographer, Hemenway, no extant copy of the manuscript exists.

7. *The Living Is Easy* (1948) and *The Narrows* (1953) were reissued in 1975 and 1971, respectively, with the resurgence of black nationalism and the women's movement. Both novels are currently in print.

8. Arvay displays an assortment of symptoms. *New York Times* reviewer Slaughter identifies her as a hysterical neurotic. Since her feelings of dejection arise from narcissistic deficiencies, I would instead identify her core problem as a narcissistic personality disorder. A manifestation of this problem would include melancholy and other neuroses. See Kohut pp. 229–238.

9. Freudian theory ascribes passivity to the female even in matters of aggression. For elaboration, see Freud, "The Economic." In Chapter 5 of *Desire and the Protocols of Race*, I argue that the character of Arvay contributes to *Seraph's* subversion of then-accepted views on the naturalness of female masochism.

10. duCille also comments on Arvay's altered speech pattern, claiming she has abandoned the speech pattern of a "cracker" and assumed the discourse of "a coquette" or "a southern belle." Moreover, she uses her newfound language to flatter Jim's ego (140).

11. For an account of the trial, see Hemenway pp. 319–325.

12. Here I adapt Castle's argument: "Even as the masquerade assumed its place in English society, it reified a sometimes devolutionary, sometimes revolutionary anti-society founded on collective gratification. Its profuse, exquisite, difficult imagery symbolized a revision, not just of the psyche, but of culture itself" (74).

13. See Chapter 5 of my *Desire and the Protocols of Race*

WORKS CITED

Bakhtin, Mikhail. *Problems of Dostoevsky's Poetics,* edited and translated by Caryl Emerson. Minneapolis: University of Minnesota Press, 1984.

Baltimore *Afro-American.* 23 Oct. 1948: pp. 1–2.

Brooks, Peter. "The Idea of a Psychoanalytic Literary Criticism," in *Psychoanalysis and Storytelling*. Cambridge, MA: Blackwell, 199, pp. 20–46.

Castle, Terry. *Masquerade and Civilization: The Carnivalesque in Eighteenth Century English Culture and Fiction.* Stanford: Stanford University Press, 1986.

Davis, Arthur. *From the Dark Tower: Afro-American Writers 1900 to 1960.* Washington, DC: Howard University Press, 1974.

duCille, Ann. *The Coupling Convention: Sex, Text, and Tradition in Black Women's Fiction.* New York: Oxford University Press, 1993.

Fanon, Frantz. *Black Skin, White Masks,* 1952, translated by Charles Lam Markmann. New York: Grove, 1967.

Faulkner, William. *The Sound and the Fury.* New York: Vintage Books, 1987.

Freud, Sigmund. "Jokes and Their Relation to the Unconscious, in *The Standard Edition of the Complete Psychological Works of Sigmund Freud,* 24 volumes, edited and translated by James Strachey. London: Hogarth, 1953–1974. VIII: pp. 7–64.

———."Remembering, Repeating and Working-Through," in *The Standard Edition of the Complete Psychological Works of Sigmund Freud,* 24 volumes, edited and translated by James Strachey. London: Hogarth, 1953–1974. XVIII: pp. 147–156.

———. "Beyond the Pleasure Principle," in *The Standard Edition of the Complete Psychological Works of Sigmund Freud,* 24 volumes, edited and translated by James Strachey. London: Hogarth, 1953–1974. XVIII: pp. 7–64.

———. "The Economic Problem of Masochism," in *The Standard Edition of the Complete Psychological Works of Sigmund Freud,* 24 volumes, edited and translated by James Strachey. London: Hogarth, 1953–1974. XIX: pp. 157–170.

———. "Female Sexuality," in *The Standard Edition of the Complete Psychological Works of Sigmund Freud,* 24 volumes, edited and translated by James Strachey. London: Hogarth, 1953–1974. XXI: pp. 223–246.

Hemenway, Robert E. *Zora Neale Hurston: A Literary Biography.* Urbana: University of Illinois Press, 1977.

Hirsh, Marianne. *The Mother/Daughter Plot: Narrative, Psychoanalysis, Feminism.* Bloomington: Indiana University Press, 1989.

Hurston, Zora Neale. "How It Feels to Be Colored Me," in *I Love Myself When I Am Laughing . . . : A Zora Neale Hurston Reader,* edited by Alice Walker. Old Westbury, NY: Feminist Press, 1979, pp. 152–155.

———. *Jonah's Gourd Vine.* 1934. New York: Harper and Row, 1991.

———. *Their Eyes Were Watching God.* 1937. New York: Harper and Row, 1990

———. *Dust Tracks on a Road.* 1942. New York: Harper and Row, 1991

———. *Seraph on the Suwanee.* 1948. New York: Harper and Row, 1991.

———. "What White Publishers Won't Print," in *I Love Myself When I Am Laughing . . . : A Zora Neale Hurston Reader,* edited by Alice Walker. Old Westbury, NY: Feminist Press, 1979, pp. 169–173.

Klotman, Phyllis. "The Black Writer in Hollywood, Circa 1930: The Case of Wallace Thurman," in *Black American Cinema,* edited by Manthia Diawara. New York: Routledge, 1993, pp. 80–92.

Kohut, Heinz. *The Analysis of the Self: A Systematic Approach to the Psychoanalytic Treatment of Narcissistic Personality Disorders.* New York: International University Press, 1971.

Lacan, Jacques. "Agency of the Letter in the Unconscious," in *Écrits: A Selection,* translated by Alan Sheridan. New York: Norton, 1977, pp. 146–178.

Lowe, John. *Jump at the Sun: Zora Neale Hurston's Cosmic Comedy.* Urbana: University of Illinois Press, 1994.

Oring, Elliott. *The Pokes of Sigmund Freud: A Study in Humor and Jewish Identity.* Philadelphia: University of Pennsylvania Press, 1984.

Roediger, David R. The *Wages of Whiteness: Race and the Making of the American Working Class.* London: Verso, 1992.

Slaughter, Frank G. "Freud in Turpentine." *The New York Times Book Review* Vol. 48 (1948): 24.

Tate, Claudia. *Desire and the Protocols of Race: Black Novels and Psychoanalysis.* New York Oxford University Press, 1997.

Wall, Cheryl A. "Zora Neale Hurston: Changing Her Own Words," in *American Novelists Revisited: Essays in Feminist Criticism*, edited by Frizz Fleischmann. Boston: G.K. Hall, 1982, pp. 370–393.

Washington, Mary Helen. "A Woman Half in Shadow," in *I Love Myself When I Am Laughing . . . And Then Again When I Am Looking Mean and Impressive: A Zora Neale Hurston Reader*, edited by Alice Walker. Old Westbury, NY: Feminist Press, 1979, pp. 7–2.

DAPHNE LAMOTHE

Vodou Imagery, African-American Tradition and Cultural Transformation in Zora Neale Hurston's Their Eyes Were Watching God

Zora Neale Hurston wrote *Their Eyes Were Watching God* in 1937 while in Haiti collecting folklore on Vodou.[1] A year later, she published *Tell My Horse,* which documents the findings from that expedition. While the history of these publications suggests that, for Hurston, folklore and fiction converge in Haiti, few critics have adequately explored that juncture. Most acknowledge Hurston's interest in Haitian Vodou, but their analyses of the impact of this belief system on her work frequently do not extend beyond perfunctory glosses. A notable exception is Ellease Southerland's essay, "The Influence of Voodoo on the Fiction of Zora Neale Hurston," published in the 1979 collection, *Sturdy Black Bridges.* Southerland's article makes an important contribution to readings of Hurston's integration of folklore and fiction. The essay discusses the appearance and significance of various "voodoo" signs, symbols and rituals in Hurston's fiction; and more specific to this paper, it identifies the use of Vodou symbolism in *Their Eyes Were Watching God* very early in the history of the novel's criticism. But Southerland does not cite her sources for certain voodoo rituals, or for the significance of various numbers and colors which appear repeatedly in Hurston's fiction. Her analysis therefore seems based on anecdotal evidence and it ignores the cultural distinctions amongst Haitian, Louisiana and other kinds of voodoo and hoodoo. These aspects of the essay contribute to the failure, or

Callaloo: A Journal of African-American and African Arts and Letters, Volume 22, Number 1 (Winter 1999): pp. 157–175 © 1999 Johns Hopkins University Press.

refusal, of succeeding generations of literary critics to further examine the cultural influences that Southerland found in *Their Eyes Were Watching God*. Some—although certainly not all—critics have categorized Hurston's study and incorporation of Vodou as an intriguing curiosity, perhaps considering it to fall within the purview of anthropology and not literature. Reading the novel within such narrow parameters, however, has resulted in a general inability on the part of Hurston's readers to identify the extent to which her use of Vodou ethnography in her literature enables her exploration of female empowerment and African-American cultural identity.

In this paper, I focus specifically on Hurston's use of Haitian Vodou imagery in *Their Eyes Were Watching God*, and I argue that the folklore enables her confrontation of various kinds of social and personal transformation. Her use of Vodou imagery enables her to analyze the relationship among migration, culture and identity that lies at the heart of the African Diaspora. In contrast to those critics who read Hurston's use of folk culture, such as Vodou, as a sign of nostalgia, I view it as her means of comprehending transformation. Within traditional cultural forms lies a structure which encourages and enables dynamic change. Therefore, Hurston's reluctance to abandon African-American tradition does not signal a rejection of modernity; rather, it becomes a vehicle for her to acknowledge modernity.

I concern myself here specifically with Vodou because *Their Eyes Were Watching God* alludes to similarities between the protagonist, Janie Killicks Starks Wood, and the Vodou goddess, Ezili. Janie's physical appearance, her romantic relationships and her interactions with the Eatonville community mirror in a multitude of ways the characteristics of that spirit (Iwa). These allusions are so embedded into the foundation of the narrative that they are virtually invisible, compelling us to ask what it was about Hurston's experiences in Haiti that compelled her to relate Vodou to her characters. Perhaps her instincts as a folklorist and writer led her to a cultural experience in which the self-expression of a displaced people comes to the fore. Perhaps because she was raised in the self-contained all-black community of Eatonville, Florida, she looked to a belief system that addressed black people's capacity for self-determination. Hurston found in Haitian Vodou a syncretic cultural production that spoke to both of those interests and more. Her anthropological research revealed that the ways in which Haitian people worked out their political, social and psychic conditions in the spiritual plane resonated with the concerns and experiences of African Americans in the United States. Because the Vodou gods' and goddesses' appearances and actions speak to the concerns and experiences of their worshippers, one finds that Vodou alludes to the heroic and the rebellious; reflects mundane jealousies, desires and hierarchies; illustrates the ravages of slavery on a collective consciousness; and provides a means of self-expression for that same collective.

Hurston was very aware of Haiti's symbolism for African Americans, and implicit references to its significance are scattered throughout the text. For example, Joe Starks dreams of a place where he can be a "big voice" and settles on Eatonville because "de white folks had all de sayso where he come from and everywhere else, exceptin' dis place dat colored folks was buildin' theirselves" (27). This reference to a place where black people live independent of white authority alludes to post-revolution Haiti, the first black independent republic in the Western hemisphere; and it underscores the revolutionary notion of a town in the United States built and run by black people. Nanny makes a similar allusion to the black republic and the collective desire for autonomy and empowerment. She dreams of "some place way off in de ocean where de black man is in power," revealing Haiti's significance as a place where the potential for black autonomy has been realized (14).

Nanny's musings also address a desire for female empowerment. For it is in that "place way off in de ocean" that she also imagines that a black woman might not have to be "de mule uh de world" (14). Anthropologist Karen McCarthy Brown writes in *Mama Lola* about the possibilities for empowerment afforded to Haitian women by Vodou:

> The adaptability of Vodou over time, and its responsiveness to other cultures and religions; the fact that it has no canon, creed, or pope; the multiplicity of its spirits; and the intimate detail in which those spirits reflect the lives of the faithful—all these characteristics make women's lives visible within Vodou in ways they are not in other religious traditions, including those of the African homeland. This visibility can give women a way of working realistically and creatively with the forces that define and confine them. (221)

Through the use of a Vodou subtext, Hurston comments on and rebels against the forces that "define and confine" black women as sexual beings, work horses and mothers. She also uses Vodou philosophy to shed light on the characters' views on poverty, class, community, and displacement. Building on the work of those critics who investigate the political implications of Hurston's cultural work, I argue that her use of Vodou imagery provides her with a vehicle for political engagement and social commentary.

Folklore, Literature and the Lure of the Primitive

In order to fully comprehend the significance of the text's Vodou imagery, it is crucial to understand the context in which Hurston wrote. I believe she submerged the Vodou images in the novel beneath more accessible folk images of the black South in a dual effort to conform to and resist popular demands for the primitive. Unlike the performance of the dozens, the telling of folk tales and other aspects of African-American folk culture which the reader can easily identify and separate from the plot, Hurston's use of Vodou is not as easily discerned. Its presence in the text has no stylistic markers, nor can we categorize the Vodou elements as mere ornaments for the central narrative.[2] Hurston's more obvious use of African-American folk culture made her vulnerable to criticisms of pandering to the then popular taste for "the minstrel stereotypes of the lazy, sensual, ignorant, laughing darky . . ." (Hemenway 154). As one of the stars of the Harlem Renaissance, courted and funded by white benefactors, Hurston juggled her literary aspirations with the often racist expectations of her patron and audience. For example, Mrs. Rufus Osgood Mason, was a generous benefactor; but "as perhaps with all patrons, . . . she expected some return on her money. In Hurston's case it was a report on the aboriginal sincerity of rural southern black folk . . . Her black guests were either primitive, or they were not being themselves" (Hemenway 107).

Many of Hurston's critics viewed this external pressure as a handicap to her literary production. H. Nigel Thomas, for example, counts Hurston as one of a school of writers (including Charles Chesnutt and Paul Laurence Dunbar) who could not meet the challenge of simultaneously satisfying the demand for "minstrel-type buffoonery" and "ensuring that [s]he did not compromise the dignity of the black race" (175). Thomas mistakes Hurston's humor for buffoonery, and fails to recognize the dignity of her lowly characters. Furthermore, his dismissal of her work arises from the notion that a successful narrative seamlessly blends folklore with fiction. Thomas marks the 1930s as, in general, a time in which African-American writers mastered the art of incorporating those elements of folklore that were necessary to their fiction, without pandering to the audience's "baser instincts" or hindering their art. From the 1930s on, black writers produced literature in which "rituals are not allowed to remain a thing apart or as caricatured quaint antics; instead they are integral aspects of the characters' struggle to survive" (175). According to Thomas, Hurston is an exception to this rule, but he fails to acknowledge that her attempts to set apart and highlight some elements of the folklore (like the stories told by the townsfolk) may be deliberate. Rather than judging the obvious seams between the novel's third person, standard English narration and its first person, African-American vernacular as a sign of Hurston's failure as a writer, it is possible to view it as an emotionally powerful juxtaposition of two very different kinds of language. Furthermore, like many other critics, Thomas does not recognize that she makes Ezili, a figure from Caribbean folklore and ritual, a central, yet nearly invisible, aspect in Janie's struggle for survival. Hurston achieves a doubled triumph over those in her audience who demanded primitive images. First, by setting apart the African-American folklore within the central narrative, she makes a case for the recognition of the literary possibilities of folklore. Second, her use of Vodou achieves the harmonious blending of folklore and fiction that Thomas holds as a standard of successful, black creative expression.

During the 1920s and 1930s, the widespread desire for the primitive extended beyond a demand for minstrel stereotypes of "happy darkies" into the world of the exotic primitive. These demands dovetailed with Renaissance writers' struggles to define what was unique to African-American culture. One way they did so was by attempting to articulate and define blacks' African heritage. But when imagining African culture's relevance to African-American culture and identity, Hurston and her contemporaries often used stereotypical images of beating drums and the jungle, feeding American society's perceptions of Africa as a savage, primal and uncivilized place. Hemenway writes:

> Such tom-tom beats were almost a cliché in Harlem Renaissance writing, and both blacks and whites became enmeshed in the cult of exotic primitivism. For the whites it was the idea that Harlem was an uptown jungle, a safari for the price of cab fare, with cabarets decorated in jungle motifs. They went to Harlem to see the natural rhythm and uninhibited grace of America's link with the heart of darkness. For the black artists it was a much more serious concern, an attempt to establish a working relationship with what Locke called in *The New Negro* the "ancestral" past. (75)

Harlem Renaissance writers' uses of African images frequently held a dual significance as expressions of a serious attempt to articulate the relevance of an African past to African-Americans' present and futures, and as a base appeal to racist demands for exotic entertainment. Hurston's literary forays into blacks' ancestral past often made use of the clichés mentioned above. In *Jonah's Gourd Vine*, for instance, and in her 1928 essay, "How It Feels to Be Colored Me," she makes prodigious use of the metaphor of the drum to invoke an ancient African heritage as the foundation of African-American identity.

One could view Hurston's turn to Vodou as another example of her exploitation of the primitive because, historically, representations of Vodou in the U.S. have been rife with clichés. For example, Eugene O'Neill's *The Emperor Jones* contains numerous stereotypes in its depiction of a voodoo cult of savages: Brutus Jones, the noble savage; the tom-toms beating incessantly in the background to foreshadow evil; and natives using black magic to depose their emperor. However, Hurston's weaving of Vodou imagery in *Their Eyes* completely evades such predictable stereotypes, delving instead into the complexities of the belief system, the culture from which it springs and the ways in which those complexities address African-American (and Afro-Caribbean) social and political concerns. The Vodou subtext represents a facet of the primitive that exceeds the scope of the plantation and jungle bunny stereotypes that dominated the Harlem Renaissance era. It links the southern folk with a Black Atlantic experience rooted in slavery, armed revolution and African spirituality.

Vodou Imagery and Female Agency

The primary Vodou element in this novel is the implicit presence of the goddess, Ezili. Hurston infuses Janie with the characteristics of two aspects of this spirit: Ezili Freda, the mulatta goddess of love, and Ezili Danto, the black goddess who is associated with maternal rage. These two spirits display attributes that are completely opposed. Freda is of an elite class; she is a mulatta, self-possessed and materialistic. Danto is working class, black and associated with motherhood. These contradictory qualities reside in one spirit, and in the case of the novel, they also lie in one body—Janie's. The tensions that stem from these oppositions reflect the conditions and desires of African Americans; and while they cannot always be assimilated or resolved, they frequently result in cultural and individual expressiveness that is dynamic and powerful. Therefore, Hurston uses Vodou imagery, in particular the image of Ezili, in order to implicitly enter a discourse on the present and future of African-American culture.

Just as all Vodou ceremonies begin with songs, dances and prayers in honor of Legba, the novel starts with an implicit invocation of him. Janie calls forth the power of Legba, the keeper of the crossroads, which is the gateway between the spiritual and material worlds, as she searches "as much of the world as she could from the top of the front steps" (11). And when she walks "down to the front gate"—the symbolic crossroads—"and [leans] over to gaze up and down the road" (11), her air of expectation invokes the potential embodied by Legba. In *Tell My Horse*, Hurston calls Legba the "opener of gates"; he symbolizes opportunity (115).[3] As Janie stands at the gate, "looking, waiting, breathing short with impatience. Waiting for the world to be made," she feels acutely this sense of opportunity (11).

This invocation of Legba, a Black Atlantic god, takes place in a text marked by its multiple references to the Christian God, most notably in its title. During the storm that erupts near the end of the narrative, the folks stranded on the muck stare into the darkness, putting themselves at the mercy of a Christian God. But throughout the narrative, as they gaze upon Janie's body, they have also been looking to a New World goddess rooted in African spirituality. Rachel Blau DuPlessis notes that "there are a number of substitutions for God made in this book, usually in the form of big talkers—'Mouth Almighty' of the rural folk, and 'I God' for Joe Stark's comic blasphemous condensation of political and economic power."[4] The temporal powers of Jody and the gossiping Eatonville folk give scant competition to the all encompassing power of God to whom Janie, Tea Cake and their friends silently appeal as they wait for the storm to arrive. But the novel refers in passing only to these false gods, and to the ultimate authority, the God who controls the potentially devastating forces of nature. This God is Ezili's primary challenger in the competition for the characters' allegiance.

Janie resembles Ezili Freda physically. In *Voodoo in Haiti,* anthropologist Alfred Mètraux describes Freda, the goddess of love, as "a pretty Antillean half-caste. . . . a personification of feminine grace and beauty. She has all the characteristics of a pretty mulatto: she is coquettish, sensual, pleasure-loving and extravagant" (110). Freda can make any man she chooses her husband, a characteristic that finds its parallel in Janie's search for a suitable mate. Janie dresses in blue (2), Freda's favorite color.[5] The description of Janie's return to Eatonville echoes Mètraux's description of Ezili's entrance into a Vodou temple. Hurston writes:

> The men noticed her firm buttocks like she had grape fruits in her hip pockets; the great rope of black hair swinging to her waist and unraveling in the wind like a plume; then her pugnacious breasts trying to bore holes in her shirt. They, the men, were saving with the mind what they lost with the eye. (2)

Mètraux writes:

> At last, in the full glory of her seductiveness, with hair unbound to make her look like a long-haired half-caste, Ezili makes her entrance to the peristyle. She walks slowly, swinging her hips, throwing saucy, ogling looks at the men or pausing for a kiss or a caress. (111)

Janie's long hair and sensuality mark her as the object of sexual desire. Although, unlike Ezili Freda, Janie does not actively solicit male attention, Freda's desire for sensuality and love blooms in Janie as she muses under the pear tree in her grandmother's garden. And finally, the celebration of love and sexuality symbolized by Freda culminates in Janie and Tea Cake's playful, loving relationship.

The text celebrates female sexuality with its sensuous prose and its positioning of Janie's quest for love at its center. By linking Janie's sexuality with Freda's, Hurston radicalizes it by associating it with the ritual of possession in which a god mounts an initiate. The goddess is said to "ride" her horse. The implicit sexuality in this terminology is self-evident and Ezili's desire for numerous "husbands" is well documented in the anthropological literature. The image of a woman, either human or spirit, "mounting" a man proves significant because it implies the woman's control over her own sexuality and over the man's pleasure as well. For Hurston, representing a woman's sexuality in full bloom is not just affirmative, it is revolutionary.

But Freda's presence also represents a desire for wealth and status, which eventually leads to conflict for Janie. After joining in a loveless marriage with Logan Killicks, Janie tells her grandmother, "Ah wants things sweet wid mah marriage lak when you sit under a pear tree and think, Ah . . ." (23). Janie's desire for "things sweet" corresponds with the mythology surrounding Ezili Freda, who also desires sweets.[6] Janie eventually satisfies that desire when she marries a man with a sweet sounding name, Tea Cake; but that only occurs when she shucks off her grandmother's belief that a secure, middle-class home should take precedence over romantic love. Nanny responds to Janie's rejection of the economically stable and physically unattractive Logan Killicks in the following way:

> If you don't want him, you sho oughta. Heah you is wid de onliest organ in town, amongst colored folks, in yo' parlor. Got a house bought and paid for and sixty acres uh land right on de big road and . . . Lawd have mussy! Dat's de very prong all us black women gits hung on Dis love! (22)

The similarities between Janie and Freda go only so far because, ultimately, Janie rejects the aristocratic ideal that Freda embodies (represented by her love of jewelry, brushes and combs, the valorization of her light skin and long hair and her preference for French over Creole, the language of the lower classes in Haiti). She laments to Pheoby the fact that "Jody classed me off"; and rejoices when she finds in Tea Cake not only romantic love, but also the connection with the folk from which she has so often been discouraged. Janie finds no satisfaction in Logan Killicks' possessions, resents the fact that Jody sits her on the front porch like "a pretty doll-baby" (28) and rejoices when Tea Cake asks her to work in the muck with all the "common" folk.

Although Janie resents being "classed off," most of the other characters crave and envy the status that comes with having material possessions and a light-skinned wife. They worship and desire the materialistic and elitist life-style represented by the mulatta Freda, which eventually proves their downfall. While most of the folk share these desires, Mrs. Turner, Janie's "visiting friend" in the muck proves the most egregious example of this mindset because her worship of Janie's mixed race features borders on self-hatred. Mrs. Turner "didn't cling to Janie Woods the woman. She paid homage to Janie's Caucasian characteristics as such" (13):

Once having set up her idols and built altars to them it was inevitable that she would worship there. It was inevitable that she should accept any inconsistency and cruelty from her deity as all good worshippers do from theirs. All gods who receive homage are cruel. All gods dispense suffering without reason. Otherwise they would not be worshipped. Through indiscriminate suffering men know fear and fear is the most divine emotion. It is the stones for altars and the beginning of wisdom. Half gods are worshipped in wine and flowers. Real gods require blood. (138–39)

Mrs. Turner worships Janie's Caucasian features like an initiate worships the Iwa—with blood sacrifices and an awareness that the gods can sometimes be arbitrary in their cruelty. This critique of Mrs. Turner's misplaced faith in whiteness is not a condemnation of Vodou, however. Rather, it is an honest assessment of the religion's tendency to respond to and reflect all of its worshippers' desires, including those that may be self-destructive. While the other characters are not as virulent in their internalized racism as Mrs. Turner, Nanny, Logan, Jody, the townsfolk and even Tea Cake show signs of being color struck and materialistic. Thus, the text's condemnation of Mrs. Turner implicitly extends to a critique of other characters who share her views.

Despite the popular tendency to worship that which Ezili Freda represents, Janie eventually rejects the elitist trappings that characterize the Iwa and embraces the working-class, folk identity of Ezili Danto. When she returns to Eatonville, the women remark on the changes in her appearance. "What she doin' coming back here in dem overhalls?—What dat ole forty year ole 'oman doin' wid her hair swingin' down her back lak some young gal?" (2). While their vituperative comments reflect their envy of Janie's appearance and wealth, the changes in her appearance reflect a profound change in Janie's self-perception and a departure from the iconography of Ezili Freda.[7] The references to Janie's "overhalls" and age place her in the province of Ezili Danto, the Petwo spirit, at the same time that her long hair and sensuality continue to align her with Freda. This passage resonates on multiple levels, positioning Janie as two kinds of women: one who benefits from and reaffirms gender, class and color biases (signified by Freda), and one who is noted for her willingness to work and for her maturity (signified by Danto).

McCarthy Brown describes Ezili Danto as an independent woman with an unconventional sexuality. She has "dark black skin" and is "not too proud to work" (229). Although the fair-complexioned, relatively well-off Janie must convince Tea Cake that she is not above working in the fields with the other migrant laborers, she soon proves to be an enthusiastic worker. Danto's black skin mirrors the blackness of the muck and that of the people in whom Janie finds fulfillment. Unlike the light-skinned Mrs. Turner who says, she "can't stand black niggers" (135), or the mulatta Ezili Freda who detests those with black skin, Janie loves Tea Cake, his dark skin and the affirmative connection with her community that blackness represents.

But Danto also has the power to destroy, which earns her the reputation of being "red-eyed," or evil. Hurston calls her "the terrible Erzulie, ge-rouge. . . . an older woman and terrible to look upon" (123).[8] That destructive force makes itself known during the hurricane, which erupts in order to convey Danto's displeasure. This spirit, who represents working-class values and an affirmative blackness, violently objects to the African Americans' deference to white cultural, racial and economic supremacy at the expense of their own autonomy. The danger of such attitudes becomes clear when the folk remain in the path of the storm, despite the warning signs they receive, because they are making "seven and eight dollars a day picking beans." In contrast to the Native Americans who know how to read the signs that nature gives them—"Saw-grass bloom. Hurricane coming," they say as they flee the Everglades—the African Americans ignore the warnings (146). They stay where they are because, "De white folks ain't gone nowhere. Dey oughta know if it's dangerous" (148). This implicit trust in white people's authority proves their downfall and results in the deaths of scores of people. Tea Cake's "possession" by the rabid dog that bites him is the most graphic example of the consequences suffered by black folks who blindly worship whiteness.

Vodou stands in this novel as a reminder of black independence and expressiveness, and the Vodou goddesses demand payment when proper attention is not paid to these principles. Janie's deferral to Tea Cake, who insists that they follow the example of the white landowners, runs against her own instincts. Her acquiescence to his will mirrors the African-American community's subordination to white authority and underscores the notion that their flaw is in the refusal to read the situation and interpret its meaning for themselves. When we first meet the young Janie, we learn that she can communicate with nature and understand its signs:

> . . . Janie had spent most of the day under a blossoming pear tree in the back-yard. She had been spending every minute that she could steal from her chores under that tree for the last three days. That was to say, ever since the first tiny bloom had opened. It had *called* her to come and gaze on a mystery. . . . She had been *summoned* to behold a revelation. (11, emphasis added)

Janie's ability to "read" nature's signs mirrors that of the Native Americans who warn her and her friends to leave before the hurricane strikes. But her unwillingness to heed her own internal barometer results in a terrible price paid to nature's forces. Karla Holloway writes in *The Character of the Word:*

> Nature has bowed to human forces throughout the novel. Here she shows that she is a power that can control, as well as be controlled. Perhaps her fury is a lesson for Janie, who has been linked with natural imagery throughout the story and who needs to learn the potential strength of her own independence. (65)

All of the folks living in the Everglades, and not just Janie, need to learn to honor their independence.

Ezili Danto makes her angry presence known at this point in the narrative. She is connected with water; a gentle rainfall signals her presence and a deluge signals her rage.[9] The hurricane is described as a terrifying and cosmic force that extracts the blood sacrifice that "real gods" demand: "Ten feet higher and as far as they could see the muttering wall advanced before the braced-up waters like a road crusher on a cosmic scale. The monstropolous beast had left his bed. The two hundred miles an hour wind had loosed his chains" (153). Danto's rage erupts as a violent reminder to the folk that their passive faith in Euro-Americans, or Christianity, to determine their fate is misguided. The events leading up to the hurricane vividly illustrate the need for self-determination in the collective black consciousness. This lesson comes too late for Tea Cake to learn; but his death is an example for other individuals. Likewise, Janie suffers for her passivity not only in losing Tea Cake, but also in having to act as the agent of his death.

Ezili Danto's brutal insistence that the folk maintain their independence defies Christian doctrine which traditionally advocated submission to authority.[10] The passiveness of the folk as they wait for the onslaught to begin underscores Christianity's traditional call for submissiveness: "They sat in company with the others in other shanties, their eyes straining against crude walls and their souls asking if He meant to measure their puny might against His. They seemed to be staring at the dark, but their eyes were watching God" (151). In contrast to this situation which forces the folk to assume a posture of defeat, Hurston saw Vodou as facilitating a peasant self-expression that often subverted authority. Her account in *Tell My Horse* of the events that take place when Gede, the peasant god of death, mounts an individual, highlights the potential threat in the Vodou tradition to upend hierarchies and disrupt social order:

> On several occasions, it was observed that Guedé [sic] seemed to enjoy humbling his betters. On one occasion Guedé reviled a well-dressed couple in a car that passed. Their names were called

and the comments were truly devastating to say the least. With such behavior one is forced to believe that some of the valuable commentators are "mounted" by the spirit and that others are feigning possession in order to express their resentment general and particular. That phrase "Parlay cheval ou" is in daily, hourly use in Haiti and no doubt it is used as a blind for self-expression. (221)

When Gede speaks through the possessed, political, economic and social injustices come under attack in ways that could never be possible in Haitian society under ordinary circumstances. If an individual pretends to be possessed by the Iwa, in effect putting on a mask of Gede, that attack becomes even more threatening than one from a possessed individual because it is a willful expression of anger, disgust or defiance.

In Gede's burlesque antics we find the most striking, but not the only, example of peasant self-expression which threatens the stability of a social order. While possession by Gede results in the subversion of class hierarchies, the presence of Ezili Freda and Danto illustrates the ways in which class identity and female agency are expressed in Haitian society (and, by extension, within Eatonville society as well). Vodou's implicit stress on self-expression echoes the novel's more explicit celebration of black expressiveness through the storytelling that takes place. Storytelling and, by extension, other forms of self-expression have the capacity to liberate Janie from the many constraints placed on her. Powerful truths about life and love exist in Janie's story, which she recounts to her friend Pheoby while they sit on the back porch of her house. Janie's story takes on a mythic dimension and her words transcend even the limitations of her own life. Mary Helen Washington aptly describes those limitations:

> One can hardly make . . . an unequivocal claim for Janie's heroic posture in *Their Eyes*. . . . Her friendship with Pheoby, occurring apart from the community, encapsulates Janie and Pheoby in a private dyad that insulates Janie from the jealousy of other women. Like the other women in the town, she is barred from participation in the culture's oral tradition. When the voice of the black oral tradition is summoned in *Their Eyes*, it is not used to represent the collective black community, but to invoke and valorize the voice of the black *male* community. (Washington 99)

While I concur that the novel primarily celebrates the black male oral tradition, I would reassert the significance of the frame story told by Janie to Pheoby. The frame story takes on the power and status of myth, which

Leslie Desmangles describes as possessing "a paradoxical capacity to express complex truths in everyday language, to use common words and familiar objects to reveal what is most sacred in life" (61). Janie's gender and race certainly circumscribe her experiences, but her story speaks to the potential she carries within. Desmangles notes that "myths are . . . powerful vehicles which can transcend the limitations of profane existence" (61). While Janie may not fully realize her voice and agency in the time frame of the narrative, her mythic tale underscores the potential which exists within all black women. Janie entrusts Pheoby with the responsibility of passing on her story and "de understandin" that goes along with it: "You can tell 'em what Ah say if you wants to. Dat's just de same as me 'cause mah tongue is in mah friend's mouf" (6). With this exhortation, the promise arises that a ritualized sharing of stories and experiences between women will develop. Pheoby will recount Janie's tale, but she will also revise it as she grows and experiences new things. She may inspire future listeners, just as Janie has inspired her. Janie's experience, her story, functions as myth for the folk, teaching them the value of self-expression and the necessity for self-determination.

Critical Schools: Tradition and Transformation

Hurston's incorporation into her novel of a religious tradition which she viewed as ancient and African does not preclude the text's relevance to the condition of modern African Americans. The Vodou intertext in *Their Eyes* actually enabled Hurston to grapple with issues which preoccupied black intellectuals in the 1920s and 1930s, such as class, gender and inter- and intraracial conflicts. Critical responses to the text failed to perceive, however, its immediate relevance to current events and modern political thought. Because Hurston positioned herself as an authority on black culture in her lifetime, she practically instigated others to attack her representations of black people and black culture for their lack of authenticity or legitimacy. Alain Locke chastised Hurston in his annual literature review for *Opportunity* magazine for creating "those pseudo-primitives whom the reading public still loves to laugh with, weep over, and envy" (18). More biting than Locke's review was the critique by the leading black novelist of the day. Richard Wright wrote that the novel, like minstrelsy, "carries no theme, no message, no thought," and functioned only to satisfy the tastes of a white audience for the simple and exotic primitive (17). Locke and Wright registered their conviction that Hurston's characters are too cartoonish, simple and docile to be real.

Locke and Wright expressed their squeamishness with Hurston's portrayal of local color during a time in which Northern black newspapers regularly instructed those in their readership who were newly arrived from the South on proper etiquette in public places. Their discomfort with her portrayal of folk characters echoed the sensitivity of many African-American intellectuals to the public's perception of black culture. In his introduction to *New Essays on Their Eyes Were Watching God,* Michael Awkward notes:

> Sensitive to the need to improve white America's perception of Afro-Americans, some powerful black intellectuals, including Locke and W.E.B. Du Bois, believing that literature represented the most effective means by which to begin to dispel racist notions that black Americans were morally and cognitively subhuman, insisted that Afro-American writers were obligated to present Afro-Americans in the most favorable—and flattering—light possible. (10)

Although Wright was subjected to similar criticisms upon the publication of *Native Son,* his review of *Their Eyes* reflects a touchiness regarding the proper strategy for depicting the African-American lower classes. Although Locke and Wright couch their criticism in a rhetoric of authenticity, they seem to object more strenuously to Hurston's seemingly apolitical depiction of poor, uneducated blacks to a presumably racist white audience.

Hurston's reputation has benefited from a surge in scholarly interest since the publication in the early 1970s of Alice Walker's essay, "Looking for Zora." To this day, however, some critics retain a residual discomfort with her often flamboyant and controversial statements about black culture. For example, in *The Black Atlantic* Paul Gilroy asserts that Hurston's romanticization of "the folk" and idealization of rural, southern black culture prevent her from acknowledging African-American cultural transformation. Gilroy's critique of Hurston assumes that the desire to preserve a sense of tradition automatically marks one as antagonistic to change. Hurston's forays into Vodou symbolism illustrate her respect for a tradition and culture which she considered ancient and African. But more importantly, her appropriation of this African diasporic tradition allowed her to participate in an ongoing dialogue about social and cultural change within black communities in the United States, which preoccupied her contemporaries during and after the Harlem Renaissance. Hurston was absolutely interested in exploring the extent and effect of cultural transformation within African-American communities; and Vodou was the primary avenue for accomplishing this exploration.

To illustrate his point, Gilroy teases out a compelling analysis of Hurston's contempt for the operatic performances of spirituals by the Fisk Jubilee Singers, focusing on her theories of authenticity and black culture:

> For Hurston, the success of the Fisk choir represented the triumph of musicians' tricks over the vital, untrained, angular spirit of the

rural folk who "care nothing about pitch" and "are bound by no rules." . . . She attacked the choir's performances as inauthentic. (91–92)

Gilroy goes on to say:

> I would emphasise that as far as this chapter is concerned, whether Hurston was right or wrong about the Fisk Singers is not the primary question. The issue which interests me more than her correctness is her strongly felt need to draw a line around what is and isn't authentically, genuinely, and really black. . . . (92)

The implied critique in Gilroy's observation is that by insisting on an authentic way of singing the spirituals, Hurston resists an inevitable and dynamic change that is an inherent part of the Black Atlantic experience. In order to make this point, he understates the desire for upward class mobility that motivated individuals and groups like the Fisk Singers to elevate a lowly folk art into "high" culture. I think it important, however, to focus on the reasons for her objections to what she considered the loss of integrity in a black cultural production. Hurston's criticism was directed primarily toward a group of formally educated African Americans who attempted to transform a rough, improvisational musical form born of illiterate blacks into an operatic, and therefore more "cultured," form of music.[11] Her refusal to see the operatic performances of spirituals as authentic stems from her resistance to an aesthetic which continued to view poor black culture as inferior, even as it attempted to rehabilitate and transform that culture for a wider audience.

While Hurston grappled with the significance and consequences of transformed cultural experiences, she was not willing to define a "New Negro" who was completely ignorant of, or free from, the influences of the past. Karla Holloway accurately notes that "Hurston's was an ancient spirit in an age that demanded modernism, that called the Negro 'new' and expected that Negro to be male" (17). Hurston refused to submit to the demands of modernism and progress without question because she feared the loss or repression of African cultural fragments. Her objection to the choir's innovations was not so much that they diluted the music's blackness with their injection of class and educational privilege; rather, she objected to the compromise, or abandonment, of the principles on which the music was based.

In an essay entitled, "Spirituals and Neo-Spirituals," Hurston describes such unique characteristics of Negro singing as "jagged harmony," disharmony, shifting keys, "broken time" and improvisation (80–81). She was very much aware that most of these musical characteristics were African in origin.

Eric Sundquist's comparison of black English and black music proves illuminating in understanding the rationale behind Hurston's supposed resistance to change. He asserts that the perceived strangeness of the language and the music (which we could also call African-ness) often led to anxiety in and ridicule from the dominant culture: "For whites' complaints about the ineffability of black dialect, which led in turn to the grotesque caricatures of minstrelsy and some plantation romance, repeated comparable observations by musicologists . . . that the intonations of the black spiritual were difficult to transcribe" (60). The elements of the spirituals that seem wrong to the ear trained in Western music (like the polyrhythms and blue notes which Hurston called broken time and disharmony) are the very elements that Hurston sought to preserve. Her critique of the Fisk Jubilee Singers was directed as much at the westernization of the spirituals at the expense of their African elements as it was towards the elegant concert halls and bourgeois performers and audience members. Hurston expressed her rejection of white cultural supremacy through her insistence on an authentic mode of performance, which Gilroy reads as a rejection of modernity. While some might argue that westernization is an inevitable and not necessarily negative cultural transformation, to do so without reservation is problematic because it does not challenge the then widely held assumption that European values were superior to and more sophisticated than African ones.

Unlike Gilroy, Hazel Carby acknowledges Hurston's investment in deflating class-driven pretensions; but like Gilroy, she finds Hurston too quick to delineate who *the* folk might be, as if such a homogenous group identity ever existed. In "The Politics of Fiction, Anthropology, and the Folk: Zora Neale Hurston," Carby notes that Hurston avoids any mention of the newly emergent northern, urban black and chooses to focus on an almost mythical South:

> Hurston was concerned to establish authenticity in the representation of popular forms of folk culture and to expose the disregard for the aesthetics of that culture through inappropriate forms of representation. She had no problem in using the term "the people" to register that she knew just who they were. But critics are incorrect to think that Hurston reconciled "high" and "low" forms of cultural production. Hurston's criticisms were not reserved for the elitist manner in which she thought the authentic culture of the people was reproduced. The people she wanted to represent she defined as a rural folk, and she measured them and their cultural forms against an urban, mass culture. (75)

Carby concludes that Hurston displaces the migration of blacks to the urban North with a nostalgic discourse about the rural South, resisting the cultural transformation that resulted from that migration. Carby stresses the need to recognize the transformation of black culture and warns against the impulse to romanticize a homogenous experience. Her critique, like Gilroy's, is facilitated by Hurston's many assertions of the genuine and authentic in black culture.[12] But Hurston's polemics do not preclude an active engagement in her literature with African-American social and cultural change.

While Carby astutely observes that, in *Their Eyes,* Janie reverses the direction of most black migrants, moving deeper South rather than North, she does not investigate the reasons for and implications of this movement.[13] She notes that Hurston situates "the southern, rural folk and patterns of migration in relation to the Caribbean rather than the northern states," viewing that migration ever southward as yet another displacement (82). Hurston's evocation of the Caribbean through Vodou, however, allows her to grapple with many of the issues being debated in cosmopolitan, intellectual circles during the Harlem Renaissance.[14]

In *Their Eyes,* Hurston comments on issues of class, gender, sexuality and cultural identity primarily through her use of Vodou imagery. The novel takes up many of the same issues being debated by her contemporaries during the 1920s and 1930s. For example, Harlem was frequently celebrated as unique because it was a gathering place for diverse people of the African Diaspora. Alain Locke writes in *The New Negro:*

> Here in Manhattan is not merely the largest Negro community in the world, but the first concentration in history of so many diverse elements of Negro life. It has attracted the African, the West Indian, the Negro American; has brought together the Negro of the north and the Negro of the south; the man from the city and the man from the town and village; the peasant, the student, the business man, the professional man, artist, poet, musician, adventurer and worker, preacher and criminal, exploiter and social outcast. Each group has come with its own separate motives and for its own special ends, but their greatest experience has been the finding of one another. (6)

In asserting that "their greatest experience has been the finding of one another," Locke minimizes any social or cultural tensions that may have existed between the different groups gathered in Harlem and celebrates Harlem as a center of African diasporic culture. This emerging and changing culture, noted for its diversity, is but one of the social transformations Carby believes Hurston should have recognized.

Locke's optimism actually was shared by Hurston, however, and is implicitly echoed in an easily overlooked passage in the novel. In it she describes how the Bahamians and Black Americans working in the Everglades overcome their initial trepidation over each other's foreignness by dancing together. The Bahamians "quit hiding out to hold their dances when they found that their American friends didn't laugh at them as they feared. Many of the Americans learned to jump and liked it as much as the 'Saws.' So they began to hold dances night after night in the quarters, usually behind Tea Cake's house" (146). The relative ease with which these groups overcome their differences suggests that national and ethnic identification can be blurred with a greater awareness and cultivation of cultural similarities, and a greater tolerance of and interest in cultural difference. So, in the midst of their dances, we cannot distinguish between American and Bahamian as they make "living, sculptural, grotesques in the dance" (147). This reference to "sculptural grotesques," African sculptures brought to life, evokes the dancers' shared ancestry.

This allusion to Africa and the passage's naive suggestion that cultural, political and economic differences can be easily eradicated by social interaction reveal that Hurston ascribed to the notion of a unified and idyllic African past. Carby and Gilroy have accurately identified Hurston's tendency to romanticize the past in this novel, yet I argue that the allusions to Vodou reveal a more complex vision of Black Atlantic cultures. Her immersion in tradition, specifically Haitian Vodou tradition, opens the novel up to politicized readings of contemporary African-American racial, gender and class politics.

Just as Locke saw the social and political potential of Harlem because it was a site of "group expression and self-determination," Hurston saw that same potential in Haitian Vodou. The elements of the text which Carby identifies as displacements to the South and to the Caribbean actually allow Hurston to explore through metaphor and symbolism the social and political concerns of African Americans in the North, South and throughout the Caribbean. Hurston was not solely interested in elevating African-American folk culture; she was also invested in collecting and recreating through fiction what black people had to say about themselves. Haitian Vodou provided Hurston with the ideal vehicle to voice African diasporic peoples' (especially women's) views on their social status and unique experiences, demonstrating that ancient tradition can effectively shape our comprehension of modern cultures that are constantly evolving.

NOTES

*I would like to thank Mitchell Breitwieser, VèVè Clark and Katherine Bassard for their careful readings of earlier drafts of this essay. I am also indebted to Cynthia Dobbs, Ann-Marie Harvey and Theresa Tensuan for their long-standing support and their many valuable suggestions for the improvement of this essay.

1. In *The Faces of the Gods*, Leslie Desmangles writes, "Thanks to Hollywood and the film industry, what average persons conjure up in their minds when they

think of *Voodoo* is a picture of witches and sorcerers who, filled with hatred, attempt to inflict diseases or even death on other persons by making wax or wooden representations of them, and perforating them with pins. Another popular image of *Voodoo* or *Hoodoo* is that of a conglomeration of exotic spells celebrated clandestinely by blacks inebriated with blood . . ." (1–2). Given that the terms, "voodoo" and "hoodoo" are saddled with misleading and defamatory meaning, I have chosen to use in this paper the Creole spelling of Vodou and other terminology related to it, except when citing sources that may spell them differently. The Creole spelling also approximates the etymological root, the Dahomean term *"vodu"* or *"vodun"* which means "spirit."

2. Trudier Harris claims that Hurston "excessively packs in folk expressions and beliefs to the extent that the excessively metaphorical folk language becomes an added character, plugging up the cracks between theme and plot, not a smoothly woven, integral part of the whole; language and story seem to have mutually exclusive functions" (6). Although the African-American folklore functions separately from, and sometimes competes with, the narrative, the Haitian folklore blends in with and extends the narrative's themes.

3. Hurston's characterization of Legba as the master of potentiality is supported by other sources. For example, Robert Farris Thompson writes that "God granted Eshu [the Yoruba manifestation of Legba] the force to make all things happen and multiply (*ashé*). . . . He is . . . the ultimate master of potentiality" (18–19).

4. References to God and god-like figures abound. Blau DuPlessis notes that "the absolute beginning of the book begins playing with title materials and meanings by opening issues about words and the Word in relation to gender and racial power. The third paragraph starts with a revisionary articulation of Biblical rhetoric, 'So the beginning of this was a woman', taking the world-creating place of Word or God" (109).

Lorraine Bethel writes, "Hurston's first description of Nanny in *Their Eyes* establishes her as a representative of the religious experience that stands at the center of Afro-American folk tradition. She is described in terms suggestive of a Christ figure. Janie makes Nanny a wreath of 'palma christi leaves,' and the words 'bore' and 'pierce' used in this passage invoke images of the crucifixion" (13–14).

Barbara Johnson and Henry Louis Gates Jr. note that "Joe Starks . . . fondly and unconsciously refers to himself as 'I-God.' During the lamp-lighting ceremony . . . Joe is represented as the creator (or at least the purchaser) of light" (73).

5. "Each *loa* has its representative colour—red for Ogu, white for Damballah, blue for Ezili etc. . . ." (Mètraux 167).

6. "Ezili being a white *loa* and a 'woman of the world' has a fondness for pale and sugary drinks" (Mètraux 176).

7. Janie's donning of the overalls can be read as a moment of symbolic transvestitism which disrupts and challenges Eatonville's social order. In *Vested Interests,* Marjorie Garber argues that "transvestitism was located at the juncture of class and gender, and increasingly through its agency gender and class were revealed to be commutable, if not equivalent. To transgress against one set of boundaries was to call into question the inviolability of both, and the set of social codes—already demonstrably under attack—by which such categories were policed and maintained" (32). The townsfolk react to Janie's transgression of class and gender boundaries, seeing the overalls as a violation of their social codes.

8. While some anthropologists mistakenly represent the Rada and Petwo spirits as symbolizing good and evil (Hurston included), the actual significance of

these two Vodou pantheons is more complicated than suggested by this binarism. McCarthy Brown writes: "The Rada spirits are sweet-tempered and dependable; their power resides in their wisdom. . . .They are intimate, familial spirits who are given family titles such as Papa and Kouzen [cousin]. . . . The Petwo spirits, in contrast, are hot-tempered and volatile. They must be handled with care and precision. Debts must be paid and promises kept, or they will badger and harass those who serve them. The power of the Petwo spirits resides in their effectivity, their ability to make things happen" (100–101).

9. "Danto's anger can exceed what is required for strict discipline. At times, it explodes from her with an irrational, violent force. Ezili Danto, like Lasyrenn, has connections with water. A gentle rainfall during the festivities at Saut d'Eau, a mountain pilgrimage site for Ezili Danto (Our Lady of Mount Carmel), is readily interpreted as a sign of her presence; but so is a sudden deluge resulting in mudslides, traffic accidents, and even deaths. . . . Thus Danto's rage can emerge with the elemental force of a torrential rain, which sweeps away just and unjust alike. This aspect of Ezili Danto might be described as an infant's eye view of the omnipotent mother" (McCarthy Brown 231).

10. Donald Petesch notes that during the period of enslavement, in sermons and catechisms, "grand moralizing gave way to immediate practical ends: the language of religion became the language of social control" (60).

11. Arnold Rampersad's assessment of the contributors to *The New Negro*, some of the most influential black intellectuals of the day, supports my suggestion that the desire to elevate the spirituals to a "higher" art form betrays a belief in the cultural inferiority of African Americans. Rampersad writes, "It is fair to say that, in the face of racial 'science,' most of the contributors to the volume accepted the notion of black racial and cultural inferiority compared to the standards of European civilization. Most also believed, however, that the African race was on the move forward, that politically, economically, and culturally, peoples of African descent around the world were engaged in the first stages of a transformation that would eventually lead to independence from Europe" (xvi). Ironically, most believed that independence from Europe could only be achieved by successfully replicating, with minor adaptations, its cultural, social and political paradigms.

12. For example, in "Spirituals and Neo-Spirituals," Hurston asserts, "There never has been a presentation of genuine Negro spirituals to any audience anywhere. What is being sung by the concert artists and glee clubs are the works of Negro composers or adaptors [sic] *based* on the spirituals" (80).

13. Carby is far from alone in perceiving the novel as being removed from history and reality. Robert Stepto writes, "The narrative takes place in a seemingly ahistorical world: the spanking new all-black town is meticulously bereft of former slave cabins; there are no railroad trains, above or underground, with or without Jim Crow cars; Matt's mule is a bond with and catalyst for distinct tribal memories and rituals, but these do not include the hollow slogan, 'forty acres and a mule'; Janie seeks freedom, selfhood, voice, and 'living' but is hardly guided—or haunted—by Sojourner Truth or Harriet Tubman, let alone Frederick Douglass" (6). What Stepto calls an "ahistorical world," Carby names a displacement. Carby remarks upon the text's avoidance of the present, while Stepto focuses on its avoidance of the past. But just as Hurston implicitly signifies on then contemporary debates and experiences, so does she signify on African-American history. One can read the fact that Logan Killicks owns not just forty, but sixty acres and a mule not as a historicism, but as an

ironic commentary on the nation's unwillingness to realize its promise to the newly emancipated slaves.

14. Deborah E. McDowell makes a similar point about Hurston's willingness to engage in political dialogue in an essay on *Moses, Man of the Mountain*. In it, McDowell discusses the ways in which the text's symbolism critiques the United States' rhetoric of liberation and reveals its hypocrisy by implicitly juxtaposing the United States' oppression of African Americans with the ideology of racial purity which fueled Germany's entry into a world war in 1939. McDowell concludes, "All too often Hurston's readers have consigned her to Eatonville and left her there on the porch. . . . Even when readers stretch her province to New Orleans and the Caribbean, the sites of her fieldwork, they often read these migrations as extensions of Eatonville, seen as the repository of black folk culture on which all Hurston's work is dependent. But reducing Eatonville and its symbolic geographic coordinates to the repositories of black 'folk' expression that Hurston mined so well regionalizes her work and ensures her removal from a more global context of cultural production and exchange" (240).

WORKS CITED

Bethel, Lorraine . "'The Infinity of Conscious Pain': Zora Neale Hurston and the Black Female Literary Tradition," in *Zora Neale Hurston,* edited by Harold Bloom. New York: Chelsea House Publishers, 1986, pp. 9–17.

Brown, Karen McCarthy. *Mama Lola.* Berkeley: University of California Press, 1991.

Carby, Hazel. "The Politics of Fiction, Anthropology, and the Folk: Zora Neale Hurston," in *New Essays on Their Eyes Were Watching God,* edited by Michael Awkward. New York: Cambridge University Press, 1990, pp. 71–93.

Desmangles, Leslie. *The Faces of the Gods: Vodou and Roman Catholicism in Haiti.* Chapel Hill: University of North Carolina Press, 1992.

DuPlessis, Rachel Blau. "Power, Judgment, and Narrative in a Work of Zora Neale Hurston: Feminist Cultural Studies," in *New Essays on Their Eyes Were Watching God,* edited by Michael Awkward, New York: Cambridge University Press, 1990, pp. 95–123.

Garber, Marjorie. *Vested Interests: Cross-Dressing and Cultural Anxiety.* New York: Routledge, 1992.

Johnson, Barbara and Henry Louis Gates, Jr. "A Black Idiomatic Free Indirect Discourse," in *Zora Neale Hurston,* edited by Harold Bloom. New York: Chelsea House Publishers, 1986, pp. 73–85.

Gilroy, Paul. *The Black Atlantic: Modernity and Double Consciousness.* Cambridge: Harvard University Press, 1993.

Harris, Trudier. *Fiction and Folklore: The Novels of Toni Morrison.* Knoxville: University of Tennessee Press, 1991.

Hemenway, Robert E. *Zora Neale Hurston: A Literary Biography.* Chicago: University of Illinois Press, 1977.

Holloway, Karla. *The Character of the Word: The Texts of Zora Neale Hurston.* New York: Greenwood Press, 1987.

Hurston, Zora Neale. "Spirituals and Neo-Spirituals," in *The Sanctified Church.* Berkeley: Turtle Island, pp. 79–84.

———. *Tell My Horse: Voodoo and Life in Haiti and Jamaica.* New York: Harper & Row, 1938.

———. *Their Eyes Were Watching God.* New York: Harper & Row, 1937.

Locke, Alain. Rev. of *Their Eyes Were Watching God. Opportunity* 1 June, 1938, in *Zora Neale Hurston: Critical Perspectives Past and Present,* edited by Henry Louis Gates, Jr. and K.A. Appiah. New York: Amistad, 1993, p. 18.

———. "The New Negro," in *The New Negro.* New York: Athenaeum, 1992, pp. 3–16.

McDowell, Deborah E. "Lines of Descent/Dissenting Lines," in *Zora Neale Hurston: Critical Perspectives Past and Present,* edited by Henry Louis Gates, Jr., and K.A. Appiah. New York: Amistad, 1993, pp. 230–240.

Mètraux, Alfred. *Voodoo in Haiti.* New York: Schocken Books, 1959.

O'Neill, Eugene. *The Emperor Jones.* New York: Random House, 1921.

Petesch, Donald A. *A Spy in the Enemy's Country: The Emergence of Modern Black Literature.* Iowa City: University of Iowa Press, 1989.

Rampersad, Arnold. Introduction. *The New Negro,* edited by Alain Locke. New York: Athenaeum, 1992, ix–xxiii.

Southerland, Ellease. "The Influence of Voodoo on the Fiction of Zora Neale Hurston," in *Sturdy Black Bridges: Visions of Black Women in Literature,* edited by Roseann P. Bell, et al. New York: Anchor Books, 1979.

Stepto, Robert B. "Ascent, Immersion, Narration," in *Zora Neale Hurston,* edited by Harold Bloom.. New York: Chelsea House Publishers, 1986, pp. 5–7.

Sundquist, Eric. *The Hammers of Creation: Folk Culture in Modern African-American Fiction.* Athens: The University of Georgia Press, 1992.

Thomas, H. Nigel. *From Folklore to Fiction: A Study of Folk Heroes and Rituals in the Black American Novel.* New York: Greenwood Press, 1988.

Thompson, Robert Farris. *Flash of the Spirit: African and Afro-American Art and Philosophy.* New York: Random House, 1983.

Walker, Alice. "Looking for Zora," in *I Love Myself When I Am Laughing . . . And Then Again When I Am Looking Mean and Impressive.* New York: The Feminist Press, 1979.

Washington, Mary Helen. "I Love the Way Janie Crawford Left Her Husbands: Emergent Female Hero," in *Zora Neale Hurston: Critical Perspectives Past and Present,* edited by Henry Louis Gates, Jr. and K.A. Appiah. New York: Amistad, 1993, pp. 98–109.

Wright, Richard. Rev. of *Their Eyes Were Watching God. New Masses* 5 October, 1937, in *Zora Neale Hurston: Critical Perspectives Past and Present,* edited by Henry Louis Gates, Jr. and K.A. Appiah. New York: Amistad, 1993, pp. 16–17.

LAURIE CHAMPION

Socioeconomics in Selected Short Stories of Zora Neale Hurston

Zora Neale Hurston sets most of her work in or near the all-black town of Eatonville, Florida,[1] which she uses to portray lifestyles of rural African Americans by showing folk customs and beliefs, communal attitudes, and voodoo practices.[2] Hurston's choice of Eatonville as setting reflects one of her major artistic philosophies, central to which is her need to celebrate African American culture. As she explains in her well-known essay "How It Feels to Be Colored Me," she realized that she was black when she was thirteen and left Eatonville to attend school in Jacksonville. Even so, she says,

> I am not tragically colored. There is not great sorrow dammed up in my soul, nor lurking behind my eyes. I do not mind at all. I do not belong to the sobbing school of Negrohood who hold that nature somehow has given them a lowdown dirty deal and whose feelings are all hurt about it. Even in the helter-skelter skirmish that is my life, I have seen that the world is to the strong regardless of a little pigmentation more or less. No, I do not weep at the world—I am too busy sharpening my oyster knife. (153)

Hurston's proclamation helps explain why much of the conflict in her works does not stem directly from relations between blacks and whites in the sense

Southern Quarterly: A Journal of the Arts in the South, Volume 40, Number 1 (Fall 2001): pp. 79–92. © 2001 Southern Quarterly/Southern Mississippi.

expressed by protest writers such as Richard Wright and Chester Himes, who use naturalism as a literary mode to expose the ills of racism.

Although critics initially objected to Hurston's works because she failed to take a political stance that focused on the plight of blacks in a racist society, during the 1970s, her works were rediscovered and fresh critical interpretations pointed out social and political concerns she addresses. [3] As these more recent assessments demonstrate, amidst portraits of rural African Americans and celebrations of blackness, Hurston frequently characterizes women who defy traditional western (white) literature and myths that depict consequences for women who step outside gender-biased social roles.[4] The large majority of the criticism focuses on her novels, her folklore studies, and her autobiography, *Dust Tracks on a Road*. However, in addition to her novels and folklore studies, Hurston was also an avid short story writer. Although her short stories were never collected during her lifetime, they originally appeared in distinguished magazines and newspapers and garnered her prestigious awards. In her short stories, as in her other works, Hurston depicts strong women who develop independence in spite of oppressive social conditions, particularly those influenced by a politics of gender-and ethnic-biased economics.[5] Hurston's characterizations of women defy traditional ideology that encourages women to remain oppressed, especially in terms of their economic status.

One of the sketches in *The Complete Stories of Zora Neale Hurston*, "The Eatonville Anthology," gives a brief overview of the characters, lifestyles, and tone used throughout the collection of sketches and short stories. Representing folktales and customs of the Eatonville community, "The Eatonville Anthology" fictionally reveals what Hurston reports from a nonfictional perspective in "My Birthplace," chapter 1 of her autobiography, *Dust Tracks on a Road:*

> So you will have to know something about the time and place where I came from, in order that you may interpret the incidents and directions of my life.
>
> I was born in a Negro town. I do not mean by that the black back-side of an average town. Eatonville, Florida, is, and was at the time of my birth, a pure Negro town—charter, mayor, council, town marshal and all. It was not the first Negro community in America, but it was the first to be incorporated, the first attempt at organized self-government on the part of Negroes in America (11).

In "The Eatonville Anthology," Hurston gives condensed versions and variations of tales told fully in other stories and introduces characters who reappear throughout her stories and in some of her other works. As Robert

E. Hemenway notes, "'The Eatonville Anthology' is the literary equivalent of Hurston's memorable performances at parties. The reader has the impression of sitting in a corner listening to anecdotes" (69). The sketch presents "pure Zora Neale Hurston: part fiction, part folklore, part biography, all told with great economy, an eye for authentic detail, and a perfect ear for dialect" (70).

As presented in *The Complete Stories*, "The Eatonville Anthology" provides a survey of themes and subjects and develops unity for all the stories and tales set in Eatonville. It becomes a sort of guide for reading the other stories in ways similar to the description of Eatonville in Hurston's autobiography. Most importantly, "The Eatonville Anthology" describes Eatonville as setting. Geographically, Eatonville sits next to Winter Park, an all-white city where upper-class northerners reside during the winter season. Many of the members of the Eatonville community work for the wealthy whites in Winter Park; thus, the "twin cities," represent opposing degrees of wealth, ultimate economic disparity, and establish, as Kathryn Lee Seidel points out, "an economics of slavery" (172).

Implied in "The Eatonville Anthology," one form of oppression Hurston demonstrates throughout the stories and tales set in Eatonville is the lack of economic opportunities for African Americans. Economic exploitation of underprivileged African Americans is apparent in "Drenched in Light," "The Gilded Six-Bits," "Sweat," and "Black Death," stories that also demonstrate gender-biased exploitation and oppression. "Drenched in Light" presents a young female protagonist whose oppression is based on gender, class, and ethnicity. Isis Watts lives with her maternal grandmother, who tries to teach her to act like a lady: "Grandma Potts felt no one of this female persuasion should . . . sit with the knees separated, 'settin' brazen' she called it; another was whistling, another playing with boys, neither must a lady cross her legs" (19). Also, as "the only girl in the family, of course she must wash the dishes" (19). Obviously, Isis is the victim of socially prescribed codes of conduct for females that force her to perform duties traditionally considered women's work. Isis violates these rules, for she sneaks a ride on a horse and whistles in defiance when Grandma Potts scolds her. However, just as Grandma Potts jumps to get a switch to spank her, her father comes home "and this excused the child from sitting for criticism" (19).

While "Drenched in Light" reveals feminist concerns, it also exposes problems created by an unequal distribution of wealth. The white lady who encounters Isis's grandmother wants to spare Isis a spanking so she asks, "You're not going to whip this poor little thing, are you?" (24). At first, the grandmother defends herself, explaining that Isis has ruined a tablecloth she cannot afford to replace. The white lady gives her a five dollar bill, says "the little thing loves laughter" (25), and asks whether Isis can accompany her to the hotel. Isis's grandmother agrees, telling her to behave herself while she is with the "white folks" (25). Significantly, Grandma Potts instructs Isis with "pride in her voice, though she strove to hide it" (25). Although her grandmother appears "proud" of her because the white lady deems her endearing, when readers consider the implied message concerning unequal distribution of wealth based on ethnicity, her "pride" demonstrates that in order to receive the five dollars, the grandmother must forgo authority and withhold from Isis retribution she strongly believes she deserves. No doubt Grandma Potts notices the condescending tone the white woman uses when she invites Isis to her hotel. She refers to her as a "little *thing*" and questions the grandmother's concern for Isis. Whether or not readers share the grandmother's notions of retribution, the more sonorous point is that Grandma Potts is both judged harshly for her treatment of Isis and forced because of economic need to act in a manner inconsistent with her convictions.

At the expense of her grandmother's authority, the white couple pay Isis to dance for them. Because of economic necessity, Grandma Potts allows Isis to accompany the white couple. Seeming never to revoke the punishments she imposes upon Isis, the grandmother must now relinquish her authority. Grandma Potts deems it inappropriate for Isis to use the tablecloth to dance in the parade watched by blacks, who do not pay Isis; but she judges it appropriate for her to use it to dance for whites, who do pay her. Obviously, the determining factor for whether Isis is allowed to frolic is economics. Hurston exposes the unequal distribution of wealth by illustrating opposing degrees of economic privilege: the Pottses can barely afford a tablecloth, but the white couple drives a Packard.

The title of the story, a phrase the white lady attributes to Isis, is ambiguous. "Drenched" has negative connotations, as though flooded, a term that might very well describe the white lady's generosity toward Isis's grandmother. Using the term "drenched," Hurston implies that the money that privileged whites offer to economically disadvantaged blacks is "drenched" in provisions and stipulations. The set-up of the final scene exposes the economic system that obviously privileges whites: a white couple rides in a luxury car, and a white lady condescends to a black woman and offers money in exchange for control of her granddaughter. Significantly, the white woman is concerned with saving Isis from what she perceives is her grandmother's anger, not with watching her dance; thus, she is not paying to be entertained but to usurp the grandmother's authority and to reinforce her own power and status.

Both when Isis's father returns and the white woman manipulates Grandma Potts, Isis escapes retribution. While in the first instance Isis is spared with no consequence to anyone, in the second instance Grandma Potts sacrifices her domestic authority in order for Isis to be absolved: in other words, when the economically advantaged whites play a role in Isis's triumph, it is a pyrrhic victory for the grandmother. While the white man and woman usurp the grandmother's power, "they represent for Isis a critical opportunity for power and freedom" (Meisenhelder 7). Noting the significance of the white man telling his wife that she has been adopted by Isis (rather than implying that the couple has adopted Isis), Susan Meisenhelder says that Isis usurps the white couple's "power for her own purposes and exercises subtle control" (7). In Isis's situation, the story supports strong girls who will no doubt develop into women who refuse to adapt to sexist or racist stereotypes, but in Grandma Potts's situation, it criticizes a social system wherein justice becomes a commodity purchased by privileged whites at the expense of underprivileged blacks.

While "Drenched in Light" shows the plight of the economically disadvantaged in terms of hierarchies based on ethnicity, "The Gilded Six-Bits" points out problems of unequal distribution of wealth within the larger black community. The story reveals a young couple whose happy marriage is threatened when the newcomer Otis Slemmons moves to Eatonville and flaunts pretentious wealth. Unaware until near the end of the story that the gold Otis flashes is fake, Missie May and Joe believe that Otis is wealthy. While Joe feels inferior to what he perceives as a wealthy man, Missie May eventually is charmed by Otis's apparent wealth.

Joe describes Otis, who has moved from Chicago to open an ice cream parlor in Eatonville, to Missie May. He tells her about his economic status, but Missie May tells Joe that she is "satisfied wid [him] jes lak [he] is" (90). Joe feels the need to compete with Otis, but because he knows he cannot compete with him financially, he desires to triumph by "possessing" a pretty wife. He says he wants to take Missie May to the ice cream parlor because Otis "talkin' 'bout his pritty womens—Ah want 'im to see *mine*" (91). After Joe takes Missie May to the ice cream parlor to meet Otis, she tells him that she noticed the "heap uh gold on 'im" and says it would "look a whole heap better on [Joe]" (91). Joe's only response is to ask, "Where would a po' man lak me git gold money from?" (91). Later, the narrator says, "It was Saturday night once more before Joe could parade his wife in Slemmons' ice cream parlor again" (92). After their first visit to the ice cream parlor, Joe reminds Missie May of both Otis's wealth and his own poverty and says, "Ah'm satisfied de way Ah is. So long as Ah be yo' husband, Ah don't keer 'bout nothin' else" (91). Before Missie May's introduction to Otis, she claims to be satisfied: afterwards, Joe makes such claims. Ironically, instead of elevating his self-esteem by showing Otis his "pretty" wife, Joe may feel further threatened because Missie May admits that this is the first time she has seen gold and that she hopes to find some while walking home.

Particularly interesting about "The Gilded Six-Bits"'s treatment of gender is its implication that men might purchase women who remain at home engaged in unpaid labor. The insult Joe gives Otis when he discovers him in bed with Missie May implies that Otis is in bed with Missie May because his wealth entitles him such privilege. Joe insults not Otis's character but his economic status: "Git into yo' damn rags, Slemmons" (93), he says, as contrasted to his earlier assessment that Otis "got de finest clothes Ah ever seen on a colored man's back" (89). Likewise, Missie May's defense for having slept with Otis is that he had promised her gold money. After Missie May and Joe have sex, Joe puts under her pillow the half-dollar Otis had given Missie May to suggest "he could pay as well as Slemmons" (96). Upon realizing that Joe is not coming home, Missie May sees no need to sweep the porch, cook breakfast, or wash and starch, chores performed "for Joe" (94). If not to engage in these duties, she asks, "why get up?" (94). In both of Joe's assumptions—that he is superior to Otis because his own wife is pretty and that women are drawn to Otis because he appears wealthy—empowerment is based on the exploitation of women. One notion suggests that a pretty wife is to be owned and "paraded" like a trophy to exhibit male status; the other implies that women desire men who can provide for them financially, a notion that assumes women are willing to sell themselves.

"The Gilded Six-Bits" criticizes both middle-class values and oppressive gender roles. As its title suggests, the story concerns deceptions of wealth. Even the physical descriptions of the setting allude to economics: "physical borders of a yard, the economic borders of a laborer's payroll, and the conceptual borders of a limited way of life" (Baum 102). Missie May's attraction to a man who might provide her with more financial security than Joe demonstrates that economics plays a role in female sexuality, an idea based on ideologies that deny women sexual pleasure. It is important to note that while Otis appears to be wealthy, Joe and Missie May are not poverty stricken, for "they had money put away. They ought to be making little feet for shoes" instead of finding shoes for a child (92). Hurston does not establish diametrically opposed dualisms, which would juxtapose Slemmons's wealth against the Banks's poverty. However, she does imply that even if Otis's gold was genuine, he would represent middle-class values which do not offer social progress in terms of the larger groups of African Americans or women. As Chinn and Dunn point out, "Through Slemmons [Hurston] criticizes the white urban, materialistic values as a whole" (779). Hurston shows that like the gold that turns out to be fake, striving for gold (whether real or not) is a fallacy counterproductive to progress toward ethnic and gender equality. Striving for material wealth also has historical implications in the story. John Lowe notes that the image of the fake gold piece next to the broken chain that Joe pulls from Otis represents "the link between historical slavery and the ideology of consumerism" (77).

Rather than depicting an adulterous woman who suffers severe consequences to affirm social agendas that instruct women to remain monogamous, Hurston's story does not center on Missie May's infidelity. Instead,

Hurston shows that economic disadvantage and adherence to middle-class values exploit Missie May's sexuality. Upon learning that Missie May has given birth to his son, Joe spends Otis's gilded half-dollar on candy for her: the product of her sexual encounter with Otis is used to purchase the symbol of Joe's reunion with Missie May. When he returns home at the end of the story, Joe leaves fifteen coins instead of the nine left at the beginning of the story; the game, he suggests, is now to be played on a higher level, one that involves competing economically for Missie May's affection. Far from taking a nonpolitical stance, "The Gilded Six-Bits" demonstrates that economics regulates Missie May's sexuality. Hurston shows Missie May as victim of a capitalistic economic structure that exploits women, who become commodities for empowered men.

Even more than "The Gilded Six-Bits," "Sweat" exposes gender oppression by revealing the plight of women in a sexist society. The protagonist, Delia, works long hours washing laundry for white customers, whose economic privilege is contrasted with Delia's economic status: not only can she not afford to hire someone to wash her laundry, but she must also wash wealthy people's laundry to provide for herself. While the story demonstrates the disparity of wealth between the wealthy Winter Park whites and the poor Eatonville blacks, the main plot of the story does not center on this form of economic exploitation, but rather upon how Delia's husband, Sykes, exploits her. Ironically, throughout the course of the story, sweat signifies Delia's exploited labor and Sykes's poisoned mental state that ultimately leads to the physical poisoning that kills him. Additionally, "Sweat" exposes gender oppression and economic exploitation by suggesting that "what goes around comes around" (Hurd 7).[5]

The story opens with a technical description of Delia's labor that reveals that she works long hours every day of the week. Early on, the narrative establishes that Sykes both physically and mentally torments Delia. Scolding him for scaring her by sliding across her knee a bullwhip that she thinks is a snake, Delia says she may die from his foolishness. More interestingly, she asks him, "where you been wid mah rig? Ah feeds dat pony" (74), informing him that the pony belongs to her and that she pays for its upkeep. He responds by reminding her that he has told her repeatedly "to keep them white folks' clothes outa dis house" and by claiming that she should not "wash white folks clothes on the Sabbath" (74). Although the argument begins with a physical scare, it soon turns to a quarrel about economics. After scolding him for scaring her, Delia reminds him that she owns the pony, the means by which Sykes leaves the house. His rebuke reveals his resentment that Delia owns the material goods he wishes to use to entice Bertha to remain his girlfriend. He promises to give Bertha the house as soon as he "kin git dat 'oman outa dere" (79). Sykes pays Bertha's rent and spends money to take her to Winter Park for dates. He promises her that he will give her whatever she wants: "Dis is *mah* town an' you sho' kin have it" (79). Significantly, when Delia sees Sykes with Bertha, he is at the store purchasing groceries for her and telling her to "git whutsoever yo' heart desires" (79). Not only does Sykes spend Delia's money on Bertha, he wants to give Delia's other possessions to her.

Delia develops from a meek woman who acquiesces to Sykes's abuse to one who defends herself both verbally and physically. Although Delia has suffered abuse from Sykes for fifteen years, she has yet to refute him. However, during this particular argument that has turned to economics, her "habitual meekness . . . slip[s]" (75), and she responds to Sykes's verbal abuse with the assertion that she has been washing clothes and sweating for fifteen years to feed him and to pay for her house. Later, when he refuses to remove the snake from the house, she says, "Ah hates you, Sykes . . . Ah hates you tuh de same degree dat Ah useter love yuh. Ah done took an' took till mah belly is full up tuh mah neck" (81). Significantly, she ends her argument by saying, "Lay 'roun' wid dat 'oman al yuh wants tuh, but gwan 'way fum me an' *mah house*" (82, emphasis added). Although the story involves a love triangle, the more important conflict is the battle between Sykes and Delia for possession of the house. Delia is much more concerned with protecting her property than she is with redeeming her marriage.

Hoping that Sykes will receive retribution for abusing her, a week before he dies, she says, "Whatever goes over the Devil's back, is got to come under his belly. Sometime or ruther. Sykes, like everybody else, is gointer reap his sowing" (76). Also, announcing that she refuses to leave her house, Delia threatens to report Sykes to the white people. Apparently, this threat scares him, for the next day he puts the snake in Delia's laundry basket. However, Delia does not depend on the "law" for justice. She seems to agree with the Eatonville community, which acknowledges both that there "oughter be a law about" Sykes and that "taint no law on earth dat kin make a man be decent if it aint in 'im" (77). Depending on forces above the law, Delia allows Sykes's retribution to come to him "naturally." Unlike the conjure that renders poetic justice in many of Hurston's works, Sykes's own action renders justice in "Sweat": the very snake he intends to bite Delia bites him instead.

Sykes's self-inflicted poisoning brings about poetic justice, as he is the victim of his attempt to kill Delia and thus gain possession of the house; but the sweat that comes from Delia's exploited labor is not self-inflicted: it is inflicted upon her by a vile social system that privileges wealthy whites. This vile social system also, to be sure, victimizes Sykes. As Lillie P. Howard points out, Sykes clearly is Delia's antagonist, but part of the reason he resents her is "because her work makes him feel like less than a man. He resents her working for the white folks, washing their dirty laundry, but he does not resent it enough to remove the need for her to do so" (67). Similarly, Lowe argues that although readers empathize with Delia, "the emasculation of the black man by a racist, capitalist society is on Hurston's mind too . . . " (74).

Critics argue whether or not Delia's refusal to help Sykes after the snake has bitten him exemplifies her spiritual downfall. Lowe says, "Delia's Christian righteousness, evident in the scene when she returns from a 'Love Feast' at church, also seems challenged by her failure to seek help for Sykes after he has been bitten by the snake at the end of the story and by her deliberate showing herself to him so he will know she knows what he attempted and that there is no hope for him" (74). Cheryl A. Wall says, "Delia makes no effort to warn, rescue, or even comfort [Sykes]. She exacts her revenge but at a terrible spiritual cost . . . The narrator does not pass judgment. Yet, how will Delia, good Christian though she has tried to be, ever cross Jordan in a calm time?" ("*Sweat*" pp. 12–13). Contrary to Wall and Lowe, Myles Hurd argues, "Because Hurston exerts quite a bit of creative energy in outlining Sykes's outrageous behavior and in subsequently punishing him for his misdeeds, Delia's virtue is too often easily overshadowed by his villainy." (13). Hurd suggests that because Sykes is a "more dramatically compelling" character than Delia, some "readers overeagerly expect Delia to counter his evil, rather than allow herself to be repeatedly buffeted by it" (14). When readers consider that the sweat, or poison, eventually seeps out of Delia's body, the title of the story suggests that she is not spiritually corrupt. Similar to the poison that kills Sykes, Delia's sweat represents both literal bodily toxins and symbolic poisons that represent the social system that has caused her to sweat. Sykes is possessed by an evil that consumes his soul and eventually kills him; however, Delia remains pure because the sweat, the toxin or poison that represents the social system that exploits her, is released from her body and does not corrupt her physically or spiritually.

In an interesting twist that parallels the snake that bites Sykes instead of Delia, at the end of the story, "the man who has loomed above her through the years now crawls toward her, his fallen state emphasized by the frame of the door and Delia's standing figure; the man who has treated her with continuous contempt and cruelty now hopes for help from her" (Baum 101). At the end of the story, Delia notices Sykes looking to her with hope; however, she also realizes that the same eye that looks to her for help cannot "fail to see the tubs" as well (85). As he lies dying, he is forced to look at the tubs, the tools of Delia's exploited labor. It is significant that while he is in the process of dying from self-inflicted poison, Sykes is forced to observe the tubs, the source of Delia's sweat, symbolizing the poisoned social system. Perhaps the tubs represent for Sykes the very property he had hoped to acquire by killing her because he is reminded of the labor Delia has exchanged for the property. Earlier, in his attempt to kill her and thus gain possession of the house, Sykes places the snake in the laundry basket, another emblem of Delia's exploited labor. Sykes's use of a tool of Delia's labor as a tool for his effort to acquire her property reminds readers that only through intense sweat, exploited labor, has Delia been able to buy a house for herself. However, Delia is determined not to allow Sykes to take possession of the house. In addition to releasing her from his emotional and physical abuse, Sykes's death releases the threat that Delia's house will be taken away from her.

The title "Sweat" refers both to Delia's hard work necessary to survive eco-nomically in a society that offers limited employment opportunities to African American women and to the emotional and physical agony Sykes's abuse causes her. As David Headon acknowledges, the story "forcefully establishes an integral part of the political agenda of black literature of this century ... [Hurston] places at the foreground feminist questions concerning the exploitation, intimidation, and oppression inherent in so many relations" (32). Breaking from literature that so often perpetuates stereotypical roles for women, "'Sweat' is in fact, protest literature" (32). Hurston simultaneously discourages those who try to reinforce sexist modes of oppression and encourages women to defy sexism by illustrating how those who abuse women are doomed.

Hurston demonstrates a similar type of damnation for men who abuse women in "Black Death," a variation of the same tale told in "Uncle Monday." "Black Death" reveals the Eatonville hoodoo man Old Man Morgan, whom Mrs. Boger seeks because Beau Diddely impregnated and refused to marry her daughter, Docia. When Mrs. Boger and Docia approach Beau about Docia's fate, he denies that Docia is pregnant: "Don't try to lie on *me*—I got money to fight ... You're lying—you sneaking little—oh you're not even good sawdust! Me marry you! Why I could pick up a better woman out of the gutter than you! I'm a married man anyway ..." (204). His claim that he is married stuns Docia; she asks him to explain, and he says, "What difference does it make? A man will say anything at times. There are certain kinds of women that men always lie to" (pp. 204–205). Beau's argument is packed with references to economic status. He says that he has the money to fight, a reminder that the legal system privileges wealth. Also, his attacks against Docia are based on class: he compares her with sawdust and says a woman found in the gutter is better than Docia.

Shocked at Beau's behavior, Docia reminds him that he promised to marry her, to which he responds, "Oh well, you ought not to have believed me—you ought to have known I didn't mean it" (205). Denying any respon-sibility whatsoever, Beau instead places blame on Docia. Instead of acknowl-edging that certain types of men lie, he reverses responsibility and says that specific types of women are lied to. He also argues that it is okay for him to lie to her, but naive of her to believe him.

Witnessing her daughter's heartache makes Mrs. Boger realize that "the world's greatest crime is not murder—its most terrible punishment is meted to her of too much faith—too great a love" (206). Her daughter's suffering also prompts Mrs. Boger to transform from woman to "cold stone ... tiger, a *female* tiger," one that seeks revenge for her daughter's suffering (206, emphasis added). Mrs. Boger visits Old Man Morgan, who already knows what she seeks; upon answering the door he asks, "How do yuh wants kill 'im? By water, by sharp edge, or a bullet?" (206). Old Man Morgan instructs Mrs. Boger to shoot the mirror when Beau's reflection appears. It is important to note that Mrs. Boger pays for Beau's death. After realizing that Beau has "robbed [Docia] of *everything*" (206), she visits Morgan, who has long ago "sold himself to the devil" (203). After she shoots the mirror, she "[flings] her money at the old man who seize[s] it greedily" (207). References to capital used in descriptions of Beau's crime against Docia and Mrs. Boger's revenge reveal that economics is as much a factor in Beau's death as hoodoo.

Economics is not the only factor in Beau's death: instead of depending on a white legal system to render justice, Mrs. Boger seeks conjure, which is practiced frequently in Eatonville. "Black Death" demonstrates that conjure is a much more reliable source of justice than the white legal system. In this regard, "Black Death" is similar to "The Bone of Contention," another one of Hurston's humorous stories. In "The Bone of Contention," a character says, "Never mind bout dem white folks laws at O'landa, Brother Long. Dis is a colored town" (218). Both "The Bone of Contention" and "Black Death" suggest that Eatonville refuses to conform to laws created by whites that maintain the political interests of the empowered. Moreover, the title "Black Death" alludes to the African American justice system practiced in Eatonville: "black" refers both to the darkness of death and to the black as opposed to the white system of justice. The story blatantly contrasts black and white customs, including methods of justice. It begins, "The Negroes in Eatonville know a number of things that the hustling, bustling white man never dreams of. He is materialist with little ears for overtones" (202). While the white coroner's "verdict" is that Beau died "from natural causes" (207), "the Negroes knew instantly" that Beau's death was the result of hoodoo and "agreed that he got justice" (208).

Docia feels mortified that Beau has spread ugly rumors about her throughout Eatonville; but after his death, Beau, whose name has romantic connotations—he is "the darling of the ladies" (207)—is now the one about whom Eatonville gossips. At the end of the story Eatonville gossips about how Beau died while wooing a woman. While chanting the "Conquest of Docia" that boasts how Docia loved and pursued him, he dies from what appears as "heart failure" (207), an appropriate punishment for breaking Docia's heart. More significantly, Hurston reveals that the black community gives retribution for sexist attitudes through its own means of justice. Although Mrs. Boger claims that the victim of unrequited love suffers more than the victim of murder, readers understand that Beau suffers much more permanently than Docia.

"Black Death" is but one example of the short stories in which Hurston reveals folklore, and hoodoo is but one of the many depictions of the cultural practices, social customs, and spiritual beliefs throughout her works. About her desire to explore experiences of rural African Americans, Hurston says,

> I was glad when somebody told me, "You may go and collect Negro-folk-lore." In a way it would not be a new experience for me. When I pitched headforemost into the world I landed in the crib of negroism. From the earliest rocking of my cradle, I had known about the capers Brer Rabbit is apt to cut and what the Squinch Owl says from the house top. But it was fitting me like a tight chemise. I couldn't see it for wearing it. It was only when I was off in college, away from my native surroundings, that I could see myself and stand off and look at my garment. Then I had to have the spy-glass of Anthropology to look through at that. (*Mules* 3)

Amidst depictions of rural African Americans, Hurston confronts issues such as the plight of women in a sexist society and the problems that surface because of unequal distribution of wealth. As these stories imply, sometimes gender and class compound to make it even more difficult to overcome obstacles. Moreover, Hurston demonstrates that oppression based on ethnicity blends with that based on gender and class, magnifying even further the difficulties of black women who are poor.[7] Whether exploited according to one or more of these social structures, Hurston depicts strong women who challenge oppression. Representative of the folklore embraced in her writing, Hurston's works also reveal that those who perpetuate these forms of oppression become the victims of their own crimes. By celebrating African American women who defy traditional norms that reinforce stereotypes and by condemning the empowered who support such stereotypes, Hurston encourages disruption of social forces that oppress African Americans, women, and the economically underprivileged.

NOTES

1. For the significance of Eatonville as setting, see Lillios.
2. Whether in broader topics or as the focus of their discussions, almost all critics allude to Hurston's portrayal of African American folklore. The following essays reflect their topics: Southerland, Stein, Faulkner, Jacobs, Kalb, and Speis-

man. Klaus Benesch looks at Hurston's use of black English and sees Janie's major conflict as her search for her African American cultural heritage. Mary O'Connor credits Hurston with establishing for women an African American literary tradition wherein talking is a tool used to blend race and gender.

3. For example, in 1974, June Jordan noted that "Wright's Native Son is widely recognized as the prototypical black protest novel. By comparison, Hurston's novel, *Their Eyes Were Watching God,* seems to suit, perfectly, the obvious connotations of Black affirmation"; she adds, however, the two traditions are not mutually exclusive: "affirmation of Black values and lifestyle within the American context is, indeed, an act of protest" (5). Similarly Alice Walker notes, "Black writing has suffered, because even black critics have assumed that a book that deals with the relationship between members of a black family—or between a man and a woman—is less important than one that has white people as a primary antagonist" (202). In 1974, S. J. Walker observed, "*Their Eyes Were Watching God* deals far more extensively with sexism, the struggle of a woman to be regarded as a person in a male-dominated society, than racism, the struggle of blacks to be regarded as persons in a white-dominated society" (520). As Pam Bordelon's 1997 title, "New Tacks on Dust Tracks: Toward a Reassessment of the Life of Zora Neale Hurston," suggests, critics continue to look for new ways to examine Hurston's works.

4. In her discussion of Hurston's autobiography and *Their Eyes Were Watching God,* Kathleen Davies alludes to the concept of a "poetics of embalmment," wherein female narrators employ "signifyin" to testify about ways they are oppressed by men and ways men are punished for such oppression.

5. From feminist perspectives, many scholars examine Hurston's women characters and look at the social issues in Hurston's works that concern women. Lorraine Bethel points out that throughout her works Hurston disrupts stereotypes of African American women portrayed by white males. Missy Dehn Kubitschek argues that Hurston's portrayal of strong and courageous black women inspired future black women writers to depict nonstereotypical black women characters. Mary Helen Washington sees Janie as a leader in her community and as a developing hero.

Similarly, Gay Wilentz suggests that Janie is one of the earliest African American women characters to develop cultural and personal identity. Cheryl Wall ("Mules and Men") and Claire Crabtree view Hurston as anthropologist/folklorist and suggest feminist issues in Hurston's works. Pearlie M. Peters examines feminist aspects of oral discourse in Hurston's works. Many scholars examine Hurston as a female autobiographer: Krasner, Fox-Genovese, Lionnet, and McKay, for example.

6. See "Sweat," edited by Cheryl A. Wall, for excellent background information and interpretations of "Sweat"; Myles Hurd makes astute observations about poetic justice in "Sweat": because Sykes justly is punished for his "outrageous behavior . . . Delia's virtue is too often easily overshadowed by his villainy" (13).

7. As Deborah K. King points out, "The triple jeopardy of racism, sexism, and classism is now widely accepted and used as the conceptualization of black women's studies" (46). However, she notes that the relationship between the three factors is more than a simple equation that adds racism, sexism, and classism. She coins the term "multiple jeopardy" to denote not only "simultaneous oppressions"

but also "the multiplicative relationships among them as well. In other words, the equivalent formulation is racism multiplied by sexism multiplied by classism" (47).

WORKS CITED

Baum, Rosalie Murphy. "The Shape of Hurston's Fiction," in *Zora in Florida*, edited by Steve Glassman and Kathryn Lee Seidel. Orlando: University of Central Florida Press, pp. 194–209.

Benesch, Klaus. "Oral Narrative and Literary Text: Afro-American Folklore in *Their Eyes Were Watching God*." *Callaloo*, 11 (1988): 627–635.

Bethel, Lorraine. "'This Infinity of Conscious Pain': Zora Neale Hurston and the Black Female Literary Tradition," in *All the Women Are White, All the Blacks Are Men, But Some of Us Are Brave: Black Women's Studies*, edited by Gloria T. Hull, Patricia Bell Scott, and Barbara Scott. Old Westbury, N.Y.: Feminist Press, pp. 176–188.

Bordelon, Pam. "New Tacks on Dust Tracks: Toward a Reassessment of the Life of Zora Neale Hurston," *African American Review*, 31 (1997): 5–21.

Chinn, Nancy, and Elizabeth E. Dunn. "'The Ring of Singing Metal on Wood': Zora Neale Hurston's Artistry in 'The Gilded Sixbits,'" *Mississippi Quarterly*, 49 (1996): 775–790.

Crabtree, Claire. "The Confluence of Folklore, Feminism and Black Self-Determination in Zora Neale Hurston's *Their Eyes Were Watching God*," *Southern Literary Journal*, 17.2 (1985): 54–66.

Davies, Kathleen. "Zora Neale Hurston's Poetics of Embalmment: Articulating the Rage of Black Women and Narrative Self-Defense," *African American Review*, 26 (1992): 147–159.

Faulkner, Howard J. "*Mules and Men:* Fiction As Folklore," *CLA Journal*, 34 (1991): 331–339.

Fox-Genovese, Elizabeth. "My Statue, My Self: Autobiographical Writings of Afro-American Women" in *Reading Black, Reading Feminist: A Critical Anthology*, edited by Henry Louis Gates Jr. New York: Meridian, 1990, pp. 176–203.

Gates. *Reading Black, Reading Feminist: A Critical Anthology*. New York: Meridian, 1990.

Glassman and Seidel, eds. *Zora in Florida*. Orlando: University of Central Florida Press, 1991.

Headon, David. "'Beginning to See Things Really': The Politics of Zora Neale Hurston," Glassman and Seidel 28–37.

Hemenway, Robert E. *Zora Neale Hurston: A Literary Biography*. Urbana: University of Illinois Press, 1978.

Howard, Lillie P. *Zora Neale Hurston*. Boston: Twayne, 1980.

Hurd, Myles Raymond. "What Goes Around Comes Around: Characterization, Climax, and Closure in Hurston's 'Sweat.'" *Langston Hughes Review*, 12,2 (1993): 7–15.

Hurston, Zora Neale. *The Complete Stories of Zora Neale Hurston*, edited by Gates and Sieglinde Lemke. New York: Harper, 1995.

———. *Dust Tracks on a Road: An Autobiography*. Philadelphia: Lippincott, 1942.

———. "How It Feels to Be Colored Me," in *I Love Myself When I Am Laughing . . . And Then Again When I Am Looking Mean and Impressive: A Zora Neale Hurston Reader*, edited by Alice Walker. Old Westbury, N.Y.: Feminist Press, 1979, pp. 152–156.

———. *Mules and Men*. Philadelphia: Lippincott. 1935.

Jacobs, Karen. "From 'Spy-Glass' to 'Horizon': Tracking the Anthropological Gaze in Zora Neale Hurston," *Novel*, 30 (1997): 329–360.

Jordan, June. "On Richard Wright and Zora Neale Hurston," *Black World*, 23 (1974): 4–8.

Kalb, John D. "The Anthropological Narrator of Hurston's *Their Eyes Were Watching God*," *Studies in American Fiction*, 16 (1988): 169–180.

King, Deborah K. "Multiple Jeopardy, Multiple Consciousness: The Context of a Black Feminist Ideology," *Signs: Journal of Women in Culture and Society*, 14,1 (1988): 42–72.

Krasner, James N. "The Life of Women: Zora Neale Hurston and Female Autobiography," *Black American Literature Forum*, 23 (1989): 113–126.

Kubitschek, Missy Dehn. "'Tuh De Horizon and Back': The Female Quest in *Their Eyes Were Watching God*," *Black American Literature Forum*, 17 (1983): 109–115.

Lillios, Anna. "Excursions into Zora Neale Hurston's Eatonville," in *Zora in Florida*, edited by Glassman and Seidel. Orlando: University of Central Florida Press, 13–27.

Lionnet, Francoise. "Autoethnography: The An-Archic Style of Dust Tracks on a Road," edited by Gates. New York: Meridian, 1990, pp. 382–414.

Lowe, John. *Jump at the Sun: Zora Neale Hurston's Cosmic Comedy*. Urbana: University of Illinois Press, 1994.

McKay, Nellie Y. "Race, Gender, and Cultural Context in Zora Neale Hurston's *Dust Tracks on a Road*," in *Life/Lines: Theorizing Women's Autobiography*, edited by Bella Brodski and Celeste M. Schenck. Ithaca: Cornell University Press, 1988, pp. 175–188.

Meisenhelder, Susan Edwards. *Hitting a Straight Lick with a Crooked Stick: Race and Gender in the Work of Zora Neale Hurston*. Tuscaloosa: University of Alabama Press, 1999.

O'Connor, Mary. "Zora Neale Hurston and Talking Between Cultures," *Canadian Review of American Studies*, Special Issue, Part 1 (1992): 141–161.

Peters, Pearlie M. "'Ah Got the Law in My Mouth': Black Women and Assertive Voice in Hurston's Fiction and Folklore," *CLA Journal*, 37 (1994): 293–302.

Seidel. "The Artist in the Kitchen: The Economics of Creativity in Hurston's 'Sweat,'" Wall., *"Sweat"* 169–81.

Southerland, Ellease. "The Influence of Voodoo on the Fiction of Zora Neale Hurston," in *Sturdy Black Bridge: Visions of Black Women in Literature*, edited by Roseann P. Bell, Bettye J. Parker, and Beverly Guy-Sheftall. Garden City, N.J.: Anchor, 1979, pp. 172–183.

Speisman, Barbara. "Voodoo As Symbol in *Jonah's Gourd Vine*," edited by Glassman and Seidel. Orlando: University of Central Florida Press, pp. 86–93.

Stein, Rachel. "Remembering the Sacred Tree: Black Women, Nature, and Voodoo in Zora Neale Hurston's *Tell My Horse* and *Their Eyes Were Watching God*," *Women's Studies*, 25 (1996): 465–482.

Walker, Alice. "Alice Walker," in *Interviews With Black Writers*, edited by John O'Brien. New York: Liveright, 1973, pp. 184–211.

Walker, S. Jay. "Zora Neale Hurston's *Their Eyes Were Watching God*: Black Novel of Sexism." *Modern Fiction Studies*, 20 (1974–75): 519–527.

Wall, Cheryl A. "*Mules and Men* and Women: Zora Neale Hurston's Strategies of Narration and Visions of Female Empowerment," *Black American Literature Forum*, 23 (1989): 661–680.

————, ed. *"Sweat": Zora Neale Hurston*. New Brunswick: Rutgers University Press, 1997.

Washington, Mary Helen. "'I Love the Way Janie Crawford Left Her Husbands': Zora Neale Hurston's Emergent Female Hero," in *Invented Lives: Narratives of Black Women, 1886–1960*. New York: Doubleday, 1987, pp. 237–254.

Wilentz, Gay. "Defeating the False God: Janie's Self-Determination in Zora Neale Hurston's *Their Eyes Were Watching God. Faith of a (Woman) Writer*" edited by Alice Kessler-Harris and William McBrien. Westport, C.T.: Greenwood Press, 1988, pp. 285–291.

DEBORAH CLARKE

"The porch couldn't talk for looking": Voice and Vision in
Their Eyes Were Watching God

"So 'tain't no use in me telling you somethin' unless Ah give you de understandin' to go 'long wid it. Unless you see de fur, a mink skin ain't no different from a coon hide." (Hurston, *Their Eyes* 7)

W hen Janie explains to her friend Pheoby the reason that simply telling her story will not suffice, why she needs to provide the "'understandin' to go 'long wid it,'" she employs a metaphor of vision: Unless you *see* the fur, you can't tell a mink from a coon. Stripped of their defining visual characteristics, the hides collapse into sameness. Recognizing visual difference, Hurston suggests, is crucial to understanding how identity is constructed: by skin and color. With this claim, she invokes new avenues into an African American tradition that has privileged voice as its empowering trope. From Phillis Wheatley's demonstration that an African can have a poetic voice, to Frederick Douglass's realization that freedom is measured by words and the ability to address a white audience, to Charles Chesnutt's presentation of the triumph of black storytelling in *The Conjure Woman*, voice has prevailed as the primary medium through which African American writers have asserted identity and humanity. Voice announced that visual difference was only skin deep, that black bodies housed souls that were, in essence, no different from those residing in white bodies. *Their Eyes Were Watching God* is very much a part of this tradition, and has inspired many fine studies on

African American Review, Volume 35, Number 4 (Winter 2001): pp. 599–613. © 2001 Deborah Clarke.

the ways that its protagonist finds a voice and a self.[1] Yet, as others have pointed out, Janie's voice is by no means unequivocally established by the end of the book. Robert Stepto was among the first to express dissatisfaction with the narrative structure and its third-person narrator; for him, the use of the narrator implies that "Janie has not really won her voice and self after all" (166). More recently, Michael Awkward has pointed out that Janie is not interested in telling the community her story upon her return (6), and Mary Helen Washington argues that Janie is silenced at crucial spots in the narrative. Carla Kaplan, reviewing the discussions of voice that the novel has inspired, examines the ways that voice is both celebrated and undermined, noting that "Hurston privileges dialogue and storytelling at the same time as she represents and applauds Janie's *refusal* to speak" (121). Clearly, Janie's achievement of a voice is critical to her journey to self-awareness, but the highly ambivalent presentation of voice in the novel indicates that voice alone is not enough. As Maria Tai Wolff notes, "For telling to be successful, it must become a presentation of sights with words. The best talkers are 'big picture talkers'" (226). For Hurston, then, the construction of African American identity requires a voice that can make you see, a voice that celebrates the visible presence of black bodies.

I would suggest that, with its privileging of "mind pictures" over words, *Their Eyes Were Watching God* goes beyond a narrative authority based solely on voice, for, as Janie tells Pheoby, "'Talkin' don't amount tuh uh hill uh beans when yuh can't do nothin' else'" (183). In contrast to Joe Starks, who seeks to be a "big voice" only to have his wish become humiliatingly true when Janie informs him that he "'big-bellies round here and put out a lot of brag, but 'tain't nothin' to it but yo' big voice'" (75), Janie seeks for a voice which can picture, which can make you see. The ability to use voice visually provides a literary space for African American women to relate their experiences in a world where, as Nanny says, "'We don't know nothin' but what we see'" (14). Thus, to expand "what we see" increases what we know. Throughout the novel, Hurston's use of visual imagery challenges dominant theories about the power hierarchies embedded in sight, long associated with white control, with Plato's rationality and logic, and, from a Freudian perspective, with male sexual dominance. She recasts the visual to affirm the beauty and power of color and to provide a vehicle for female agency.

In so doing, Hurston opens up different ways of conceptualizing the African American experience. Responding to the long history of blacks as spectacle—from slavery to minstrelsy to colonized object—she offers the possibility of reclaiming the visual as a means of black expression and black power. Controlling vision means controlling what we see, how we define the world. Visual power, then, brings political power, since those who determine what is seen determine what exists.[2]

In recent times, the Rodney King beating trial highlighted the significance of this power, when white interpretation sought to reverse the apparent vision presented by the video of the assault. Commenting on the trial, Judith Butler writes that the "visual field is not neutral to the question of race; it is itself a racial formation, an episteme, hegemonic and forceful" (17). Zora Neale Hurston recognized this, anticipating what Houston Baker terms the "'scening' of the African presence" as a means of silencing that presence (42). As opposed to the King jurors, who learned not to see what was presented, Hurston's Janie makes readers "see" her story, and thus takes control of both the visual field and its interpretation. Visual control is not, obviously, the answer to racist oppression: Had the jurors "seen" what happened to Rodney King, it would not have undone his beating, and Hurston fully realized that black bodies bear the material evidence of racial violence (indeed, Janie's perceived beauty—her long hair and light skin—results from an interracial rape). But by taking visual control, Hurston looks back, challenges white dominance, and documents its material abuse of African Americans.

She thus manages to present a material self that can withstand the power of the gaze, transforming it into a source of strength. In establishing a rhetoric of sight, Hurston ensures that black bodies remain powerfully visible throughout the novel, particularly the bodies of black women.[3] As Audre Lorde has noted, visibility is the cornerstone of black female identity, "without which we cannot truly live":

> Within this country where racial difference creates a constant, if unspoken, distortion of vision, Black women have on one hand always been highly visible, and so, on the other hand, have been rendered invisible through the depersonalization of racism. Even within the women's movement, we have had to fight, and still do, for that very visibility which also renders us most vulnerable, our Blackness. . . . And that visibility which makes us most vulnerable is that which also is the source of our greatest strength. (Lorde 42)

In attempting to reclaim visibility, Hurston focuses not just on rendering black bodies visible, but also on redeeming the "distortion of vision" of which Lorde speaks. Neither is an easy task, for Janie's visible beauty makes her vulnerable to both adoration and abuse, and the ability to see does not come readily. As the title of the novel indicates, Hurston is interested in far more than the development of one woman's journey to self-knowledge; she seeks to find a discourse that celebrates both the voices and the bodies of African Americans. By emphasizing "watching God," she foregrounds sight.

The existing theoretical work on vision is both useful and limiting for one seeking to understand Hurston's use of visual language. While various feminist theorists such as Braidotti, Haraway, and Keller have contributed greatly to our understanding of the topic, joining film theorists Mulvey, Doane, and Silverman, their work does not always take race sufficiently into account, though Jane Gaines reminds us of the racial privilege inherent in the gaze: "Some groups," she remarks, "have historically had the license to 'look' openly while other groups have 'looked' illicitly" (25). Some African American theorists such as Fanon, Wallace, and hooks do engage issues of visibility, but it is surprisingly under-examined in African American literary and film theory despite the fact that the visual is critical to black female identity, the source, Lorde insists, of black women's vulnerability and strength. Michelle Wallace has noted that "black women are more often visualized in mainstream American culture . . . than they are allowed to speak their own words or speak about their condition as women of color" (*Invisibility* 3). Hurston takes this visualization and turns it into a source of strength and a kind of language, thus redeeming visibility and establishing voice. While vision has long been associated with objectivity, this objective position has been assumed to be raceless (white) and sexless (male). Hurston exposes these dynamics, and in so doing lays the groundwork for a kind of vision that embodies blackness as both body and voice. The visible presence of Janie's material body reflects the complex historical and cultural forces which have created her and offers her a unique, individual identity. The visual, then, allows for a negotiation between the post-structuralist argument that identity is largely a construction and the concerns, particularly by nonwhites, that such a position erases individual identity and presence just as non-white peoples are beginning to lay claim to them. Awareness of the visible brings together the "politics of positioning," of who can look, with a recognition of the political and psychological significance of the gaze and with the "real" presence of a material body and individual self (Braidotti 73).

Hurston's insistence on the importance of visual expression, of course, stems largely from racism's disregard for African American individuality. In "What White Publishers Won't Print," Hurston explains the American attitude toward blacks as "THE AMERICAN MUSEUM OF UNNATURAL HISTORY. This is an intangible built on folk belief. It is assumed that all non-Anglo-Saxons are uncomplicated stereotypes. Everybody knows all about them. They are lay figures mounted in the museum where all may take them in at a glance" (170).[4] By characterizing the white American perspective as that of museum-goers, Hurston suggests that the non-white population becomes mere spectacle, "lay figures" to be taken in "at a glance" by white eyes. We generally see this power dynamic in operation when black bodies are displayed. In minstrel shows, as Eric Lott points out, "'Black' figures were there to be looked at, shaped to the demands of desire; they were screens on which audience fantasy could rest, and while this purpose might have had a host of different effects, its fundamental outcome was to secure the position of white spectators as superior, controlling figures" (140–141).

The dynamic still exists. Steven Speilberg's 1997 film *Amistad,* for example, opens with an extended display of naked black bodies and offers its black cast few words, inviting the public to view blackness rather than listen to it.[5] One is defined by how one is seen. For African Americans, this leads to a condition of "hypervisibility," in which "the very publicness of black people as a social fact works to undermine the possibility of actually seeing black specificity" (Lubiano 187). We need only look to Frantz Fanon for confirmation: ". . . already I am being dissected under white eyes, the only real eyes. I am *fixed.* . . . I feel, I see in those white faces that it is not a new man who has come in, but a new kind of man, a new genus. Why, it's a Negro!" (116). The racist power of visibility thus seems daunting, but Hurston not only takes on the challenge of reclaiming the visual as racially affirmative, she does so in response to a masculinist tradition in which visual power so often objectifies women. Her fiction reveals that, even in the context of a black community, the ability to see "black specificity" may be impaired, particularly when the specific individual is a woman. Hurston, a student of Franz Boas, who pioneered the participant-observer model of anthropological study, recognized the need for looking closely and carefully.[6]

Their Eyes opens with almost an anthropological tone, presenting us with a group of people who have been "tongueless, earless, eyeless conveniences all day long" (1). After spending their days erased by white eyes as a specific presence, they become talkers and lookers. In order to regain human identity after "mules and other brutes had occupied their skins," they need to speak, listen, and see. It is important to note that Hurston equates all three sensory apparati; she does not privilege the verbal over the visual. Just as Pheoby's "hungry listening" helps Janie tell her story, so Janie's keen vision provides her with a story to tell. This vision is far different from one which "glances" at objects in a museum; such a way of seeing merely replicates white erasure of everything but skin color. Hurston seeks a uniquely African American vision, a way of seeing that both recognizes color and sees beyond it. But being black does not automatically confer, for Hurston, visual ability. In fact, visual language is predominately associated with women in her work. As Michelle Wallace has observed, "Gender is as important as 'race' to understanding how 'invisibility' has worked historically in all fields of visual production" ("Race" 258). Initially, the "big picture talkers" are male in this novel, and much of the talk centers on impressing and evaluating women. Janie's first appearance in Eatonville causes Hicks to proclaim his plans to get a woman just like her "'Wid mah talk'"(34). Hurston's challenge is to redeploy the language of the visual in ways that do not simply re-evoke the objectification of women of any color by situating them as objects of the male gaze.

In a culture that has so long defined black people as spectacle and black women as sexualized bodies, one needs to transform and redeem the potential of vision. While the visual certainly holds the threat of objectification, it can also serve as action—both personal and political. bell hooks argues that, for blacks, looking can be viewed as an act of resistance. She asserts that "all attempts to repress our/black peoples' right to gaze . . . produced in us an overwhelming longing to look, a rebellious desire, an oppositional gaze." With this gaze African Americans declared, "Not only will I stare. I want my look to change reality" (116). Looking becomes an act charged with political resistance, a way to reconfigure the world and its power dynamics.[7] One must look, then, at African American writing as a means of challenging the power of the white gaze. We need to employ what Mae Henderson terms a new "angle of vision" (161), a means of looking back, of seeing without objectifying. To analyze Hurston's "angle of vision," I would argue, necessitates bringing together a wide range of theoretical perspectives, for seeing and being seen are highly complex acts in her fiction, acts which place individuals within an intricate web of personal and historical forces.

In Hurston's work, looking is more than a confrontational challenge. Her fiction is replete with examples of women's need to look, see, understand, and use language visually. In "Drenched in Light," an autobiographical story which recalls Hurston's descriptions of her childhood days, Isis, "a visual minded child," "pictur[es] herself gazing over the edge of the world into the abyss" (942). She escapes punishment for her many mischievous actions by impressing a white lady as being "drenched in light" (946); her strong visual force marks her as a child destined for creative accomplishment. Delia, the protagonist of "Sweat," prefigures Janie in her use of visual metaphors to re-evaluate her marriage. "She lay awake, gazing upon the debris that cluttered their matrimonial trail. Not an image left standing along the way" (957). This visual realization grants Delia the strength to defy her abusive husband. "The Gilded Six-Bits" presents the story of Missie May, unable to see through the shining currency to recognize its meager value; this mis-sight leads her to an affair with the man who owns the false coins, nearly ruining her marriage. Interestingly, her husband Joe finally forgives her when her son is born and turns out to be "'de spittin image'" (995) of Joe himself. Only visual proof of paternity can erase his anger.

Jonah's Gourd Vine, in many ways a pre-text for *Their Eyes,* examines many of the same issues of voice and identity with a male protagonist. But though John Pearson, like Janie Crawford, struggles to establish a self, he does not employ her rhetoric of sight. In fact, his white boss specifically associates him with blindness as an explanation for John's lack of foresight:

> "Of course you did not know. Because God has given to all men
> the gift of blindness. That is to say that He has cursed but few with

vision. Ever hear tell of a happy prophet? This old world wouldn't roll on the way He started it if men could see. Ha! In fact, I think God Himself was looking off when you went and got yourself born." (86)

Not only is John a result of God's blindness, but John consistently fails to see his way, particularly in failing to pick up on Hattie's use of conjure tricks to entrap him into a second marriage. The vision in the novel belongs to his first wife, Lucy. She is the one whose "large bright eyes looked thru and beyond him and saw too much" (112). Lucy, far more self-aware and perceptive than John, harnesses the power of vision so successfully that her visions live on after her death. Interestingly, when John finally does attain a degree of vision, it proves highly ambiguous and problematic, leading to his death when he drives his car into a railroad crossing: "He drove on but half-seeing the railroad from looking inward" (167). Lacking Lucy's ability to put her visual power to practical use, John fatally blinds himself to his surroundings and pays the ultimate price for his inability to see. Here Hurston sets up her paradigm: Vision must be embodied, one must see outwardly as well as inwardly.

Hurston establishes the full power of the visual in *Their Eyes Were Watching God*. Initially subjected to the defining and objectifying power of a communal gaze, Janie, unlike John Pearson, learns to employ vision in ways that are self-affirming rather than self-sacrificing. Returning to Eatonville at the novel's start, Janie finds herself in a position very familiar to her: the object that all eyes are upon. When she approaches, the people are full of hostile questions to which they "hoped the answers were cruel and strange" (4). But when she keeps on walking, refusing to stop and acquiesce to their voyeuristic desires, talk becomes specularization: "The porch couldn't talk for looking." The men notice her "firm buttocks like she had grape fruits in her hip pockets; the great rope of black hair swinging to her waist and unraveling in the wind like a plume; then her pugnacious breasts trying to bore holes in her shirt." The women focus on the "faded shirt and muddy overalls." Looking at her body, the men see her as sexed; for the women, gazing on her apparel, she is gendered. In both cases, it seems, Janie vanishes. The men define her as female body parts and the women deny her feminine identity. While the female resentment of her attire may seem less intrusive than the male x-ray vision, both looks constitute "mass cruelty" (2). Yet having set up Janie as spectacle, Hurston then illuminates the positive potential of vision in the ensuing interchange with Pheoby. Here, the visual takes on a different tone. Just as voice, according to Kaplan, becomes a kind of double-edged sword, so can vision—particularly when shared between friends—both specularize and affirm. Pheoby tells Janie, "'Gal you sho looks *good*. . . . Even wid dem overhalls on, you shows yo' womanhood'" (4). What she sees is presence, not absence. To look like a woman is to look good, a way of visualizing which does not fixate on sexual anatomy but which allows for materiality. She *shows* her womanhood, a far different sight than that gazed upon by the men, who see not Janie's presence but their own desire, desire which her body is expected to satisfy.

The materiality of Janie's body as an object of desire has, of course, determined much of her history. Her first husband, Logan Killicks, presumably wants to marry her based on what he sees, though her own eyes tell her something very different: "'He look like some old skullhead in de grave yard'" (13). But her vision lacks authority; despite what her eyes tell her, she is married off to him, defeated by Nanny's powerful story of her own oppression which seems to give her the right to impose her will upon Janie. Having "'save[d] de text,'" Nanny uses language to desecrate Janie's vision of the pear tree (16). Joe Starks, Janie's next husband, is likewise attracted to her beauty: "He stopped and looked hard, and then he asked her for a cool drink of water." This time, Janie does not submit passively to this specularization, and tries to look back, to return the gaze, pumping the water "until she got a good look at the man" (26). But her look still lacks the controlling power of the male gaze, what hooks calls the ability to "change reality." At this point, Janie has difficulty even seeing reality, as is evidenced by her inability to see through Joe Starks. She takes "a lot of looks at him and she was proud of what she saw. Kind of portly, like rich white folks" (32). What Janie sees is whiteness, and her valuation of this sets her on a path that will take twenty years to reverse. Looking at Joe's silk shirt, she overlooks his language of hierarchy, his desire to be a big voice. She has privileged the wrong kind of sight, a vision that fails to see into blackness and thus fails to see through language.

Still, Janie is not entirely fooled. Joe does "not represent sun-up and pollen and blooming trees, but he spoke for far horizon. He spoke for change and chance" (28). Janie thus gives up a vision she has seen—that of the pear tree—in favor of one she can only imagine: horizons, chance, and change. In allowing herself to be swayed by his language, she fails to notice that his rhetoric is that of speech, not vision. Joe only speaks; he does not see. Consequently, Janie's own vision deteriorates even further. Having initially recognized that Joe does not represent "sun-up and pollen," she later manages to convince herself that he does: "From now on until death she was going to have flower dust and springtime sprinkled over everything. A bee for her bloom" (31). Stubbornly, she tries to force Joe into her vision, possibly to justify running off with him. Convincing herself to see what is not there leads Janie into an unequal marriage in which she is expected to sit on a "high chair" (58), an infantilizing position where she can overlook the world and yet also be subjected to its envious eyes.

But Joe has a problem, for while he wants to put Janie on display in order to reap the benefit of reflected glory as her owner, this is precisely the position which is threatened by the eyes of other men. He wants her to be both present and absent, both visible and invisible, a task he attempts to accomplish by insisting that she keep her hair tied up in a head rag because he sees the other men not just "figuratively wallowing in it" (51) but literally touching it, and she "was there in the store for *him* to look at, not those others" (52). Joe wants to engage privately in scopophilia within a public forum, without subjecting Janie herself to this public gaze. Once she is fixed by gazes other than his own, he loses his exclusive ownership of her body. As Lorde notes, while visibility entails vulnerability, it can also be a source of great strength, a characteristic Joe certainly does not want to see in Janie. But the situation reflects more than Joe's concern about Janie's gaining cultural power; Janie's visibility also invokes a classic Freudian scenario. Laura Mulvey, in her groundbreaking psychoanalytic study "Visual Pleasure and Narrative Cinema," notes that the female figure, beyond providing pleasure for the looker, also implies a certain threat: "her lack of a penis, implying a threat of castration and hence unpleasure. . . . Thus the woman as icon, displayed for the gaze and enjoyment of the men, the active controllers of the look, always threatens to evoke the anxiety it originally signified" (21). Indeed, Joe's greatest anxiety is not focused on Janie's body but on his own. He wants to have the dominant position, but without being visually objectified by the viewers. "The more his back ached and his muscle dissolved into fat and the fat melted off his bones the more fractious he became with Janie. Especially in the store. The more people in there the more ridicule he poured over her body to point attention away from his own" (73–74).

But the racial situation problematizes this notion of woman as icon, which presumes looking to be a masculine act. The cultural permutations of the significance of the gaze within the African American community challenge a strictly Freudian reading. If looking is an act of political defiance, it cannot be exclusively associated with black masculinity, particularly given the long history of black female activism and resistance. When Janie challenges Joe, she does so not just to defend her female identity—"'Ah'm uh woman every inch of me'" (75)—but also to protest against Joe's almost constant oppression. Joe, with his prosperity and seemingly white values, fails to realize that his mouth is not all-powerful, that, despite his favorite expression, "I god," he is not divine. His centrality as mayor and store owner renders him even more vulnerable to specularization than Janie, and he falls prey to a kind of reversed Freudian schema of the gaze which entails serious repercussions for his political power.

Having set up the dynamics of the body as visualized object, Joe becomes its victim, as Janie linguistically performs the castration of which she is the visual reminder. As she tells him publicly, "'When you pull down yo' britches, you look lak de change uh life,'" her pictorial language renders it impossible for him to deny the vision she creates. He tries to erase the image by questioning her speech. "'Wha—whut's dat you said?'" It doesn't work, however, for Walter taunts him, "'You heard her, you ain't blind.'" This comment highlights the interconnection between hearing and seeing; to hear is to see. And yet, given the words of her insult, Joe might as well be blind, for Janie has, in fact, revealed his lack of visual difference. By not using a visual metaphor in this case, she emphasizes that there is nothing there to see. She bares his body to the communal gaze, not only denying his masculinity but displaying his lack to other men: "She had cast down his empty armor before men and they had laughed, would keep on laughing" (75). Feminized by the visual dynamics that he has established, Joe dies, unable to withstand the gaze which erases his masculinity and identifies him as empty armor. Not only is it impossible for him to continue as mayor under these circumstances, it is impossible for him to continue. Joe has no life once denied both sexual and political power.

Though Hurston uses the visual to expose the vulnerability of a phallocentrism which abuses women, she also recognizes its empowering potential. In transforming the visual into a tool of female power, Hurston reclaims the power of the visual as a vehicle for examining African American women's experiences. After all, if one erases vision, one erases race, which is culturally visualized by the physical body, the sign of visual difference. As Michelle Wallace notes, "How one is seen (as black) and, therefore, what one sees (in a white world) is always already crucial to one's existence as an Afro-American. The very markers that reveal you to the rest of the world, your dark skin and your kinky/curly hair, are visual" ("Modernism" 40). Racial visibility as a marker of difference allows black women to "show" their womanhood.

Yet, as Joe's experience makes clear, this must be a particular kind of vision, a way of seeing which expands rather than limits understanding. Despite Joe's entrapment in his own gaze, the novel is replete with examples of the affirmative quality of the visual. Janie's attempts to define a self originate with the act of looking. Her "conscious life" begins with her vision of the pear tree, leading to her sexual awakening. Having felt called to "gaze on a mystery" (10), she beholds a "revelation" in the bees and flowers. She seeks her own place in the picture, searching for "confirmation of the voice and vision." Looking down the road, she sees a "glorious being" whom, in her "former blindness," she had known as "shiftless Johnny Taylor." But the "golden dust of pollen" which "beglamored his rags and her eyes" changes her perspective (11). Johnny Taylor's kiss, espied by Nanny, sets Janie's course in motion. Whether or not Johnny Taylor represents a better possibility is both impossible to determine and irrelevant; what matters is Janie's realization that her fate is linked to her vision, though the recognition will lead her astray until she learns effectively to interpret what she sees.

This vision, after her mistake in mis-seeing Joe Starks, is finally fulfilled when she meets Tea Cake, a man who is willing to display himself rather than subject others to his defining gaze. When Janie says, "'Look lak Ah seen you somewhere,'" he replies, "'Ah'm easy tuh see on Church Street most any day or night'" (90–91). By denying any anxiety in thus being viewed, Tea Cake transforms sight from a controlling, defining gaze into a personal introduction, demystifying himself by inviting inspection. In fact, Tea Cake cautions her about the importance of looking closely in the ensuing checkers game, challenging her claim that he has no right to jump her king because "'Ah wuz lookin' off when you went and stuck yo' men right up next tuh mine. No fair!'" Tea Cake answers, "'You ain't supposed tuh look off, Mis' Starks. It's de biggest part uh de game tuh watch out!'" (92). His response underscores the importance of watching, of using one's vision not to fix and specularize but to see and think, to understand. Consequently, Janie realizes that he "could be a bee to a blossom—a pear tree blossom in the spring" (101), a man who can confirm her initial vision. She defines him with visual metaphors: "He was a glance from God." This metaphor highlights Tea Cake's connection to the visual; he recognizes the need to combine voice with understanding, remarking that Janie needs "'tellin' and showin''" (102) to believe in love.

But Janie does not need simply to find a man capable of assimilating voice and vision, she needs to learn for herself how to formulate a self which is not predicated upon oppression. She finds the task particularly challenging because her racial identity is founded upon invisibility, upon her inability to see herself. The photograph which reveals her color, her difference, divides her from her previous notion of the identity of sameness: "'Before Ah seen de picture Ah thought Ah wuz just like de rest.'" To be black is to be not just different but absent, for Janie looks at the photograph asking, "'Where is me? Ah don't see me'" (9). Both blackness and femininity are culturally predicated upon lack; thus Janie needs to learn to show her womanhood and to find visible presence in blackness. Priscilla Wald has suggested that Janie's problem with seeing herself stems from her "white eyes": "The white eyes with which Janie looks see the black self as absent, that is, do not see the black self at all" (83). This is a particularly important point, for it indicates that Janie needs not just vision, but black vision—black eyes. Vision, which initially divides her from herself, must then provide the means for re-inventing a self, one in which racial identity adds wholeness rather than division. To deny either her blackness or her whiteness is to deny the specificity of her being, for her body is the site of the physical evidence of white oppression and a partially white origin. The answer is not to retreat into colorlessness but to reconstitute the definition of the self into something that acknowledges the conditions of her physical being: the visible evidence of her whiteness and her blackness, the heritage of slavery and sexual abuse.

Janie takes the first step toward acquiring this visual sense of self in response to Joe's oppression. "Then one day she sat and watched the shadow of herself going about tending store and prostrating itself before Jody, while all the time she herself sat under a shady tree with the wind blowing through her hair and clothes" (73). She sees the self that prostrates itself before Jody as her shadow, and this realization acts on her "like a drug," offering an escape from an oppressive life. In order to move from passive spectator to active doer, however, she needs to take that vision further. The act of seeing must become active and affirmative before she can re-integrate the disparate parts of her identity into one unified whole. As Andrew Lakritz has written, "Some of the most powerful moments in Zora Neale Hurston's writings occur when a fig-ure in the narrative is represented as watching events unfold, when such acts of looking become constitutive of the entire question of identity" (17). But looking itself does not automatically constitute identity; one must learn how to do it. Barbara Johnson's much cited analysis of Janie's recognition of her division into inside and outside also can be viewed as an experience in learn-ing to use the visual. Johnson identifies Janie's realization that the spirit of the marriage has left the bedroom and moved into the parlor as an "externaliza-tion of the inner, a metaphorically grounded metonymy," while the following paragraph where Janie sees her image of Jody tumble off a shelf "presents an internalization of the outer, or a metonymically grounded metaphor." This moment leads Janie to a voice which "grows not out of her identity but out of her division into inside and outside. Knowing how not to mix them is know-ing that articulate language requires the co-presence of two distinct poles, not their collapse into oneness" (Johnson 212). If, indeed, the moment leads her to voice, it does not lead to a voice of self-assertion, as Janie remains silent under Joe's oppressive control for several more years.

I would suggest that the moment does not engender Janie's voice so much as it moves her toward a way of visualizing her experience which will, in time, lead her toward a picturing voice. In imagining her marriage as living in the parlor, she creates, as Johnson notes, a metonymy. But her metaphor of Joe as statue is also a metaphor infused with vision:

> She stood there until something fell off the shelf inside her. Then she went inside there to see what it was. It was her image of Jody tumbled down and shattered. But looking at it she saw that it never was the flesh and blood figure of her dreams. Just something she had grabbed up to drape her dreams over. In a way she turned her back upon the image where it lay and looked further. She had no more blossomy openings dusting pollen over her man, neither

any glistening young fruit where the petals used to be. . . . She had an inside and an outside now and suddenly she knew how not to mix them. (67–68)

The significance of this moment lies not just in Janie's recognition of the division between inside and outside but also in the ability to turn her back on the image and "look further." No longer content with surface vision, Janie is learning to "look further," a necessary precondition for finding an expressive voice.

Joe's death offers her further opportunity to use this knowledge as she fixes her gaze upon herself. Janie goes to the mirror and looks "hard at her skin and features. The young girl was gone, but a handsome woman had taken her place" (83). This scene illustrates why vision is so crucial to Hurston's work. Recalling Butler's comment that the "visual field" is a "racial formation," one sees Hurston establishing precisely that. In looking hard at her "skin and features," Janie looks hard at her interracial body, seeing it now not as different but as handsome. She uses her own vision to find beauty and value in her visually inscribed racial identity. She then burns her head rags, symbol of Joe's attempts to deny her beauty and to hide her from the communal gaze while subjecting her to his own. Displaying her abundant hair, presumably another indication of her racially mixed heritage, brings her still closer to an affirmation of her visual self, a self that celebrates rather than denying the mark of race—of both races. Kaja Silverman asserts that the "eye can confer the active gift of love upon bodies which have long been accustomed to neglect and disdain. It can also put what is alien or inconsequential into contact with what is most personal and psychically significant" (227). Even before Janie gains the aid of Tea Cake's loving eye, her own eyes confer love upon her body as she begins to assimilate what has often seemed an alien world into her own psyche.

Janie transforms her understanding of color so that the sting of her original recognition of her photograph, "'Aw! aw! Ah'm colored!'" (9), can be alleviated and reversed by recognizing the visual beauty of color. The evening she meets Tea Cake, she watches the moon rise, "its amber fluid . . . drenching the earth" (95). This scene reveals the darkness of night to be full of color, transcending the stark blackness of the sky and whiteness of the moon. Hurston thus presents color as a full range of variation and beauty. Janie starts wearing blue because Tea Cake likes to see her in it, telling Pheoby not only that visual mourning should not last longer than grief, but that "'de world picked out black and white for mournin'" (107–108). By specifically associating mourning with black and white, Hurston subtly suggests that going beyond the color binary moves one from grief to happiness, from mourning and loss to fulfillment. She further challenges the black-white binary with the episode after the storm in the Everglades, when Tea Cake is forcibly conscripted into burying bodies. The white overseers insist that the workers "'examine every last one of 'em and find out if they's white or black'" (162). This ridiculous and horrific command inspires Tea Cake to comment, "'Look lak dey think God don't know nothin' 'bout de Jim Crow law'" (163). The suggestion that God needs the aid of coffins to "see" racial difference again highlights the absurdity of seeing the world only in terms of black and white. By tying vision so intricately to race, Hurston offers a way out of the oppositional hierarchy of both.[8]

Thus Hurston destabilizes the visual racial binary, and Janie learns a new respect for color and for her own image. She restores the image that was desecrated by the photograph, when Tea Cake tells her to look in the mirror so she can take pleasure from her looks. "Fortunately," says Silverman, "no look ever takes place once and for all" (223). As Hurston well understands, looking is not a static activity. To "transform the value," as Silverman puts it, of what is seen, one needs to use one's life-experience in order to see it better. Having stood up to her husband, survived the gossip implicating her in his death, taken over the business, and dared to consider a lover, Janie learns to transform her gaze into one that accepts and values her own image.

After learning to use her vision to value herself, Janie is ready to take the next step: using vision to find God. The title episode of the novel reveals the full importance of the power of sight and of being an active looker; watching God is an active rather than a passive enterprise.

> They sat in company with others in other shanties, their eyes straining against crude walls and their souls asking if He meant to measure their puny might against His. They seemed to be staring at the dark, but their eyes were watching God. (151)

Like Alice Walker in *The Color Purple*, Hurston re-visions the old white man with a long beard. Instead, one approaches God not just in darkness but by looking *through* darkness, to see God where others see blackness. In so doing, she enables a kind of vision that deifies darkness, replacing the emptiness with presence, presence in blackness. At the height of the storm, Janie tells Tea Cake, "'If you kin see de light at daybreak, you don't keer if you die at dusk'" (151). Since she can "see" the light in darkness, neither it nor death holds any fear for her. By having her characters watch God in darkness, Hurston redefines rationalist and masculine control of the gaze, transforming scopophilia into spirituality. Her enabled gaze does not make women specularizable, for it takes place in darkness; rather, it makes God viewable and blackness visible. Similarly, in Toni Morrison's *Paradise*, the midwife Lone, trying to find out what the men plan to do to the women at the convent, sits in the dark to read the signs: "Playing blind was to avoid the language God spoke in. He did not thunder instructions or whisper messages into ears. Oh, no. He was a liberating God. A teacher who taught you how to learn, to see for yourself" (273). Learning how to see—particularly, learning how to see in darkness—takes on special meaning for African American women. One comes to God not through light but through the ability to see in the dark.

But Hurston's world is not solely visual; material bodies exist tactily as well as visually, and color is not always beautiful, as the historical forces of slavery and oppression can be read on Janie's body. She is the product of two generations of rape, one of them interracial. She suffers physically for her interracial body when Tea Cake beats her to display his ownership in the face of Mrs. Turner's theories of Janie's superiority due to her light skin. The bruises, of course, are clearly evident precisely because of that light skin, as Sop-de-Bottom enviously remarks, "'Uh person can see every place you hit her'" (140). These marks inscribe both visually and physically the full implications of her racial identity as well as the violence that brought it into being. Just as black women cannot ignore the visual, neither can they escape the tactile, a physical language which highlights the material racist and sexist abuse of the body.[9] As Sharon Davie argues, Hurston's bodily metaphors "acknowledge the tactile, the physical, which Western culture devalues" (454). But Hurston does more than acknowledge the tactile; she *reveals* it. In Hurston's world, the mark of violence is seen, making the tactile visual. Though she celebrates the power of vision, she has no illusions that it can erase or replace the discourse of violence and racism. Rather, it documents, for all to see, the effects of brutality.

Janie's act of killing is an act of physical self-defense to protect the body that Tea Cake has restored to her. Yet even this highly tactile response has a visual component. She waits for a sign from the sky, a visual indication that God will relent and spare Tea Cake's life, but "the sky stayed hard looking and quiet" (169). I find it telling that this is a daytime supplication, as Janie seeks to find a message "beyond blue ether's bosom," waiting for a "star in the daytime, maybe, or the sun to shout." This daylight sky appears much less accessible to her searching eyes than the blackness of the storm. The God sought in darkness evokes a reaffirmation of love, but this light (skinned?) God forces murder. Lack of visual contact spells doom, and Tea Cake's vision consequently suffers to the point where the "fiend in him must kill and Janie was the only thing living he saw" (175). Thus Tea Cake's death both saves Janie's physical body and erases his false vision.

Her final test involves learning to integrate voice and vision in a different form of self-defense. The trial scene reconstitutes Janie as speaker rather than object. The spectators are there not to watch but to listen. Janie's verbal

defense succeeds because she "makes them see," a phrase repeated three times
in six sentences:

> She had to go way back to let them know how she and Tea
> Cake had been with one another so they could *see* she could never
> shoot Tea Cake out of malice.
> She tried to make them *see* how terrible it was that things were
> fixed so that Tea Cake couldn't come back to himself until he had
> got rid of that mad dog that was in him. . . . She made them *see* how
> she couldn't ever want to be rid of him. (178; emphasis added)

Despite critical concern with the narrator replacing Janie's voice at this
crucial moment, we must recognize that Janie has made them see, as she
has already made the reader see, that voice at this moment is subordinate
to the ability to visualize, an effect that may be heightened by Hurston's
deflection of Janie's story. We don't need to hear her, since we can see her
story. She manages to refute the implications of the black male spectators,
that "'dem white mens wuzn't goin tuh do nothin' tuh no woman dat look
lak her'" (179), and they turn their anger against Mrs. Turner's brother who
puts "himself where men's wives could look at him" (181). But Janie's looks
have not been directed at him; she has been too busy learning to visualize
to waste time specularizing.

Consequently, she returns home to discover "'dis house ain't so absent of
things lak it used tuh be befo' Tea Cake come along'" (182). Having learned
to make presence out of absence, she can now not only re-visualize Tea Cake,
whose "memory made pictures of love and light against the wall," but can
also call "in her soul to come and see" (184). In thus successfully employing a
visualized voice, Janie becomes both spectator and participant in her own life.
To speak the body, for an African American woman, means to recognize its
visual racial difference as well as affirming its sexual identity. Hurston's mind-
pictures and seeing-voices reclaim the physical world of pear trees and the
beauty of the visible presence of blackness. As Hurston herself noted, pictorial language is of primary importance in black discourse, where everything
is "illustrated. So we can say that the white man thinks in a written language
and the Negro thinks in hieroglyphics" ("Characteristics" 24). By filling Janie
"full of that oldest human longing—self revelation" (*Their Eyes* 6), Hurston
presents a text of "revelation"—with all of its visual implications. Her hieroglyphics reflect a community of people whose world is their canvas and whose
lives and bodies are pictured in living color.

She thus provides a model for reconciling voice and vision, for transforming black bodies from museum pieces or ethnographic objects into
embodied voices, by recasting spectacle as visual, a move away from passive

sensationalism to active participation. Hortense Spillers notes of the Du Boisian double-consciousness that "it is also noteworthy that his provocative claims . . . crosses [sic] their wires with the specular and spectacular: the sensation of looking at oneself and of imagining being seen through the eyes of another is precisely performative in what it demands of a participant on the other end of the gaze" (143). In Hurston's hands, looking is indeed a performative act. In fact, it becomes a linguistic performance which affirms bodily presence, reversing Fanon's claim that, in the white world, "consciousness of the body is solely a negating activity" (110). Hurston, as Priscilla Wald so aptly puts it, "redesignates 'color' as performance in a process that draws her readers into the dynamics of 'coloration'" (87). Through the use of hieroglyphics, she reconstitutes women as active and colored performers. Vision, so often a means of fixing and silencing African Americans, can also provide the means to foreground the body without surrendering the voice. As the title of Hurston's novel indicates, her concern goes beyond presenting an individual woman's journey to self-awareness; her accomplishment is nothing less than redefining African American rhetoric, rendering it verbal and visual.

NOTES

1. Along with several studies cited within the text of my article, the following represent only a few of the many fine analyses of various aspects of voice and language in *Their Eyes:* Bond; Brigham; Callahan; Gates, "Zora"; Holloway; Kubitschek; McKay; Racine; Wall.

2. For more on the political power of the visual, see Rosi Braidotti, especially 73.

3. In this, Hurston differs markedly from Ralph Ellison, who focuses not so much on attaining vision as on the implications of invisibility. Whereas Ellison documents in intricate detail the confines of being invisible, Hurston examines the process of learning to see and be seen.

4. Indeed, in film theory, as Miriam Hansen points out, "an aesthetics of the glance is replacing the aesthetics of the gaze" (135). This reflects a move from the intensity of a gaze to the glance, "momentary and casual" (50), according to John Ellis, who notes that, with a glance, "no extraordinary effort is being invested in the activity of looking" (137). While this may result in a less controlling and hegemonic situation, it can also, as Hurston indicates, illustrate a lack of deep perception.

5. Film, both popular and documentary, has long specularized black bodies. According to Fatimah Tobing Rony, early-twentieth-century ethnographic films "incessantly visualized race" (267).

6. I am indebted to Lori Jirousek's 1999 Penn State dissertation "Immigrant Ethnographers: Critical Observations in Turn-of-the-Century America" for better understanding the significance of Boas to Hurston's fiction.

7. Indeed, vision can offer a challenge to the links which Homi Bhabha has traced between the scopic drive and colonial surveillance (28–29).

8. As Donna Haraway has suggested, "Vision can be good for avoiding binary oppositions" (188).

9. Again, we see further evidence in Morrison's work in Beloved's scar and Sethe's "tree"; like Hurston, Morrison demands that one read the body visually.

Works Cited

Awkward, Michael. *Inspiring Influences: Tradition, Revision, and Afro-American Women's Novels*. New York: Columbia University Press, 1989.

Baker, Houston A., Jr. "Scene . . . Not Heard," in *Reading Rodney King, Reading Urban Uprising*, edited by Robert Gooding-Williams. New York: Routledge, 1993, pp. 38–48.

Bhabha, Homi K. "The Other Question . . . The Stereotype and Colonial Discourse," *Screen* 24, 6 (1983): 18–36.

Bond, Cynthia. "Language, Speech, and Difference in *Their Eyes Were Watching God*," in *Zora Neale Hurston: Critical Perspectives Past and Present*, edited by Henry Louis Gates Jr., and K. A. Appiah. New York: Armistad Press, 1993, pp. 204–217.

Braidotti, Rosi. *Nomadic Subjects: Embodiment and Sexual Difference in Contemporary Feminist Theor*. New York: Columbia University Press, 1994.

Brigham, Cathy. "The Talking Frame of Zora Neale Hurston's Talking Book: Storytelling as Dialectic in *Their Eyes Were Watching God*," *CLA Journal* 37, 4 (1994): 402–419.

Butler, Judith. "Endangered/Endangering: Schematic Racism and White Paranoia," in *Reading Rodney King, Reading Urban Uprising*, edited by Gooding-Williams. New York: Routledge, 1993, pp. 15–22.

Callahan, John F. *In the African-American Grain: The Pursuit of Voice in Twentieth-Century Black Fiction*. Urbana: University of Illinois Press, 1988.

Davie, Sharon. "Free Mules, Talking Buzzards, and Cracked Plates: The Politics of Dislocation in *Their Eyes Were Watching God*," *PMLA*, 108 (1993): 446–459.

Doane, Marianne. *The Desire to Desire: The Woman's Film of the 1940s*. Bloomington: Indiana University Press, 1987.

Ellis, John. *Visible Fictions: Cinema, Television, Video*. Boston: Routledge & Kegan Paul, 1982.

Fanon, Frantz. *Black Skin, White Masks: The Experiences of a Black Man in a White World*, translated by Charles Lam Markmann. New York: Grove, 1967.

Gaines, Jane. "White Privileging and Looking Relations: Race and Gender in Feminist Film Theory," *Screen*, 29, 4 (1988): 12–27.

Gates, Henry Louis, Jr., "Zora Neale Hurston and the Speakerly Text," in *Southern Literature and Literary Theory*, edited by Jefferson Humphries. Athens: University of Georgia Press, 1990, pp. 142–169.

Gates and Appiah, eds. *Zora Neale Hurston: Critical Perspectives Past and Present*. New York: Armistad Press, 1993.

Gooding-Williams, ed. *Reading Rodney King, Reading Urban Uprising*. New York: Routledge, 1993.

Hansen, Miriam. "Early Cinema, Late Cinema: Transformations of the Public Sphere," in *Viewing Positions: Ways of Seeing Film*, edited by Linda Williams. New Brunswick: Rutgers University Press, 1995, pp. 134–152.

Haraway, Donna. "Situated Knowledges: The Science Question in Feminism and the Privilege of Partial Perspective," in *Simians, Cyborgs, and Women: The Reinvention of Nature*. London: Free Association Books, 1991, pp. 183–201.

Henderson, Mae G. "Response" to Baker's "There Is No More Beautiful Way: Theory and the Poetics of Afro-American Women's Writing," *Afro-American Literary Study in the*

1990s, edited by Baker and Patricia Redmond. Chicago: University of Chicago Press, 1989, pp. 155–163.

Holloway, Karla F. C. *The Character of the Word: The Texts of Zora Neale Hurston*. Westport, Conn.: Greenwood Press, 1987.

hooks, bell. *Black Looks: Race and Representation*. Boston: South End Press, 1992.

Hurston, Zora Neale. "Characteristics of Negro Expression," in *Negro: An Anthology*, edited by Nancy Cunard, edited and abridged by Hugh Ford. New York: Ungar, 1970, pp. 39–46.

———. "Drenched in Light," in *Zora Neale Hurston: Novels and Stories*. New York: Library of America: *1995*, pp. 940–948.

———. "The Gilded Six-Bits." in *Zora Neale Hurston: Novels and Stories*. New York: Library of America: 1995, pp. 985–996.

———. *Jonah's Gourd Vine*, in *Zora Neale Hurston: Novels and Stories*. New York: Library of America: 1995, pp. 1–171.

———. "Sweat," in *Zora Neale Hurston: Novels and Stories*. New York: Library of America: 1995, pp. 955–967.

———. *Their Eyes Were Watching God*. New York: Harper, 1990.

———. "What White Publishers Won't Print," in *I Love Myself When I Am Laughing . . . And Then Again When I Am Looking Mean and Impressive*, edited by Alice Walker. Old Westbury: Feminist Press, 1979, pp. 169–173.

———. *Zora Neale Hurston: Novels and Stories*. New York: Library of America, 1995.

Johnson, Barbara. "Metaphor, Metonymy and Voice in *Their Eyes Were Watching God*," in *Black Literature and Literary Theory*, edited by Henry Louis Gates, Jr. New York: Methuen, 1984, pp. 205–219.

Kaplan, Carla. "The Erotics of Talk: 'That Oldest Human Longing' in *Their Eyes Were Watching God*," *American Literature*, 67, 1 (1995): 115–142.

Kubitschek, Missy Dehn. "'Tuh de Horizon and Back': The Female Quest in *Their Eyes Were Watching God*," *Black American Literature Forum*, 17 (1983): 109–115.

Lakritz, Andrew. "Identification and Difference: Structures of Privilege in Cultural Criticism," in *Who Can Speak?: Authority and Critical Identity*, edited by Judith Roof and Robyn Wiegman. Urbana: University of Illinois Press, 1995, pp. 3–29.

Lorde, Audre. *Sister Outsider*. Trumansburg, N.Y.: Crossing Press, 1984.

Lott, Eric. *Love and Theft: Blackface Minstrelsy and the American Working Class*. New York: Oxford University Press, 1993.

Lubiano, Wahneema. "Don't Talk with Your Eyes Closed: Caught in the Hollywood Gun Sights," in *Borders, Boundaries, and Frames: Cultural Criticism and Cultural Studies*, edited by Mae Henderson. New York: Routledge, 1995, pp. 185–201.

McKay, Nellie. "'Crayon Enlargements of Life': Zora Neale Hurston's *Their Eyes Were Watching God*," in *New Essays on Their Eyes Were Watching God*, edited by Michael Awkward. Cambridge: Cambridge University Press, 1990.

Morrison, Toni. *Paradise*. New York: Knopf, 1998.

Mulvey, Laura. *Visual and Other Pleasures*. Bloomington: Indiana University Press, 1989.

Racine, Maria J. "Voice and Interiority in Zora Neale Hurston's *Their Eyes Were Watching God*," *African American Review*, 28 (1994): 283–292.

Rony, Fatimah Tobing. "Those Who Squat and Those Who Sit: The Iconography of Race in the 1895 Films of Felix-Louis Regnault," *Camera Obscura*, 28 (January 1992): 263–289.

Silverman, Kaja. *The Threshold of the Visible World*. New York: Routledge, 1996.

Spillers, Hortense J. "'All the Things You Could Be by Now, If Sigmund Freud's Wife Was Your Mother': Psychoanalysis and Race," in *Female Subjects in Black and White: Race*,

Psychoanalysis, Feminism, edited by Elizabeth Abel, Barbara Christian, and Helene Moglen. Berkeley: University of California Press, 1997, pp. 135–158.

Stepto, Robert. *From Behind the Veil.* Urbana: University of Illinois Press, 1979.

Wald, Priscilla. "Becoming 'Colored': The Self-Authorized Language of Difference in Zora Neale Hurston," *American Literary History,* 2, 1 (1990): 79–100.

Wall, Cheryl. "Zora Neale Hurston: Changing Her Own Words," in *American Novelists Revisited: Essays in Feminist Criticism,* edited by Fritz Fleischmann. Boston: G. K. Hall, 1982, pp. 371–393.

Wallace, Michelle. *Invisibility Blues: From Pop to Theory.* New York: Verso Press, 1990.

———. "Modernism, Postmodernism and the Problem of the Visual in Afro-American Culture," in *Out There: Marginalization and Contemporary Cultures,* edited by Russell Ferguson, Martha Gever, Trinh T. Minhha, and Cornel West. Cambridge: MIT Press, 1990, pp. 39–50.

———. "Race, Gender, and Psychoanalysis in Forties Films: *Lost Boundaries, Home of the Brave, and The Quiet One,*" in *Black American Cinema,* edited by Manthia Diawara. New York: Routledge: 1993, pp. 257–271.

Washington, Mary Helen. "'I Love the Way Janie Crawford Left Her Husbands': Emergent Female Hero," in *Critical Perspectives Past and Present,* edited by Henry Louis Gates Jr., and K. A. Appiah. New York: Armistad Press, 1993, pp. 98–110.

Wolff, Maria Tai. "Listening and Living: Reading and Experience in *Their Eyes Were Watching God,*" edited by Gates and Appiah, pp. 218–229.

Young, Lola. *Fear of the Dark: "Race," Gender and Sexuality in the Cinema.* New York Routledge, 1996.

Chronology

1901?   January 7, Zora Neale Hurston born in the all-black town of Eatonville, Florida, to Lucy Ann and John Hurston, a carpenter and minister, and the mayor of Eatonville.

1915   Leaves home and begins working as a maid and wardrobe girl for Gilbert and Sullivan's traveling troupe, which eventually brings her to Baltimore, Maryland. There, she enters the Morgan College Preparatory School.

1918   Graduates from the Morgan College Preparatory School. Enters Howard University.

1919–24   Studies at Howard under Lorenzo Dow Turner and Alain Locke, who encourage her in her writing.

1920   Receives an associate degree from Howard University.

1921   "John Redding Goes to Sea," Hurston's first published short story, appears in *The Stylus*.

1924   "Drenched in Light" published in *Opportunity* (edited by Charles S. Johnson).

1925   "Spunk" published in *Opportunity*. Granted a scholarship to Barnard College. Moves to New York, and into the center of the Harlem Renaissance.

1925–27   Studies anthropology under Franz Boas (whom she calls "Papa Franz").

1926   "Muttsy" published. Hurston, Langston Hughes, and Wallace
        Thurman found the short-lived avant-garde magazine *Fire!!*. They
        regard themselves as rebels, reacting against black leaders such as
        W. E. B. Du Bois and Alain Locke, who urge that all creative work
        emphasize the problems between races. Depicting blacks only in rela-
        tion to white oppression is itself exploitative, Hurston, Hughes, and
        Thurman say; their first responsibility is to their art.

1927   Hurston undertakes first anthropological field research, going to
        Alabama for Carter G. Woodson and the Association for the Study of
        Negro Life and History to interview Cudjo Lewis, an ex-slave. Results
        published as "Cudjo's Own Story of the Last African Slaves" in the
        Journal of Negro History. A low point in Hurston's career: though the
        article includes material of her won, it has since been revealed that it
        also draws heavily on, perhaps plagiarizes Emma Langdon Roache's
        Historic Sketches of the Old South, published in 1914. *Great Day*, a play,
        published. Contract signed with the patron Mrs. Rufus Osgood Mason
        (whom Hurston calls "God-mother"). Mrs. Mason supports Hurston in
        anthropological field work in Eatonville, Florida, Alabama, Louisiana,
        and the West Indies from 1927 to 1932; she insists on owning all of
        Hurston's material and on approving all uses of it, as she feels Hurston
        cannot be trusted to manage it properly. Marriage to Herbert Sheen for
        four months, after a relationship of six years.

1928   Receives B.A. from Barnard College.

1930   "Dance Songs and Tales from the Bahamas" published. Works with
        Langston Hughes on a play, *Mule Bone*, of which only the third act is
        published. They quarrel over who is to receive credit for the body of
        the work, a conflict that is never clearly resolved.

1931   "Hoodoo in America" published. Returns to interview Cudjo Lewis
        and writes a full-length (unpublished) work based on his life.

1933   "The Gilded Six-Bits" published.

1934   Receives a Rosenwald Fellowship. *Jonah's Gourd Vine*, Hurston's first
        novel, published. It is praised for its use of folklore and is criticized for
        its lack of a statement on the effects of racism on Southern blacks.

1935   *Mules and Men* published, an anthropological study of the folklore of
        American blacks. It is the result of intensive participatory research
        into ceremonies and rituals and is the first such study written by a
        black woman. It, too, is praised for its contribution to the knowledge
        of folklore but is criticized for its lack of political statement.

1936   Receives a Guggenheim Fellowship. Uses it to study folklore in the West Indies.

1937   "Fannie Hurst" published. *Their Eyes Were Watching God* published, perhaps Hurston's most artistically successful work, which was written in seven weeks after a devastating love affair.

1938   *Tell My Horse* published, the first major work on Caribbean folklore.

1939   *Moses, Man of the Mountain* published. Marriage to and separation from Albert Price III, a man several years Hurston's junior. She wrote that her romantic affairs failed at the point when she was expected to give up her work and assume a more traditional role as a wife.

1942   "Story in Harlem Slang" published. *Dust Tracks on a Road*, Hurston's autobiography, published. It is her most commercially successful publication thus far (though perhaps not a factually accurate representation of her life).

1943   "The Pet Negro System," "High John de Conquer," and "Negroes Without Self-Pity" published.

1943–46 In this period, Hurston has trouble obtaining funding for her prospective research, as study of blacks in Central America.

1944   "Black Ivory Finale" and "My Most Humiliating Jim Crow Experience" published.

1945   "Beware the Begging Joints" and "Crazy for this Democracy" published. Stricken with a gall-bladder and colon infection, a condition that becomes chronic and affects her ability to support herself.

1947   Sails for British Honduras, partially financed by an advance from the novel *Seraph on the Suwanee*.

1948   *Seraph on the Suwanee* published, her first and only novel depicting the lives of whites. Arrested on a morals charge involving a young boy. She was out of the country at the time of the supposed offence and the boy turns out to be psychologically disturbed. The unsubstantiated charges are dropped, and she is cleared; but the press, especially the black press, sensationalizes the case. Overwhelmed, she returns to the South, working for a short time as a drama instructor at North Carolina College and as a scriptwriter for Paramount Pictures.

1950   "The Conscience of the Land" and "What White Publishers Won't Print" published. Discovered by a newspaper reporter working as a maid for a wealthy white woman in a fashionable section of Miami.

She claims that she is researching an article on domestics, but she is living in squalor.

1950–60 Occasional publications during this period, contributions to such journals as *American Legion Magazine*, seem to indicate a growing political conservatism; or an attitude formed growing up in a secure, all-black community. She opposes the 1954 Supreme Court desegregation decision *Brown v. Board of Education*, saying that desegregation implies a degradation of black teachers, students, and schools.

1951   "I Saw Negro Votes Peddled" published.

1955   Scribner's rejects a manuscript.

1959   Writes and asks Harper and Brothers if they would be interested in publishing a book she is working on, "A Life of Herod the Great." Enters the St. Lucie County Welfare Home in Florida.

1960   Dies without funds to provide for her burial, a resident of the St. Lucie County Welfare Home. She is buried in an unmarked grave in a segregated cemetery in Fort Pierce, Florida.

1973   Alice Walker places a gravestone in the cemetery where Hurston is buried, unable to pinpoint the exact location of the grave.

Contributors

HAROLD BLOOM is Sterling Professor of the Humanities at Yale University. He is the author of thirty books, including *Shelley's Mythmaking* (1959), *The Visionary Company* (1961), *Blake's Apocalypse* (1963), *Yeats* (1970), *A Map of Misreading* (1975), *Kabbalah and Criticism* (1975), *Agon: Toward a Theory of Revisionism* (1982), *The American Religion* (1992), *The Western Canon* (1994), and *Omens of Millennium: The Gnosis of Angels, Dreams, and Resurrection* (1996). *The Anxiety of Influence* (1973) sets forth Professor Bloom's provocative theory of the literary relationships between the great writers and their predecessors. His most recent books include *Shakespeare: The Invention of the Human* (1998), a 1998 National Book Award finalist, *How to Read and Why* (2000), *Genius: A Mosaic of One Hundred Exemplary Creative Minds* (2002), *Hamlet: Poem Unlimited* (2003), *Where Shall Wisdom Be Found?* (2004), and *Jesus and Yahweh: The Names Divine* (2005). In 1999, Professor Bloom received the prestigious American Academy of Arts and Letters Gold Medal for Criticism. He has also received the International Prize of Catalonia, the Alfonso Reyes Prize of Mexico, and the Hans Christian Andersen Bicentennial Prize of Denmark.

DEBORAH G. PLANT is associate professor of English at South Florida University. She wrote *Every Tub Must Sit on Its Own Bottom: The Philosophy and Politics of Zora Neale Hurston* (1995).

DANIEL J. SUNDAHL is professor of English at Hillsdale College. His volumes of poetry include *The Small Logics* (2000), *Hiroshima Maidens* (1994), and *Loss of Habitat* (1993).

DOLAN HUBBARD is professor and chair of the English and language arts department at Morgan State University. He wrote *The Sermon in the Making of the African American Literary Imagination* (1994) and has edited *Recovered Writers/Recovered Texts: Race, Class, and Gender in Black Women's Literature* (1994) as well as works by W E. B. Du Bois and Langston Hughes.

WILLIAM M. RAMSEY is professor of English at Francis Marion University. His book of haiku, *This Wine,* was published in 2002.

GORDON E. THOMPSON is professor of English at City College of New York.

JOHN LOWE is professor of English at Louisiana State University. He has written *Jump at the Sun: Zora Neale Hurston's Cosmic Comedy* (1994) and edited *Bridging Southern Cultures: An Interdisciplinary Approach* (2005).

SUSAN E. MEISENHELDER is a professor of English, emeritus, at California State University, San Bernardino. She is author of *Hitting A Straight Lick with a Crooked Stick: Race and Gender in the Work of Zora Neale Hurston* (1999) and *Wordsworth's Informed Reader: Structures of Experience in His Poetry* (1988).

MICHAEL AWKWARD is Gayl A. Jones Collegiate Professor of Afro-American Literature and Culture at the University of Michigan. He wrote *Soul Covers: Rhythm and Blues Music and the Struggle for Artistic Identity: Aretha Franklin, Al Green, Phoebe Snow* (2007) and *Scenes of Instruction: A Memoir* (2000).

MICHELLE JOHNSON is assistant professor of Anthropology at Bucknell, specializing in the religious and cultural practices of the Mandinga people.

CLAUDIA TATE was professor of English and African-American studies at Princeton University. Her books include *Black Women Writers at Work* (1983), *Domestic Allegories of Political Desire: The Black Heroine's Text at the Turn of the Century* (1992) and *Psychoanalysis and Black Novels: Desire and the Protocols of Race* (1998).

DAPHNE LAMOTHE is professor of English at Smith College, where she teaches African-American literature.

LAURIE CHAMPION is an assistant professor of English at San Diego State University, Imperial Valley. She is co-editor of *Contemporary American Women Fiction Writers, An A-Z Guide* (2002) and *American Women Writers,*

1900-1945: A Bio-Bibliographical Critical Sourcebook (2000), among other works.

DEBORAH CLARKE is associate professor of English and Women's Studies and Director of the American Studies program at the University of Missouri, St. Louis. She is author of *Robbing the Mother: Women in Faulkner* (1994) and *Driving Women: Fiction and Automobile Culture in Twentieth-Century America* (2007).

Bibliography

Awkward, Michael. *Inspiring Influences: Tradition, Revision, and Afro-American Women's Novels.* New York: Columbia University Press, 1991.

Bone, Robert. *The Negro Novel in America.* New Haven: Yale University Press, 1958.

Bontemps, Arna. *The Harlem Renaissance Remembered.* New York: Dodd, Mead, 1972.

Brawley, Benjamin. *The Negro Genius.* New York: Dodd, Mead, 1937.

Byrd, James W. "Zora Neale Hurston: A Novel Folklorist." *Tennessee Folklore Society Bulletin,* 21 (1955): 37–41.

Campbell, Josie P. *Student Companion to Zora Neale Hurston.* Westport, Conn: Greenwood Press, 2001.

Christian, Barbara. *Black Women Novelists.* Westport, Conn: Greenwood Press, 1980.

Cooke, Michael G. *Afro-American Literature in the Twentieth Century.* New Haven: Yale University Press, 1984.

Croft, Robert W. *A Zora Neale Hurston Companion.* Gainesville: University Press of Florida, 2002.

Davis, Arthur P. *From the Dark Tower: Afro-American Writers, 1900–1960.* Washington, D. C.: Howard University Press, 1974.

Ford, Nick Aaron. *The Contemporary Negro Novel: A Study in Race Relations.* College Park, Md.: McGrath Publishing, 1936.

Gates, Henry Louis, Jr. *Black Literature and Literary Theory.* New York: Methuen, 1984.

Gayle, Addison, Jr. *The Way of the New World: The Black Novel in America.* Garden City, N.Y.: Anchor Press, 1975.

Giles, James R. "The Significance of Time in Zora Neale Hurston's *Their Eyes Were Watching God.*" *Negro American Literature Forum* (Summer 1972): 52–60.

Gloster, Hugh M. "Zora Neale Hurston: Novelist and Floklorist." *Phylon*, 4 (1943): pp. 153–159.

Harris, Trudier. *The Power of the Porch: The Storyteller's Craft in Zora Neale Hurston, Gloria Naylor, and Randall Kenan.* Athens, Ga.: University of Georgia Press, 1996.

Hemenway, Robert E. *Zora Neale Hurston: A Literary Biography.* Chicago: University of Illinois Press, 1977.

———. "Folklore Field Notes from Zora Neale Hurston." *The Black Scholar*, 7 (1975–76): pp. 30–46.

Holloway, Karla F. C. *The Character of the Word: The Texts of Zora Neale Hurston.* New York: Greenwood Press, 1987.

Howard, Lillie P. *Alice Walker and Zora Neale Hurston: The Common Bond.* Westport, Conn.: Greenwood Press, 1993.

Johnson, Yvonne. *The Voices of African American Women: The Use of Narrative and Authorial Voice in the Works of Harriet Jacobs, Zora Neale Hurston, and Alice Walker.* New York, N.Y.: Peter Lang, 1988.

Jordan, June. "On Richard Wright and Zora Neale Hurston: Notes Toward Balancing Love and Hatred," *Black World*, 23 (August 1974): p. 5.

Kaplan, Carla. *Zora Neale Hurston: A Life in Letters.* New York, N.Y.: Doubleday, 2002.

Kilson, Marion. "The Transformation of Eatonville's Ethnographer." *Phylon*, 33 (1972): pp. 112–119.

Kunitz, Stanley, and Howard Haycraft. *Twentieth-Century Authors.* New York: H. W. Wilson, 1972.

Lowe, John. *Jump at the Sun: Zora Neale Hurston's Cosmic Comedy.* Urbana: University of Illinois Press, 1994.

Meisenhelder, Susan E. *Hitting a Straight Lick with a Crooked Stick: Race and Gender in the Work of Zora Neale Hurston.* Tuscaloosa: University of Alabama Press, 1999.

Neale, Larry. "A Profile: Zora Neale Hurston," *Southern Exposure*, 1 (Winter 1974): pp. 160–168.

Patterson, Tiffany Ruby. *Zora Neale Hurston and a History of Southern Life.* Philadelphia, Penn.: Temple University Press, 2005.

Perry, Margaret. *Silence in the Drums: A Survey of the Literature of the Harlem Renaissance.* Westport, Conn.: Greenwood Press, 1976.

Peters, Pearlie Mae Fisher. *The Assertive Woman in Zora Neale Hurston's Fiction, Folklore, and Drama.* New York, N.Y.: Garland, 1998.

Plant, Deborah G. *Every Tub Must Sit on Its Own Bottom: The Philosophy and Politics of Zora Neale Hurston*. Urbana: University of Illinois Press, 1995.

Pratt, Theodore. "A Memoir: Zora Neale Hurston: Florida's First Distinguished Author." *Negro Digest* (February 1962): p. 54.

Rambeau, James. "The Fiction of Zora Neale Hurston." *The Markham Review*, 5 (Summer 1976): pp. 61–64.

Rayson, Ann. "The Novels of Zora Neale Hurston." *Studies in Black Literature*, 5 (Winter 1974): pp. 1–11.

Rosenblatt, Roger. *Black Fiction*. Cambridge: Harvard University Press, 1974.

Schraufnagel, Noel. *From Apology to Protest: The Black American Novel*. Deland, Fla.: Everett-Edwards, 1973.

Southerland, Ellease. "Zora Neale Hurston." *Black World* 23 (August 1974): pp. 20–30.

Starke, Catherine Juanita. *Black Portraiture in American Fiction*. New York: Basic Books, 1971.

Thurman, Wallace. *Infants of the Spring*. New York: MacCauley Company, 1932.

Tischler, Nancy M. *Black Masks: Negro Characters in Modern Southern Fiction*. University Park: The Pennsylvania State University Press, 1969.

Turner, Darwin. *In a Minor Chord*. Carbondale: Southern Illinois University Press, 1971.

Walker, S. Jay. "Zora Neale Hurston's *Their Eyes Were Watching God:* Black Novel of Sexism." *Modern Fiction Studies*, 20 (1974–75): pp. 519–527.

Wall, Cheryl A., Sandra M. Gilbert, and Susan Gubar. *Women in the Harlem Renaissance*. Bloomington: Indiana University Press, 1995.

Washington, Mary Helen. "The Black Woman's Search for Identity." *Black World*, 21 (August 1972): pp. 69–75.

West, M. Genevieve. *Zora Neale Hurston and American Literary Culture*. Gainesville: University Press of Florida, 2005.

Williams, Sherley Anne, Ruby Dee, and Jerry Pinkney. *Their Eyes Were Watching God*. Urbana: University of Illinois Press, 1991.

Acknowledgments

"The Folk Preacher and Folk Sermon Form in Zora Neale Hurston's *Dust Tracks on a Road*" by Deborah G. Plant, *Folklore Forum*, Volume 21, Number 1 (1988): pp. 3–19. © 1988 Folklore Forum/CCC. Reprinted by permission of Folklore Forum/CCC.

"Zora Neale Hurston: A Voice of Her Own/An Entertainment In Herself" by Daniel J. Sundahl, *Southern Studies: An Interdisciplinary Journal of the South,* Volume 1, Number 3 (Fall 1990): pp. 243–255. © 1990 Southern Studies / Northwestern State University. Reprinted by permission of Southern Studies / Northwestern State University.

"' . . . Ah said Ah'd save de text for you': Recontextualizing the Sermon to Tell (Her)story in Zora Neale Hurston's *Their Eyes Were Watching God*" by Dolan Hubbard, *African American Review,* Volume 27, Number 2 (Summer 1993): pp. 167–178. © 1993 Dolan Hubbard. Reprinted by permission of the author.

"The Compelling Ambivalence of Zora Neale Hurston's *Their Eyes Were Watching God*" by William M. Ramsey, *Southern Literary Journal,* Volume 27, Number 1 (Fall 1994): pp. 36–50. © 1994 Southern Literary Journal/UNC Press. Reprinted by permission of Southern Literary Journal/UNC Press.

"Projecting Gender: Personification in the Works of Zora Neale Hurston" by Gordon E. Thompson, *American Literature: A Journal of Literary History, Criticism, and Bibliography,* Volume 66, Number 4 (December 1994): pp.

229

737–763. © 1994 Duke University Press. Reprinted by permission of Duke University Press.

"From Mule Bones to Funny Bones: The Plays of Zora Neale Hurston" by John Lowe, *The Southern Quarterly: A journal of the Arts in the South*, Volume 33, Numbers 2–3 (Winter–Spring 1995): pp. 65–78. © 1995 Southern Quarterly/ Southern Mississippi. Reprinted by permission of Southern Quarterly/Southern Mississippi.

"Conflict and Resistance in Zora Neale Hurston's *Mules and Men*" by Susan E. Meisenhelder, *Journal of American Folklore*, Volume 109, Number 433 (1996): pp. 267–288. © 1996 American Folklore Society.

"Zora Neale Hurston," by Michael Awkward and Michelle Johnson in Kopley, Richard, ed. *Prospects for the Study of American Literature: A Guide for Scholars and Students*. New York: New York University Press, 1997; xvi, p. 347. © 1997 New York University Press.

"Hitting 'A Straight Lick with a Crooked Stick': *Seraph on the Suwanee*, Zora Neale Hurston's Whiteface Novel" by Claudia Tate, *Discourse: Jouranl for Theoretical Studies in Media and Culture*, Volume 19, Number 2 (Winter 1997): pp. 72–87. © 1997 Wayne State University Press.

"Vodou Imagery, African-American Tradition and Cultural Transformation in Zora Neale Hurston's *Their Eyes Were Watching God*" by Daphne Lamothe, *Callaloo: A Jouranl of African-American and African Arts and Letters*, Volume 22, Number 1 (Winter 1999): pp. 157–175. © 1999 Johns Hopkins University Press. Reprinted by permission of Johns Hopkins University Press.

"Socioeconomics in Selected Short Stories of Zora Neale Hurston" by Laurie Champion, *Southern Quarterly: A Journal of the Arts in the South*, Volume 40, Number 1 (Fall 2001): pp. 79–92. © 2001 Southern Quarterly/Southern Mississippi. Reprinted by permission of Southern Quarterly/Southern Mississippi.

"'The porch couldn't talk for looking': Voice and Vision in *Their Eyes Were Watching God*" by Deborah Clarke, *African American Review*, Volume 35, Number 4 (Winter 2001): pp. 599–613. © 2001 Deborah Clarke. Reprinted by permission of the author.

Index